Peter Marinello was bc
front-page headlines at the age of 19 with his record
transfer of £100,000 from Hibernian to Arsenal. He also
played for Portsmouth, Motherwell, Canberra City in
Australia, Fulham, Phoenix Inferno in the USA, Hearts
and Partick Thistle in a career that ran from 1967 to 1984.
He now lives in Bournemouth with his wife Joyce and
manages a local Sunday football league parks team.

Will Price, who worked with Peter Marinello on this book,
was born in Lambeth, London and brought up in Derby,
where he had the good fortune to see Brian Clough and
Dave Mackay win league titles in the 1970s. He now lives
in Bournemouth with his wife Alison and children Dan,
Joe, James and Sarah, while working in the sports depart-
ments of the *Daily Mirror* and the *People*.

Fallen Idle

FIGHTING BACK FROM THE BOOZE, SWINDLES AND DRUGS THAT RIPPED MY LIFE APART

PETER MARINELLO

with Will Price

headline

The right of Peter Marinello to be identified as the Author
of the Work has been asserted by him in accordance with the
Copyright, Designs and Patents Act 1988.

First published in 2007
by HEADLINE PUBLISHING GROUP

First published in paperback in 2007
by HEADLINE PUBLISHING GROUP

1

Cataloguing in Publication Data is available from the British Library

ISBN 978 0 7553 1558 1

Typeset in Palatino by Avon DataSet Ltd,
Bidford-on-Avon, Warwickshire

Career statistics compiled by Jack Rollin

Printed and bound in Great Britain by Clays Ltd, St Ives plc

HEADLINE PUBLISHING GROUP
A division of Hachette Livre UK Ltd
338 Euston Road
London NW1 3BH

www.headline.co.uk
www.hodderheadline.com

To Joyce, for putting up with me all these years,
and my dad – the best barman I ever knew

Contents

Acknowledgements

I would like to thank the following:

Will Price, my ghost writer. I could never have told my story fully without Will's constant help, encouragement and – most importantly – friendship. He is a true football fan. I wasn't keen to reveal all the pain, heartache and disappointment to begin with, but Will frequently reassured me that it was a tale worth telling . . . along with some great highs, of course.

Arsenal Football Club. My 'second family' in many ways and I will never forget the personal financial assistance given to me by Frank McLintock and Bob Wilson when I was at my lowest ebb, or the enduring friendship of Sammy Nelson, Eddie Kelly and Charlie George. I must also thank Brian Hornsby and the late Bill Graves for involving me in the Arsenal ex-professional and celebrity charity team. They never knew how much those matches meant to me and kept me sane. I missed playing so much, and they gave me something to look forward to.

George Best and Jimmy 'Jinky' Johnstone – the two players I looked up to most. If I had come anywhere near their standards consistently, I would have been delighted.

Everyone at Headline, who have had such faith in me, particularly David Wilson, Rhea Halford, Helena Towers and Jack Rollin.

Eric Coombes, a long-standing friend in local amateur football through sunshine and rain, who has seen our clubs dominate parks football and get chopped down to size once or twice.

Ladbroke's and Coral bookmakers – for keeping a couple of welcoming offices within walking distance of my home, and the camaraderie of my fellow punters.

"I squandered my talent. I pissed most of it against the wall. I'm the guy who wrote the manual of How Not To Do It."

Prologue

Desperate men resort to desperate acts, and nobody was more desperate than me when a gun was whipped out and pressed hard against the temple of the man who had conned me out of £110,000.

My wife was in a psychiatric unit and I was on the dole after losing my home, two pubs plus a nightclub in disastrous business ventures and being forced to flee Scotland for the south coast of England with my two sons to escape creditors and a gangster I had dubbed 'Benny from the Bronx'.

I snapped when there was no sign of the taxi booked to drive me and my sons to the airport for a flight to Spain, where my business partner was supposed to have invested that £110,000 in a bar. There was no taxi, no flight, no bar. Nothing but a string of broken promises. I had entrusted my entire life savings to a character who had calmly ripped me off. Now it was payback time. I wanted my money back and I wanted revenge for years of uncertainty, bitter frustration and anguish as my life had gone downhill from the glamour and glitz of professional football and five-star luxury on a raft of booze to a tramp-like, hand-to-mouth existence in lodgings. There was my poor wife to consider and the boys, of course, but when you hit rock bottom strange things can happen.

An underworld figure I knew in London was happy to commit murder for £30,000, but suggested I got involved in his venture smuggling diamonds and drugs instead, while I couldn't afford more than £120 for a pistol. My intentions might have been murderous, but I would settle for a knee-capping. I was prepared to do the crime and serve my time in prison.

Accompanied by my minder, Adam, a giant Cockney, we unearthed a devastating trail of deceit and fraud before cornering our quarry behind the changing rooms of a rugby ground.

It was time for the gun to come out to play.

CHAPTER 1

An Edinburgh Boy

I always thought I was the one supposed to do the shooting when I was running down the wing, not the maniac with homicidal tendencies who turned an air rifle on me. Mind you, those Edinburgh derbies between my Saughton housing estate, near the prison, and our deadly rivals a mile and a half away in Broomhouse, renowned as the home of hard men, always tended to be bitterly contested affairs, even if most of us were still in short pants and wearing plimsolls, or 'gutties' as we called them, on our feet. When I was about eight years old we played a version of football known locally as 'take-ons', involving anything from four-a-side to a couple of dozen of us charging about. I was leading the Broomhouse bruisers a merry dance on this particular occasion when I suddenly felt a sharp, stabbing pain less than an inch below by right eye. I was bleeding, and one of the older youths on our side studied the damage with the practised air of an experienced surgeon before announcing knowledgeably, 'Airgun!'

Who knows how my life might have changed course had that shot been fractionally higher? One thing I am certain of: it has never been dull – and that wasn't the first time a gun was going to get me into trouble. I count myself fortunate to have crashed through life without any kind of physical defect or permanent handicap, despite my magnetic attraction to trouble.

I must confess I've sometimes had cloudy vision regarding which path to take for the best, and certainly haven't always taken the correct decision, but Grandpa Marinello, who hailed from Naples, clearly saw his future in Scotland. He emigrated from Italy, via some time working in Germany, in the 1920s with my granny, who grew up as a girl in Florence. Scotland was popular with Italians at the time, and many settled north of the border to lead industrious lives running fish and chip shops and cafés. My father, Peter, was the eldest of seven sons – my uncles Freddie, Eddie, Paul, Leno, Andrew and Johnny – plus one daughter, Anna, who they all adored. My mum, Theresa, is of Irish descent from a huge family, and I was brought into the world on 20 February 1950 at Edinburgh Royal Infirmary. I was a first child, and two sisters for me, Anna and Theresa, were to follow.

I was proudly bundled up and taken home to our two-bedroomed prefab on the outskirts of the city, into which Dad would travel to earn his living. He was a barman of the old school, collar and tie at all times if you please, and worked for over forty years at Twisses, later renamed the Old Coach Inn, in the Canonmills district. An honest, simple man, he was good at his job.

It was a very tough, working-class upbringing in Saughton, but I would never call it deprived. From about six until I was twelve, I clearly recall family holidays at Butlins, Ayr, with Mum entering me for the Tarzan contest, where I simply had to get up on stage in a pair of swimming trunks and parade my little body. I must have been a natural showman, even then, because I was crowned camp Tarzan on three occasions, as well as winning a boxing competition or two. How times have changed. Can you imagine the outcry today from the 'pc' brigade if a holiday camp ran anything as sexist as a Tarzan show, or as 'dangerous' as boxing for children. Needless to say, all the boys enjoyed both immensely and lived to tell the tale.

Saughton was neighbourly, a nice community, very open and honest, even if some folk barely had two ha'pennies to rub together, and I always had a loving family to turn to when I could be prised away from my true first love, playing football. We lived at the start of a big horseshoe-shaped row of prefabs, with gardens front and back. Mind you, my back garden was never likely to detain me for long once I understood what pleasures were to be located on the other side of our fence – the local school playing fields. That's where it first dawned on me that I possessed some talent after kicking a hole through the fence for the speediest of entrances to this sporting arena, and I was looked after well by older guys, such as Jimmy Ferguson and Rab Burnett. Some of the bigger boys threatened us whippersnappers with physical violence if we didn't fancy a 'take-on' but those threats barely registered with me, because I was always up for it.

Barely 300 yards away lived the Souness family with their three sons, Gordon, Billy and young Graeme, who was three years younger than me. Neither Gordon nor Billy were really interested in football, but that did not prevent Billy and me becoming good pals. As for Graeme Souness, I have thoroughly enjoyed watching him progress from that teak-tough midfield player with Liverpool, Sampdoria and Rangers to a top-flight Premiership manager with the little matter of fifty-four Scotland caps thrown in.

There were to be occasions when ambition flickered briefly for me, and I would have given anything for one cap, yet there were times when my life was in such turmoil that the mere business of surviving the day was more important. But was it all my fault? I'll leave that for you to decide.

As far as football in the blood goes, Uncle Johnny had trials at St Mirren, while Leno reckoned during the Second World War he played for a Scottish side at left-back against an England Select featuring Tom Finney and Stanley Matthews, a legendary character who was to enter my life briefly in a quite remarkable fashion. Dad said he had been a goalkeeper, but at no great level.

Given my Italian–Irish parentage, I could hardly be raised anything else but Roman Catholic. I was duly baptised and briefly became an altar boy, serving at Mass and regularly attending church on Sundays until I was eighteen, when I rather got out of the habit. Religion was encouraged at home, rather than shoved down our throats. We did, however, live on the side of Edinburgh from which the Protestant club, Heart of Midlothian, drew their backing. In Saughton, at the age of nine or ten, it was advisable to be a Hearts supporter if you didn't want a battering from the local toughs. We lived a fifteen-minute bus ride away from a part of town known as Gorgie and the Hearts ground of Tynecastle. It was there I sometimes ventured to worship the likes of Dave Mackay, Alec Young, who left in 1960 for Everton where he became known as the Golden Vision, and Gordon Smith, after witnessing the end of the era featuring the famous Terrible Trio of Alfie Conn, Willie Bauld and Jimmy Wardhaugh. Great players, one and all, and an influence on me, even though I wouldn't class myself as a Hearts regular – finances dictated I couldn't attend many games.

I can't have been much more than ten when we left the prefabs, after Dad bought a house in Canonmills, near the city centre, which was more convenient for his work, but I still attended my junior school, St Joseph's in Broomhouse, having learned to read and write at Stenhouse primary school. A spot of 'light relief' brought me huge embarrassment one afternoon when I was there. We'd spent the lunchtime playing football, what else, and at 1–1 with just a few minutes left I was desperately in need of a pee. A dash inside would certainly have meant the end of the game for me, so I quickly unbuttoned my trousers and went, there and then, behind a goalpost. Almost immediately, a bell rang which summoned the entire school, maybe 300–400 pupils, to the main hall, and we were all asking each other excitedly what was happening. The headmaster, Dr Gaffney, summoned me up on stage and I went, proud as Punch, because I knew he was going to congratulate me on being selected to play for Edinburgh schoolboys. He did that, but then made a reference to me peeing in public, which brought a flush to my cheeks the colour of Hearts' shirts and a punishment of 200 lines: 'I must always use the boys' toilet in school when necessary.' I fear Dr Gaffney would have been horrified by some of my antics on the piss in later life.

The world sure is a small place at times. A few years ago, my wife, Joyce, and I were in America, staring out at the sunset over the Grand Canyon, when a voice behind us asked, 'Excuse me, you're from Scotland, aren't you?' We got chatting, and it only turned out to be Dr Gaffney's son.

A really impressive pass mark in the eleven-plus would have seen me transferred to Holy Cross Academy, but that wasn't to be, and instead I moved to St Anthony's Secondary School, which was closer to our new house, yet notorious as a hard place with more than its fair share of naughty boys. St Anthony's also meant a fairly rapid change in my allegiances. I swapped my support of the maroon of the Hearts jerseys for the green of Hibernian,

Edinburgh's Catholic professional football club. My abiding recollection of the school was of a St Trinian's for boys, where the bell at the end of the day sounded twenty minutes earlier than anywhere else because the authorities wanted us packed up and well on the way home before the chance arose to tackle any unfortunate rival pupils. St Anthony's was a massive school with ten classes in the first year, ranging from IT1 to IT10 according to ability. I was placed in IT4 and, intellectually, I suppose I would have to class myself as average, yet attentive. I liked geography best, could turn in a useful English essay when the mood took me and was good at arithmetic when it came to figures, but the long-suffering teachers might as well have been speaking a foreign language when their lessons turned to algebra and geometry. Practical subjects, such as woodwork and metalwork, left me equally cold.

I enjoyed a stroke of good fortune when I crossed the path of Mr Cannon, who became my form teacher. He taught geography, and also encouraged me a tremendous amount at football. He was a great guy who arranged for me to take quite a lot of time off school for football training with various clubs. He once told me, quite emphatically, 'You will be a professional footballer, Peter, but there's no guarantee you will ever get selected for representative schoolboy teams because it's all a bit of a fix. The teachers in charge look after their own there.' Despite that early warning about favouritism, I was destined to play for Edinburgh schoolboys and later graduated to the Scottish youth team with that A-star footballer Kenny Dalglish.

I was a happy, settled boy with loads of friends and football-mad. We got on with our unremarkable lives. Of course, I had porridge for breakfast, and Dad would frequently dish up spaghetti and meatballs with tons of garlic on Sundays before we went visiting, either to my Italian grandma with her lovely, long black hair, or to see my mum's sisters. I looked forward to these outings in particular, and they frequently ended with me coming away ten to fifteen shillings richer. My aunts spoiled me rotten, but the money never lasted long – an early warning of the shape of things to come – swiftly invested as it was in sweeties and comics. Oor Wullie and The Broons in the *Sunday Post* were particular favourites, along with the *Dandy* and *Beano*. I loved all the characters and would have been perfectly at home with the Bash Street Kids . . . terrorising Lord Snooty!

But a serious career in football was beginning to beckon . . . and it was soon *Roy of the Rovers* stuff for me.

CHAPTER 2

Snubbing Stanley Matthews

I can never see a bar of Cadbury's chocolate without being reminded of the thin line between success and failure in football, the rewards winning can bring and the bitter taste of coming second.

I must have been all of eight years old when St Joseph's reached the final of the Edinburgh School Inspectors Cup, an occurrence which would have had me leaping for joy under normal circumstances. The problem was our opponents were my old school, Stenhouse, and the mates I still mucked around with really rubbed my nose in it big time, winning 2–1 in front of 500 assorted parents and family members before they were awarded their shiny silver winners' medals. All the St Joe's team received was a bar of Cadbury's chocolate each. Even for a kid of eight, that supposed 'treat' tasted bitter. I ate up, mind you – we didn't waste things in the Marinello family.

Stenhouse were the top side in the city and had quite a sprinkling of good players who went on to become professionals with Hearts, Hibs and Rangers. We were basically a bunch of ragamuffins, but nobody could beat us for heart and effort. What gave the final an extra edge was the Catholic v. Protestant element. As I'd already been a pupil at Stenhouse, it was deadly serious for me that I performed well, which I did, and we gave the hot favourites a good game. Only losing by the odd goal was something of a moral victory.

Two years later I was picked to play on the right wing for Edinburgh schoolboys at primary school level and was good enough to play for them for two years. Most boys had just the one season before moving on to big school, but I got in twelve months early. I was that good: very quick and with the ability to go past opponents. Playing with the older lads from an early age brought my game on in leaps and bounds. I found it all quite easy and maybe I was a wonderkid. The truth of the matter is that I just loved football: I lived for it, and it didn't matter whether I was playing for Edinburgh schoolboys, St Joseph's or Salvesen boys' club.

Our city boasted two cracking boys' football clubs, Salvesen and Tynecastle, both with excellent reputations for unearthing raw talent and nurturing it into something of interest to Scotland's professional outfits. They were the main feeder clubs for Hibs and Hearts, naturally. I joined Salvesen, and my first little brush with professionalism smacked of bigotry because a Rangers scout travelled over specifically from Glasgow to watch me in a school match and left the moment he was informed I was a Catholic – very definitely the 'wrong denomination' in those sectarian days at Ibrox.

As well as Salvesen, I trained during the week at Crossroads boys' club under the care of Eric Gardner, a great character who was later awarded the MBE and OBE for his services to youth football and various other projects, and Dougie Love. Dougie was one of Edinburgh's most cherished football personalities; he was still helping out at the Ian St John coaching camps at the age of seventy-five. I was gaining a reputation as being a bit useful with my feet, and that was enhanced the day my friend John Murphy and I beat John Greig, captain of Rangers and Scotland no less, in a little two-a-side game when he dropped into Crossroads with his nephew Mervyn Jones, although I shouldn't imagine John Greig lost a moment's sleep over the result.

John Murphy went on to join Hibs before me. He and I formed part of a little clique of lads who hung out together between the ages of thirteen and eighteen. I was in the thick of it, and the rest of the gang, with the clubs they joined, included Sandy Jardine (Rangers), Jimmy Brown (Hearts), Murray McDermott, who went on to keep goal for various professional clubs, Jim Steele (Dundee and later Southampton, where he starred in the team that beat Manchester United in the 1976 FA Cup final), David Ross (also Dundee) and Ian Cruikshank, who went on to join Hearts but never made it into the first team ranks. David was a clever inside-left who liked to stroll around a bit in the manner of George Graham at Arsenal, and I remember when he announced he'd had enough of football and fancied going into stocks and shares. We thought David was mad, absolutely stark raving bonkers. The last I heard of Mr Ross, he was a millionaire with substantial property interests in both Edinburgh and the London borough of Kensington – so obviously that was a really bad move!

I continued to be a mainstay in the Edinburgh school-boys team while I was a pupil at St Anthony's and recall one year tackling a Glasgow side containing Willie Carr, who went on to enjoy a very good career in England with Coventry City. First up, Glasgow came to Hearts' big stadium at Tynecastle for a match on grass, which they won. The return in Glasgow was staged, if that's the right word, on this horrible brown-dirt pitch, but I was happy to muck in, and we put in a considerably improved display to force a draw. No footballer worth his salt should ever use the state of the pitch as an excuse for a poor perform-ance – George Best would still have been an absolute genius had he played his entire career on cobblestone streets. And I was beginning to develop my balance and ball control to an extent that was catching the eye of the people who mattered.

I detected a certain rivalry between George Smith, the chief scout at Hibs, and his second-in-command, David Dalziel. They both independently asked me to come down to Easter Road to train with the club's part-timers on Tuesday and Thursday nights for £3 a week, money which they informed me was for 'expenses'. Although Hibs were a professional club, they had plenty of room for part-time players and had maybe sixteen or seventeen on the books. Men such as Alan Cousin, a schoolteacher from Dundee, and George McNeill, an athletic left-winger who won Edinburgh's famous Powderhall Sprint. George was electric when he got into his stride and competed a fair bit in Australia, where there was a lucrative market for professional runners. In fact, he was so good I would have backed him to have given Allan Wells, another of Edinburgh's famous sporting sons, a very good run for his money had the pair of them been contemporaries.

Now, many of these part-timers were fully grown men and regular reserve-team players, while I was just this small, slightly built schoolboy. The manager, Jock Stein, who later acquired legendary status in charge of Celtic and the Scotland national team, took one look at me and shook his head. Fortunately, it wasn't that he didn't fancy me as a player, he just didn't fancy seeing me taken home in an ambulance if I tried any fancy footwork out on the pitch training against the hard men. Jock had two small goals painted on facing walls, twenty-five yards apart, in the car park, and I spent hours playing 'wally', shooting against one goal then turning to strike a shot in the opposite direction. When I'd tired of that, Jock had one of his coaches make me dribble through a line of cones or right around the perimeter of the pitch. For two years at Hibs, I don't think I ever faced a physical opponent – just bricks and those plastic cones.

Between thirteen and fifteen, I was pretty normal and strait-laced. All I knew was sport. I wasn't particularly interested in girls and drinking – that came a few years later, as did my love of music and fashion. Saturday night might have been all right for dancing if you were a bit older, but it invariably found me watching the Edinburgh Monarchs speedway team if they were at home.

My money rose to £6 a week, and I was itching to join the groundstaff the day I turned fifteen and join my friend John Murphy and other lads recruited from all over Scotland. My fifteenth birthday came and went with no sign of the present I desired above all. Hibs were still perfectly happy for me to train twice a week with them, but I was getting more than a little cheesed off. I yearned to get my foot on the first rung of the professional ladder and thought no job on earth could be better than that of the apprentice footballer, sweeping the terraces of litter after a game, cleaning the first-team boots and doing some rudimentary painting. Not quite the aspirations of would-be footballers now, I suspect.

Salvesen were eager to form an attachment with an English club in 1965. They already had links established with Dundee when the invitation came from Port Vale to travel down to the Potteries and take on their youth team. Quite what the Vale youngsters were expecting, I don't know, but we were undoubtedly one of the best sides in Scotland for our age and ran out comfortable winners, 6–1. I had a decent game, although I didn't score. That was a foretaste of my career to come, I suppose. I was never greedy enough to want to score all the time and grab the headlines. Even at fifteen, I was your typical winger. I would beat two or three defenders before laying the ball on for the centre-forward to finish. If I could do that half a dozen times in ninety minutes, I was perfectly happy. Sometimes, the sheer lung-bursting effort of avoiding a late tackle and getting to the goal-line to put in a cross would leave me a bit knackered, and I wouldn't be that accurate with the delivery.

Back home after the trip, the Salvesen manager, Peter Mackay, came calling to casually inform the Marinello family to expect a personal visit from the Port Vale manager, none other than Stanley Matthews. I had, it seemed, created a very favourable impression with one of the greatest players the game has known. Peter said he had been told that Sir Stan, as he was to become, had been scouring England for a young winger . . . and that I was that player. My first reaction was that Peter had to be joking. Then I experienced blind panic. I didn't want to play hundreds of miles away in a totally alien environment. Salvesen had been superbly looked after on our trip to the Potteries, and the hospitality had been fantastic, but Stoke-on-Trent won't ever win any beauty prizes. It didn't exactly look like Fun City to me, and I strongly suspected I would quickly become homesick. I wanted to play for Hibs. That's where my heart was.

Within a matter of days, a handsome black Jaguar saloon car swung into our tidy cul-de-sac near Edinburgh city centre, and out climbed Stanley Matthews. The curtains were twitching, the neighbours were popping their heads in and out, small boys clambered around requesting autographs and my mum offered Mr Matthews more tea and cake than he could safely tuck away in a month of Sundays. I was totally in awe of him on that first visit, and when he sensed my reluctance to sign for Port Vale, he suggested I come down initially for a fortnight. I said no. He could have asked me a million times and the answer would always have been the same. My heart was set on Hibs.

Talks reached a stage where he offered me a £3,000 signing-on fee plus £40 a week, which was twice what my father was earning, and a hell of a good wage in the sixties. To put it in perspective, since leaving school at the age of fifteen with no O-levels whatsoever, I had been working for £3.10 a week in the post room of The Royal Highland and Agricultural Society of Scotland. Everything was geared to their annual show at Ingliston, and I certainly earned my money, given the amount of envelopes I had to address and stamps I was required to lick. But I wasn't complaining, they treated me well – better than I treated Stanley Matthews, certainly. Three times he drove that Jaguar north to our house and three times he drove away disappointed. On the final occasion, I was too embarrassed to even leave my bedroom and come downstairs to see him while my mum and dad urged me to sign. I suspect they were beginning to feel sorry for him. Mr Matthews looked pig-sick and reiterated what Peter Mackay had said. He had been all over England, and I was a natural right-winger who looked to beat people, and he wanted to groom me, and he was so disappointed with my response.

Looking back, it might have been better if I had gone. I could have learned a hell of a lot from a man like him, the maestro. He might have made me 100 per cent better. Playing on the wing like I did and trying to beat defenders who want to kick you is the hardest thing in the game. You put your credibility on the line every ninety minutes and sometimes you meet a full-back who is not just good, but very good. Stanley Matthews spent the prime years of his professional playing career putting one over the best full-backs the world had to offer, bewildering the good ones and leaving the average ones dazed and confused.

I should have had the balls to join him at Port Vale but I wanted Hibs, yet it seemed at one stage they didn't want me, and George Smith and David Dalziel started to get a bit worried. Then Peter Mackay made contact out of the blue with the news that the Chelsea manager, Tommy Docherty, had been in touch, fancied me and wanted me to come to London for a trial. Some football agents today may work in dark and devious ways, setting up deals on their mobile phones, but there was a refreshing honesty about the way business was conducted forty-odd years ago, as I hope these two handwritten letters I kept from Chelsea in July, 1966 demonstrate:

4 Mossyde Avenue
Port Glasgow

Scotland
9-7-66
Phone Port Glasgow 41622

Dear Peter,

I am writing this note at the airport after being on the phone to Mr Docherty. Sorry about the delay in having you down to London but would you please phone me at Stamford Bridge Grounds on Monday morning 10.15. Phone number 5545 Fulham. Reverse charge and ask for Mr Morris. I would like to have you down on Wednesday for a couple of days now as you know we have already fixed Brian Wilson for Chelsea. I would expect to have you signed before you go back home. The Wilsons are expected to go back home on Friday or Saturday. Anyway phone me on Monday morning and if you are interested I will book a plane flight for you for Wednesday. Cheerio just now.

Yours sincerely,
Dan Morris
Chief Representative, Chelsea Football Club

Montana Hotel
67 Gloucester Road
London SW7
Phone Knightsbridge 7654

Dear Peter,

Your flight ticket to London has been booked for you and you can collect it at the airport terminal office on George Street on Wednesday morning at about 9.30am. This will ensure that it won't be delayed in the post. Your flight I believe will be at 11.25am but check up on this when you go to collect your ticket. Brian Wilson is enjoying himself here in London. I will be at the London Airport to meet you.

Yours sincerely,
Dan Morris
Chief Representative, Chelsea Football Club

The Chelsea connection was music to Salvesen's ears because boys' clubs were more or less guaranteed some sort of unofficial financial compensation, anything from £300 up to £1,000, if one of their lads made the grade and signed professional forms. Hibs were duly informed that, unless they made me an offer immediately, I was signing for Chelsea. That wasn't strictly true, but it certainly had the desired effect. Jock Stein had left and gone to Celtic by then, to be replaced by Bob Shankly, brother of Liverpool legend Bill. I mentioned that I'd turned down a £3,000 signing-on fee to join Stanley Matthews at Port Vale, but Hibs thought that matching that generous offer was a bit rich, and I spent less than five minutes with the chairman, W. P. Harrower, who owned a chain of bookies. He beat me down to £1,000 and gave me a genuine Royal Bank of

Scotland £100 note there and then as the first of ten instalments to swell my £12-a-week pay packet on the groundstaff.

The Royal Highland and Agricultural Society of Scotland were disappointed to be losing me. I know that for a fact, because they offered me a pay rise of £1 a week to stay, bless them!

Suddenly, I felt like a millionaire with the world at my feet. Signed by my beloved Hibs, I had a £100 note burning a hole in my back pocket and celebrated in style by hitting Edinburgh's most fashionable clothes emporiums. I like to think I was already a sharp dresser, or 'trendy' as the term was then, and the clobber at Jaeger was a personal favourite. I was also a regular fixture at all the record stores, where I stocked up on the latest hit singles. After a few of those £100 instalments, I must have possessed half a dozen suits at £50 a throw off the peg, yet none of them fitted me properly because I was so slender. I knew exactly where Ray Davies was coming from when he penned the lyrics to the Kinks' big hit of the era, 'Dedicated Follower of Fashion'. That was me, all right.

I was a mod with a Beatle haircut and splashed out on all the up-to-date gear plus shoes, lots of lovely shoes. As for pop, I was a member of the Elvis Presley fan club, loved the Beatles and the Rolling Stones as well as Tamla Motown, the Drifters and Dusty Springfield. I still remember the first '45' I ever bought: 'The Locomotion' by Little Eva. That haircut soon grew a touch too long for Bob Shankly's liking and, the day after I'd been to visit the barber, he demanded to know when I was going to have a trim. Style, to Bob, was all short back and sides, but the times were changing. He was quick to sing my praises, though, and always said I would be the first of the youngsters to break through. Bob told anyone who cared to listen that I was a winger of the old school, a ball player who could dribble through a defensive minefield, much in the manner of Stanley Matthews. Just hearing that name could make me shudder a little with embarrassment, rather than pride, because something at the back of my mind told me I should have been serving my apprenticeship under the guidance of the Master in the Potteries.

A little fledgling international recognition soon arrived, however, and I enjoyed two years playing for the Scottish youth team with the likes of Kenny Dalglish, Martin Buchan, Willie Carr, John O'Hare and John McGovern.

Life couldn't be better, and I was especially keen to turn up for work after Hibs had entertained Celtic or Rangers at Easter Road. Sweeping the terraces, I would invariably find silver, £5 and £10 notes and the odd half-bottle of whisky that had fallen out of a supporter's coat pocket. I wasn't too familiar with the hard stuff then, but by the time I had turned sixteen my clique certainly liked a beer. After a reserve match on a Saturday we would get as many pints as possible down our necks before the barman called last orders at ten to ten. This was the life ... or so I thought.

CHAPTER 3

Teenage Kicks

Some of my teenage refuelling habits were first class, even if they were the cause of a little friction at the Marinello family dining table. Three or four times a week, Mum would serve me up a prime steak, frequently a juicy sirloin, while my poor sisters, Anna and Theresa, had to make do with tinned corned beef as often as not. Talk about the blue-eyed boy!

Orders were orders, though, and for a couple of years from the age of fourteen I was more than happy to follow the dietary advice of Alfie Nicholl, a family friend who trained the Powderhall Sprint athletes. I suppose you could call my rise to footballing fame 'meteoric', and for that Alfie deserves a great deal of the credit. I was already quick when he began to coach me twice a week at Saughton enclosure, where the football pitch was surrounded by a running track. It was through Alfie that I picked up a job with Freddie Whitten, the foreman for a building firm in Edinburgh and the father of my great friend Peter Whitten, later to become my best man. That first summer when I was a member of the Hibs ground-staff, I also spent six weeks building up my muscles, fetching and carrying on site for Freddie as a glorified teaboy. I collected the labourers' midday sandwiches and pies one moment, made a powerful brew the next before turning my hand to some heavy-duty cement-mixing and hod-carrying. The powers that be at Easter Road were none too pleased when they found out how I had been supplementing my summer income of £12 a week from them, concerned that I might have done myself a mischief and picked up an injury.

By the time I parted company with Alfie and his stable of sprinters, he had put a good three yards on me in terms of pace and I could clock 10.3 seconds over 100 yards. We would round off the session with him massaging my legs before I'd pay him with my mum's money for the steak he had picked up from the butcher and which he insisted would be of enormous benefit. I needed to be pretty quick, too, in the dressing-room in the mornings, laying out all the kit for the first team and reserve professionals. As one of half a dozen groundstaff boys, it was my job to ensure their shirts, shorts, tracksuit tops and bottoms, plus appropriate footwear, were ready and waiting for the big men when they breezed in around ten o'clock. The players each had three pairs of boots, two with rubber and leather studs, and one we called 'snow boots'. These were basically American-style baseball boots, yet quite useless for playing in the snow itself. This, remember, was 1966, and major sporting arenas with undersoil heating were virtually unheard of. Matches in Scotland generally went ahead in deep mid-winter come hell or high water after the snow had been rolled away, and the players were used to performing ballets on ice and frosty surfaces. Easter Road was usually reserved for the major business of matches, so we trained at a variety of places, reached either in a minibus or by jogging through the streets.

When I turned professional at seventeen, my money increased to £20 a week, and Saturday nights were more fun than ever for my clique of Edinburgh youngbloods, plus Sandy Jardine, who was carving out a reputation for himself at Rangers. We used to get a wee bit of hassle in those days from local teenagers who resented our status or our clubs, or took exception to both. I don't imagine they were too impressed either with the way the local female talent gravitated in our direction. The wife of comedian Chic Murray took mercy on us and offered us the exclusive use of a function room at their hotel in Morningside. We were delighted to take up temporary residence in the hotel, installed a record player along with a first-choice collection of local girls and had our drinks sent up by rope and pulley from the lounge bar. There was no rush for final orders at 9.50 p.m., because this was a hotel rather than a bar, and we revelled in the special treatment before heading out on the town around 10.30 p.m. for discos and clubs such as The Place, Friscos, Romanos and McGoos.

Our cosy drinking den was rumbled all too soon, however: we were shopped to our employers when we invited some others up and things got out of hand. Instead of the usual four or five of us, there were twenty revellers partying away. I remember standing head down in front of Bob Shankly in his office, being torn off a strip like some naughty schoolboy. I felt guilty and owned up to overstepping the mark. Yes, I was drinking under-age, but it was a big thing among me and my mates if you could get served with a pint of heavy or lager when you were sixteen. It never quite tasted the same when you turned eighteen. Shankly softened after his initial outburst, marked my card and said, 'Look, Peter, Edinburgh is not that big a place, son. We get calls every week regarding players if they're out drinking and misbehaving. I'm not telling you not to have a drink after the game, but try and be less conspicuous.'

I would maybe go out drinking once during the week for a heavy session, but I would be home in bed by midnight, and it had no effect on me in the morning. Saturday nights were a different matter, however, and we really got stuck into the booze. This was par for the course. I was influenced by the older players. Instead of being different as a youngster among older team-mates, I just graduated to become one of them, I suppose. The prevailing attitude was 'live for the day': money was there to be spent.

One particular Saturday night is etched indelibly on my mind. How could I ever forget the first time I saw Joyce

Murray? She was a beautiful blonde of Italian descent (her mum was a Di Angelo) and was destined to become Mrs Marinello, my lifelong companion and mother of our two sons, Paul and Jon. We'd been playing away, at St Johnstone as I recall, and, as was our habit, we dashed back to Edinburgh, changed into some casual gear and went out on the town for as much beer as we could get down our necks before closing time. The Morningside hotel function room was out of bounds now, so we started off in a little local bar in Broughton, where I disgraced myself by being a bit sick over my nice new suit, having rushed my first four or five pints. I went home for a wash and to change into something fresh and a little more casual before catching up with the rest of the gang at Friscos.

Joyce caught my eye and captured my attention more or less immediately while Peter Whitten, who used to knock around with the group, made a beeline for her pal. I think Joyce knew I played for Hibs, and I wasn't backwards in coming forward, surprising her when I pinned her against a wall and started flashing the cash to impress her. A tidy wad of £10 notes was fished from my hip pocket, all for a round of four Coca-Colas. Over the top? Just a touch. Most of the discos were unlicensed, so the culture was to drink as much as your body could stand in the pubs before joining the queues to get into the clubs, which, as you can imagine, became horrendous after 10 p.m. As for Joyce, she told me later that she thought I was just a flash git, but she couldn't be certain just how good-looking I was because she didn't have her contact lenses in. Then it was on to the dance floor, where I was quite self-conscious despite all the alcohol. I may have had twinkling toes on a football pitch, but I wasn't the smoothest operator you've ever seen when it came to tripping the light fantastic. The evening came to a chaste conclusion with me and Peter dropping the girls off home by taxi before the cabbie took us on to Logie Green, where he lived in a cul-de-sac backing on to mine. Joyce thought the taxi was a welcome touch of class and rewarded me for my chivalry with her telephone number. Normally, she couldn't afford more than the last bus home.

The following Tuesday I met Joyce again for our first proper date at the Edinburgh Odeon, where one of us saw Barbra Streisand and Omar Sharif in *Funny Girl* – and the other didn't. Poor Joyce. Her contact lenses were hurting her like hell; she'd taken them out for the occasion and was too vain to wear her glasses.

Joyce belonged to a big family. Two of her uncles ran an ice cream factory, and I swiftly got the nod of approval from her dad, Jackie, which was just as well. He was a powerful character who had seen plenty of action during the Second World War in the desert with the air force and was now working as a postman and semi-professional drummer in a band. Then there was Joyce's mum, Laura, and younger sister, Janice.

Joyce and I were soon going steady, seeing each other three or four times a week – but never on a Sunday. That was strictly for the boys. We met at a local hotel for a two-hour lunchtime session on the beer, went home for a roast dinner and then drank the evening away. I very rarely suffered from hangovers and had no trouble handling my drink. All told, on a 'good' Sunday, I would maybe get through four or five pints of lager plus half a dozen Bacardis – the vodka didn't kick in until later in life. I was always home by 11 p.m., or midnight at the very latest. And I always managed to get in a solid shift of seven or eight hours' sleep. I was seventeen, but nobody batted an eyelid at my drinking. It was just part of the culture, and I certainly could see no harm in it. If there had been a father figure at the club, warning me to put a brake on my input, I would no doubt have laughed in his face, as you do, of course, when you're a teenager who thinks he knows it all.

We always trained on the Monday morning, and if it had been a good result on the Saturday, the work wasn't so rigorous. If we'd had a bad result, it was harder, but nothing to compare with what was in store for me later in my career. The first-team players quickly accepted me as one of their own, and, after I'd been a full-time professional for only a year, Bob Shankly gave me my league debut, away to Raith Rovers at Stark's Park. I never knew I was playing until we were in the dressing-room, forty-five minutes before kick-off. Bob wasn't a great talker; he simply said, 'You're playing today, Peter. Go out and enjoy yourself, beat your full-back and get your crosses in.' Everything happened so quickly; I didn't know what to think. I hadn't even played that many reserve games, so my debut wasn't overdue. I didn't have any nerves, I was purely happy that I had ninety minutes of football in front of me that afternoon, rather than watching from a seat in the stands. Easy come, easy go. That was me, to a tee.

The Raith game followed a handful for the third team and no more than a couple of dozen in the reserves. Alex Scott, who had played for Rangers and Everton, was the man whose number seven shirt I inherited. He had been very fast but was nearing the end of his career. The Hibs team of that era was packed with quality footballers, men such as Joe McBride, Peter Cormack, Pat Stanton, John Blackley, Colin Stein and Pat Quinn, who was serenaded from the terraces with lyrics from the Manfred Mann hit: 'Come all without, come all within, you'll not see nothing like the Mighty Quinn.' Football and pop culture were starting to collide head-on.

Dominant were two larger-than-life characters in Jimmy O'Rourke and Eric Stevenson, who, along with Willie Hunter, were members of the 'social committee'. You always knew the moment Jimmy clocked on for work in the morning, accompanied by a barrage of jokes and surprises. One of the favourite stunts he pulled on unsuspecting newcomers was to give them the telephone number of Edinburgh Zoo on a scrap of paper along with the name Mr C. Lyon and tell the wet-behind-the-ears rookie, 'You'd better ring this fella, he's already called here four times.' I often wonder how long it was before the patience of the zoo receptionist was strained and snapped by those requests to speak to a C. Lyon! Jimmy had a nickname for everybody and called me 'Nello the elephant', or just plain 'Nello' for short, while our keeper,

Willie Wilson, a bit overweight but nevertheless very sound, was dubbed 'Tubby Morton' in recognition of his similarity to the fictional Melchester Rovers custodian of that name in the *Roy of the Rovers* cartoon strip. Although Jimmy was perfectly happy to dish it out, he couldn't always take the humour when it was directed at him. Jimmy's eyes could give him the appearance of a wee Chinaman, and I once danced in front of him, singing the Goons' nonsense rhyme 'Ying tong iddle I po', which caused him to chase me, threatening strangulation – and worse. Mind you, Jimmy got his own back for that in spectacular fashion the night he arranged for me to lose my virginity, but we'll come to that in due course.

Eric's nickname was 'Brian Phelps' after the British Olympic gold medal-winning diver, and the tricky left-winger regularly won eight or nine penalties a season by haring into the penalty area at full tilt and collapsing as if he'd been hit by a train. Until referees cottoned on to this act after a few seasons, Eric was so adept at conning his way to spot-kicks, he made today's top 'fall guys' look like third-rate amateurs. Eric's other great claim to infamy is that he taught me how to drink, seriously. Hibs were a very sociable side who trained hard and drank hard. I'd been strictly a lager man to start with until I was introduced to that old smoothie, Mr Bacardi. 'Win or lose, have some booze', that was our creed – particularly after midweek matches, when we'd locate a bar which offered the opportunity for a lock-in and stay drinking there until the wee small hours. Eric took me under his wing when I was sixteen going on seventeen and he must have been thirty-ish and coming towards the end of his career. He probably felt he could pass on the benefit of his experience.

Four days after my debut against Raith, I was an instant success at Easter Road in a 3–0 victory over Dundee United on the bone-chilling afternoon of Saturday 6 January 1968, after which the *Edinburgh Evening News* gushed:

> Here is a guaranteed star of the future. Peter Marinello fitted into the team as though he had been a member of the attack for years. And, in addition to showing brilliant footwork, he produced a couple of beautifully judged through balls which split the United defence. I'd say he shows more ability than Jimmy Johnstone at a comparable age, and there is nothing wrong with his temperament.

Pat Quinn scored the first goal before Colin Stein, fresh from changing his footwear to something suitable for the icy conditions, added two more.

As an indication of how much football has been sanitised and generally cleaned up, United's ageing full-back Jimmy Briggs was actually applauded in the press for resisting the temptation to give me a thorough clogging and chopping me down to size. One critic reckoned: 'The veteran Taysider played Marinello extremely fair, even when the youngster was waltzing through in the latter stages. Many full-backs wouldn't have stood for it! It was good to see the youngster getting a chance to beat his man. Well done, Jimmy!' Strange that. Throughout my career I never once earned praise for making a full-back look good.

Immediately after that match, there was a rather sterner United due in town – the mighty Leeds United of Billy Bremner, Norman Hunter and Jack Charlton – for a European Fairs Cup tie. Hibs had made the third round in sensational fashion, achieving the near-impossible by overturning a 4–1 drubbing away to Napoli by thrashing the Italians 5–0 in the return leg in front of our own delirious fans. Now hopes were high in Edinburgh of another impressive feather in our cap because Don Revie's tough, ultra-professional English side were travelling from Elland Road with only a slender 1–0 lead for company. Willie Waddell's opinion was always worth respecting. The Rangers legend turned his hand to journalism in his later years and, previewing our Battle of Britain in the Scottish *Daily Express*, he ventured:

Outside-right Marinello played only his second first-team match on Saturday, but despite his inexperience I feel Bob Shankly will blood him in Europe, whether Alex Scott is fit or not. Marinello is the most brilliant youngster I have seen in many years, and he revealed such confidence in his own ability that Shankly can have no doubts about plunging him into what will be a red-hot tie.

So it was a source of major disappointment and frustration that I didn't see action against Leeds from nearer than my place on the substitutes' bench as Hibs were held 1–1, and Leeds won their fight for a place in the quarter-finals, although I thought we were the superior side over two legs. I had thought I was definitely starting that night, but Alex got the nod instead of me. Bob must have thought I was too young, even though I was on fire. Dear old Bob, he never filled my head with any complicated mumbo-jumbo about football. He just used to say, 'Go oot and run rings roon' them.' Full credit to Shankly, he never pegged me down on the right wing but, rather, granted me the licence to wander and cause damage wherever I fancied. I think that suited my style much better. Mind you, in his final match in charge, memorable for me running into a succession of dead ends, Bob's half-time rant incorporated the withering view: 'Bloody hell, Peter. We need two balls out there today – one for you and one for the rest of the team.'

There's a first time for everything, yet I don't imagine many sportsmen, or women for that matter, have been the subject of a live sex show when they've lost their virginity – let alone been kidnapped! It was 1968, the Swinging Sixties for some, I was eighteen and still a 'good' Catholic boy, though not for the want of trying, when Hibs were sponsored by a tobacco company to tour Africa after the season ended. So it was we faced a four-match itinerary: three games in Nigeria and one in Ghana just at the outbreak of the Biafran War. Very helpful, that.

My delicate state of sexual naivety became known to team-mate Jimmy O'Rourke, who took it upon himself to organise a nice little surprise – a late and overdue eighteenth birthday present, I believe he termed it. After a night's extremely cheap beer-drinking in Lagos, we returned to our luxury hotel, and I suddenly found myself shoulder-charged sideways through a door to find a lady of the night on the bed awaiting company, my company. She was a big, gorgeous girl in her twenties. How could I resist? Roared on by a crowd of half a dozen team-mates, I duly 'scored'. The lads stayed in the room the whole time after setting up a semi-circle of chairs around the bed. They were shouting things like 'Go on, my son' and 'Do the business' – although she was doing the business, astride me. I'd had a few drinks, which had loosened me up, and there was no sense of nerves or embarrassment. I had no inhibitions, in fact, and it was all over – bar the shouting – from start to finish in well under ten minutes, to a generous round of applause. The lads all chipped in maybe £20, tossing notes and coins on the bed, and my lover, who had been considerably more energetic than me, had a big smile on her face as she scooped up her clothes along with the money and repaired to the toilet to get dressed before leaving. She must have been laughing all the way to the bank, because £20 sterling in Nigeria then was a small fortune.

As for the kidnapping, that came about when our tour courier, a colossus and the spitting image of Ugandan dictator Idi Amin, took us to an island off Accra in Ghana for the day. The afternoon started bizarrely enough with a friendly fixture against a bunch of Russian sailors, who had emerged from a submarine. It was light-hearted, knockabout stuff, played in bare feet on the sandy beach. Most of our lads were just disappointed not to get an invitation back on board for some serious vodka-sampling when the Russians left. Then we spotted some canoes moored nearby and started messing around with them until the owners, clad only in loincloths and wearing tribal facial tattoos, emerged from a clearing in the jungle. Amused they were most certainly not, and I thought it was even less funny when I was suddenly snatched and frogmarched a good 200 yards away down the beach. The local fishermen, it seemed, were convinced we had damaged their boats and they indicated that, unless Hibernian Football Club were prepared to foot the bill for repairs, they could kiss goodbye to Peter Marinello. 'Bloody hell,' I thought, 'these guys are serious.' I had been restrained, both my hands firmly tied behind my back, as they drew my attention to the damage to the canoes, pointing and saying one word over and over again which I am sure translated into 'pay'. Quite what my fate would have been I shudder to think, and it took O'Rourke and co. – typically stingy Scots – forty minutes of haggling until they came up with the readies and my ordeal was over. Thanks a bundle, lads.

It was an extraordinary tour, not exactly helped by one African newspaper insisting that, far from being a football club, we were British soldiers in disguise, and it was quite unnerving when, travelling to one fixture, we were confronted at several checkpoints by youths as young as fourteen wielding sub-machine guns, intent on thoroughly searching our coach for any evidence we might be military men rather than sportsmen. Another match required us to travel in an army plane flying so low we almost brushed the treetops. 'Gotta do it this way, mister,' the pilot casually informed us. 'Otherwise we'll be spotted by radar and get shot down.' Some of the poverty I saw on that trip was unbelievable, diabolical, but the lads gave away lots of money to beggars and orphans, while others did their bit for the local economy, purchasing a new watch every day!

I was already a budding celebrity before the 1968–69 campaign kicked off, and Hibs travelled down to the Midlands for a friendly at Birmingham City, FA Cup semi-finalists the previous season. We were under severe first-half pressure, but the whole mood of the match was transformed when I replaced Alex Scott at the interval and started running at the City defenders. That lifted the team as a whole, and we went on to win 2–0, with goals from Peter Cormack and Allan McGraw. I was never interested in the cult of 'me', just content in the knowledge that my presence had lifted the team and put us in the perfect frame of mind for a great Scottish League Cup adventure, which began a few days later. Further on during that run, I seized the back-page headlines in a 3–0 home win over Raith Rovers with a couple of goals in the space of five second-half minutes.

We were an exciting young team, but our development was not helped in any way by the departure of Colin Stein. He was a massive personality who had blasted his way into the first team at eighteen and made scoring goals, lots of them, look easy. He was only twenty-one when he became the first £100,000 transfer between Scottish clubs, when he left for Rangers in October 1968. Bob Shankly was sick of selling his best players, and that was the final straw, forcing him, as he saw it, to resign. Bob had previously enjoyed enormous success as manager of Dundee, leading them to the league championship in 1962 and masterminding a heady European Cup adventure the following season which only ended in defeat in the semi-finals by AC Milan after Cologne, Sporting Lisbon and Anderlecht had been sent packing. But, crucially, he had seen stars such as the young Jimmy Gabriel, Ian Ure and Alan Gilzean sold against his wishes, and he once memorably chastised the board of directors, telling them, 'You lot would sell our groundsman if you got an offer.' When history started repeating itself at Easter Road, he decided he'd had enough.

As for me, it was a telling sign of things to come.

Another stand-out memory was facing Celtic, and Tommy Gemmell in particular, in the Scottish League Cup final in the spring of 1969. That Celtic side was awesome, as you would expect for a collection of men who had won the European Cup by beating Inter Milan two years previously. Despite the result, a 6–2 drubbing for Hibs, I produced a very decent display against Gemmell. I couldn't believe all the jokes he kept cracking that afternoon at Hampden Park, no doubt attempting to disturb my concentration. I thought I was playing against Danny Kaye, the American comic, but Celtic had the last laugh because, despite the fact that I gave Gemmell a bit of a chasing, too many of my crosses ended up in the ultra-safe hands of their goalkeeper, John Fallon, while I could grudgingly appreciate the brilliance at the other end of their winger, Jimmy Johnstone, who was absolutely blinding. That final against the recent champions of Europe, or, to be strictly accurate, my performance in it, made me realise I had the talent and ability to make it as a footballer. I could show flashes of bloody arrogance, I trained hard and I could party even harder but I never missed a day's training through anything but injury and genuine illness.

I didn't have the slightest inkling that the 1969–70 campaign would be my last at Hibs when we kicked off with a 3–0 defeat at Ayr United. It was a totally false start, not at all representative of our collective ability, and a magnificent seven straight wins later Hibs were sitting proudly on top of the Scottish First Division. At home we disposed of St Mirren 2–0, Partick 5–1, Raith 3–1 with the help of a goal from me, then Morton 1–0 as the Easter Road attendances leaped by 50 per cent. If that was good, our results on the road were even more impressive that autumn. The mighty Celtic were conquered 2–1 at Parkhead on 13 September, then we proved ourselves masters of Edinburgh in a 2–0 triumph over Hearts at

Tynecastle before travelling to face Rangers on 11 October.

I sensed Willie Waddell didn't know whether to laugh or cry after we had triumphed 3–1 at Ibrox to go top of the league. Three times I streaked through the middle of a Rangers defence that barely knew which way to turn and I scored two goals in a victory that acclaimed our arrival as a major force – and my arrival as the hottest property in Scottish football. It was great, really great, to beat Rangers at Ibrox. And the way we did it was even more pleasing. I was a bit nervous until I scored the first goal but after that I was brimming with confidence. The whole team played their socks off, and we fully deserved to win.

Willie Macfarlane had replaced Bob Shankly as manager and he predicted we would win, simply because he felt we possessed superior players, and Waddell told his readers in the Scottish *Daily Express*: 'Just how true that was, I did not appreciate until I had seen the Young Lions of Easter Road give Rangers a lesson in all the finer arts of the game. For Rangers did not have players like Marinello, Stanton, Jones, Blackley and Stevenson. Not since the days of the Famous Five have Hibs had such a galaxy of footballing stars. And the brightest of these was Marinello.' He reckoned I was the most exciting footballing personality to hit Scotland for a long, long time – another George Best in the making, full of confidence and brimming over with talent.

If I had a pound for every time I've been compared with George over the years, I would be an extremely wealthy man. I admit it was a burden. I always wanted to be Peter

Marinello, an entertaining footballer pure and simple, and not labelled the 'Second George Best'. Of course, there were similarities – long hair, carrying the ball at speed, taking players on, fashion, wine, women and song to excess. I had to smile when one wag in the London press reckoned I never even became the 'First Peter Marinello' because I failed to realise my full potential. Life can be cruel at times, as I know to my cost. I heard, too, that George drank because he was shy, although he was supremely confident on the park. That sounds very much like me. Like George, I've always stuck away more than my fair share of booze, but it never killed me, and I still enjoy a good drink from time to time.

Scotland manager Bobby Brown was there to watch me at Ibrox, although he had already selected his squad to face West Germany in a World Cup qualifier in Hamburg, and Waddell, happy to champion me in the press, added: 'All the finer points of the game are there. All the skill one looks for in an international. What a tragedy that a player with such talent should be on the sidelines as Scotland face a vital World Cup commitment in 10 days' time.' The Rangers result didn't go down too well with the bookies, and there were a few dark rumblings from turf account- ants in Glasgow and Edinburgh because a lot of money had been wagered on Hibs to win, while Rangers at home to anyone bar Celtic in those days were always installed as favourites. The legendary 'Slim' Jim Baxter had returned from Sunderland to more or less wind up his career with the Gers and presented a distressing sight that day. He was 'slim' only in talent – the rest of him had mushroomed, and Jim, a notoriously heavy drinker, was clearly unfit and looking the worse for wear.

Rangers away proved to be my absolute high spot, however. I was struggling with a damaged ankle now and missed the next two matches as we were held 2–2 at Kilmarnock and stumbled to defeat by a solitary goal at St Johnstone. Still, I had impressed Brown sufficiently to be called up by Scotland for the last and now meaningless World Cup qualifier against Austria in Vienna. The national side had gone down 3–2 to the Germans, a result which laid to rest any chance we had of reaching the finals in Mexico the following summer. Now was the time to introduce some fresh young faces, thought Brown – and that's why I was selected in a pool of twenty-two players alongside fellow newcomers Willie Johnston, the Rangers winger, and Manchester United's Francis Burns, who had achieved the not inconsiderable feat of replacing Scotland legend Paddy Crerand in the first team at Old Trafford. I had my fingers crossed I would be picked, but it was still a thrill to hear the news confirmed. Delighted though I was, the joy was muted by the ankle injury, although Hibs assured Bobby that I would be fit for action in the Prater Stadium. I didn't make it, Scotland lost 2–0 to Austria on 5 November, and by the following April, when the Home International series rolled around again and I was at Arsenal, I think Bobby had lost interest in me.

I suspected my time might be coming to an end at Hibs one particular Thursday after a lot of newspaper speculation, suggesting as much. I was nursing the injury and feeling thoroughly pissed off with life after Macfarlane had found out that I'd been out drinking while I was unable to train for two or three weeks. So when Eric Stevenson called to ask, 'Are you coming for one, or what, son?' I jumped at his kind offer to drown my sorrows. One became twenty-six Bacardis apiece. Eric held court at the Saxe-Coburg Hotel in Edinburgh, where he knew the owner, and a fair few other bars were taken into account, from what I can remember. Eric was a clever winger and someone I looked up to, but I suppose I was easily led, not for the first time in my life. Peter Cormack, who was to leave for Nottingham Forest in March 1970 for £80,000, and Willie Hunter tried their level best to keep me on the straight and narrow. Eric had played with Willie Macfarlane, knew him well and said the manager wouldn't stand in the way of a move. The fact of the matter is Hibs knew they could get £100,000 for me and the club didn't want me coming back from injury in less than peak condition in case it scuppered their chances of selling me. But I hadn't been thinking about a transfer, I didn't want to leave.

It was the deep frustration of being out with that ankle injury that led to an acceleration in my drinking for a spell. I would go into the club for treatment at 10 a.m. and by two o'clock in the afternoon I would be chasing pints of lager with Bacardi in a hotel bar until 7 p.m. about three times a week. Basically, I let my fitness slip. Peter Cormack, in particular, preached the virtue of hard training, and I would join him for voluntary extra work in the afternoons if I wasn't drinking. That sounds very noble, doesn't it? The truth of the matter is that extra training for me did not amount to very much more than firing balls from all angles into Peter, who worked at bringing them under control. He was more dedicated than me off the pitch and didn't drink that much. Other afternoons were idled away in snooker halls and frittered away in bookies by both Peter and myself. He was red hot on the green baize, would give me a start of twenty-five points and still have the game and my money in his pocket before the colours. The manager, meanwhile, was worried I was in danger of becoming uncontrollable and that my lifestyle was erratic. I was just coming back from injury and Hibs did nothing to discourage speculation that I was available – if the price was right.

I scored a goal, the only one of the match, at Dundee United in my comeback on 15 November after we had been under the cosh, and Joe McBride suddenly found a pass to set me free. Then my market value increased when I was picked to play for Scotland Under-23s at home against France. We won 4–0 with a couple of goals apiece from John O'Hare and Peter Lorimer, but I was restricted to a brief appearance as a substitute in place of Aberdeen's Davie Robb.

Back in domestic action, I played in a thrilling 4–3 home win over Ayr before making my fourteenth and final league appearance of the season for Hibs on 27 December 1969 in a 1–0 defeat at Dundee as speculation I would soon be moving reached a crescendo. It was a good Hibs team, and if players such as Colin Stein, Cormack and myself had stayed, the Old Firm would have felt a definite shift of power to the east of the country. But you could never say that Hibs were going to keep their players, not on gates of around 9,000, despite finishing third in the league, as they did come the end of the season behind champions Celtic and runners-up Rangers. At that time, if anybody looked like becoming anything, he was going to be transferred because the club needed money.

I honestly didn't want to leave Hibs, but I was a success, and, like my idol George Best, I had got there too quickly: that success had come easily, too easily. I was still training hard but, by Christmas 1969, probably drinking too much, too often. And I was still not yet out of my teens.

CHAPTER 4

Me and My Shadow

Everything changed with that ankle injury. The problem started when I got a kick in a pre-season friendly match which I shrugged off as a mistimed tackle, rather than anything malicious. That sort of thing was a common occurrence, given my pace and the habit I had of taking the ball very close to defenders before whipping it away from under their noses. Another kick merely served to aggravate the problem. The injury was diagnosed as ligament damage, and my haste to return to the team prompted further trouble. Hibs were flying high at the top of the league after I'd help them beat Rangers. I sensed something special might be in the air at Easter Road and I desperately wanted to be a part of it.

Our trainer, physiotherapist, launderette manager and virtual chief cook and bottle-washer was Tom McNiven, good when it came to restoring players' fitness, although a bit old-fashioned and set in his ways. Many of the top professionals in Scotland would make a beeline for Archie Campbell in Dalkeith if they were injured. Archie had a brilliant reputation, although he frequently had his patients screaming in agony because his preferred mode of treatment was to dig his fingers right into the source of the trouble and get a literal 'feel' for the root cause of the problem. I was happy to put up with that, but Tom's nose was put out of joint when he got wind of it, and my 'disloyalty', if you can call it that, was duly reported back to Willie Macfarlane, who had already made his mind up that I was more trouble than I was worth.

Peter Cormack often gave me a lift in his car from the bottom of the street where I lived at No. 10 Logie Green Road with my parents and sisters, or I would just as happily cover the three-mile journey to the ground by bus. This particular morning I missed Peter and was stationed at the bus stop, waiting to travel in for treatment from Tom McNiven, when a car sounded its horn driving past and pulled up twenty yards down the road. I hobbled off to investigate and discovered the driver was none other than Arthur Duncan, the Partick Thistle winger I'd lined up against earlier in the season.

'What brings you to this neck of the woods, Arthur?' I asked innocently.

'Really, don't you know?' he grinned. 'I'm going to the ground. Jump in. I've come for signing talks – and I heard you are on the way to Arsenal.'

For a fleeting moment, it crossed my mind that Hibs

would be better than ever with me flying down one wing and Arthur patrolling the other, before sickening reality hit me like a punch in the stomach. I never wanted to leave the club, and this was the first piece of concrete evidence that I was going to be transferred, and suddenly lots of things began to fall into place. For several weeks now I had been aware of a shifty-looking guy wearing a hat pulled down over his eyes skulking in the doorways late at night near my house. I thought he was a bit creepy, especially as he was there one time when I strolled home at two in the morning after a particularly boisterous night on the tiles. The guy in the shadows was like some kind of spy from *The Third Man*. He might have been employed by Hibs – but now I strongly suspected he was connected with me moving.

Speculation had reached fever pitch in the month I'd been out with that dodgy ankle. If truth be told, my form had tailed off before the injury, although not dramatically, and now there was massive speculation in the newspapers that Manchester United, Tottenham and Arsenal were all interested in me. Many people, in fact, had Spurs marked down as front-runners – but they weren't quick enough off the mark when it came to negotiating with Hibs.

It was approaching the Christmas/New Year period, when the games came thick and fast, and it was clear I would need another two or three weeks to get fully fit. Stories started filtering back to the boss that I wasn't looking after myself properly off the pitch, that some of my nocturnal activities were not in the best interests of the club. If Hibs wanted rid of me, better sooner than later.

My world was changing, rapidly. My relationship with Joyce reached a sudden crisis when her dad, Jackie, decided to cash in his lot as an Edinburgh postie and accepted the invitation of the £10-a-head assisted passage to emigrate to Australia. I'm not sure Joyce's mum Laura was too keen on the prospect of upping sticks and moving to the other side of the world to start a new life in a suburb of Sydney, while my lovely Joyce was torn between her family and me. And as for me, I was on my way out of Edinburgh too – to London. Joyce was only eighteen. I sympathised greatly with her jumble of emotions and decided to force the issue when I laid it on the line quite simply: 'Don't go to Australia, Joyce. I love you. Let's get married instead.' Nothing had been planned. Like so much of my life, that proposal just sort of happened – but I have never regretted it for one minute.

Rumours were rife in both Edinburgh and London that I was on my way to Highbury when George Smith, the Hibs chief scout, and I slipped in the back door at Edinburgh airport, or Turnhouse as it was then known, and I was smuggled on to a plane bound for Heathrow at roughly the same moment Hibs were telling anyone who cared to listen that I was going nowhere.

Arsenal always did everything in five-star style when I was there, whether it be luxury hotels or the chauffeur-driven car despatched to convey George and me to Highbury. The ground was swarming with press when we arrived and, again, I felt like a fugitive on the run as I was bundled through a side entrance to be met by a director. It was all a bit of a pantomime, with Arsenal denying any knowledge of my presence. I might have looked out of place, but George didn't. In fact, he might very well have been mistaken for a club director himself, with his immaculate collar and tie, slicked-back hair and Sean Connery brogue. He cut the very image of an Old Etonian, but he was in awe of everything to do with Arsenal. I was ushered into a room where we were joined by the club captain and Northern Ireland skipper, Terry Neill. Remember, I was basically just a young lad and not very streetwise, so that's why I at first confused Terry with Bertie Mee, the manager. All the Irish blarney came pouring out from Terry, who really did have the gift of the gab as he sold Arsenal to me lock, stock and barrel. I thought, 'Bollocks, I'll just sign for them,' but there was a nagging problem. I didn't really want to go but, equally, I'm one of those guys who didn't like to let anyone down. I've always been the man who can't say no.

The club doctor arrived to give me a thorough examination. I was a right slip of a lad at 10 st 2 lb and whippet-thin with it, although I had good thighs on me and could run like the wind. I recall the doc smiling as he turned to Bertie and announced, 'We're paying £100,000 for the player, and there's nothing of him, but he's sound.' With that, Bertie casually asked me if I fancied joining in a training match about to start between the first team and reserves. That was no problem as far as I was concerned – I wasn't frightened of giving an audition right there and then and was loaned a pair of snowboots with rubber soles which suited me down to the rock-hard ground. Mind you, all hell would have broken loose had I picked up an injury and put the deal in jeopardy – or worse. The conditions were very much to my liking, and after forty minutes Bertie hauled me off, declaring: 'That's fine, son. You've done enough.'

I was far from impressed by my future team-mates on the evidence of those forty minutes, however. Arsenal looked distinctly average, a bit of a collection of mid-table mediocrities, to be honest. There was this sticking point, too. I thought if Hibs were getting £100,000 out of the deal, the least they could do was put their hands in their pockets and give me some of that money. After all, the transfer was never initiated by me, it was their doing.

Joining Arsenal was a strange transfer from start to finish. I made it plain that I wasn't signing anything until I'd had some money from Hibs, even though the Gunners were giving me £5,500 to join them on a three-year contract with a three-year option. I was just like a piece of meat, at least that's the way it felt. I had given Hibs excellent value in over fifty games all told, and now it was time for them to give me something in return.

George and I flew back on the 6.10 p.m. plane to Edinburgh after looking at a property in Barnet which the club thought I might fancy. We were accompanied by Arsenal's chief scout, Gordon Clark, a lovely man from Derbyshire who was later largely instrumental in bringing such gifted young Irishmen as Liam Brady, David O'Leary and Frank Stapleton to London N5. It dawned on me that Gordon might well have been the character spying on me in Logie Green, but, in any event, he wasn't coming home with me that night and stayed in a hotel in Edinburgh city centre instead.

The morning dawned, and I marched straight down to Easter Road and told the manager Willie Macfarlane straight, 'I don't want to go, but I know you're getting £100,000 for me, so I'm only signing for Arsenal if you give me £1,500.' Willie was in an awkward position and was pushing for me to go because he'd already agreed to shell out £55,000 for my replacement, Arthur Duncan, and was loath to sanction any extras for me. Still, a meeting with W. P. Harrower was hastily convened at which the chairman appeared rather nonplussed, and he muddied the waters still further by telling me, 'If you don't want to go, then don't go, Peter,' but I think they agreed to give me £1,000, and the manager claimed, 'Peter, three months ago you were worth £150,000, but you're getting a bit uncontrollable.' Uncontrollable was a bit thick as far as I was concerned, but he was entitled to his opinion, and Arthur would give him less trouble.

Still, nothing was cut and dried. There was speculation that Hibs feared Partick might suddenly up their asking price for Arthur if they knew my transfer had gone through at £100,000, and also that the club didn't want my move to damage their gate for the New Year's Day derby with Hearts.

Manchester United had been showing an interest, and

the following day I was due to fly back to London once more to meet the Tottenham manager, Bill Nicholson. George and I were actually in the taxi heading for Turnhouse, and he must have sensed my unease because he asked, 'Do you really want to see Spurs, Peter?'

'No,' I replied. 'Let's get it done with Arsenal.' I liked Gordon Clark, he was understandably dead keen on me joining the Gunners, and it was a combination of his faith in my ability and Terry Neill's rampant enthusiasm that swung it.

I thought I had my head screwed on and my feet on the ground, but what did I know? I was just a working-class boy with a talent for football from a humble Edinburgh prefab, and nothing had prepared me for a fantasy world in London.

CHAPTER 5

Arsenal's Best Man

I officially became Arsenal property for £100,000, the club's first six-figure purchase, on Friday 2 January 1970, accompanied by a wave of publicity and the inevitable comparisons with George Best at Manchester United. We were both slim, young, dark-haired wingers with an eye for fashion and a talent to entertain and excite crowds. The difference was that George was a genius, and my genius lay in attracting trouble. Rolf Harris was top of the hit parade with 'Two Little Boys'. Enough said.

Uncle Leno and George Smith accompanied me on the flight south, only this time our travel plans weren't cloaked in secrecy, and I entered through the front door into the famous marble hall at Highbury – or was it Hollywood? – after signing autographs for a smattering of young boys as the television cameras rolled and a posse of photographers snapped away merrily. It felt crazy, almost as if I was potholing and there was only one way to go. 'Well, I cannae go back to Hibs now,' I thought before taking a deep breath in Bertie Mee's office and scribbling my name on a rather more significant document than the page of a child's autograph book. The manager made it abundantly clear that he was signing me with the future in mind. I would have to fight for my place, and he cautioned that I'd find it very different from Scottish football, where afternoon training was the exception rather than the rule. The warnings all washed over my head in the general euphoria and the anticipation of training and playing my first match. I was still young and learning the game. I never paid much attention to what Bertie said to me at the time. I thought I'd just get in the team, take it from there and play it off the cuff. I was never privy either to how Hibs and Arsenal carved up my additional money, but my signing-on fee magically increased from £5,500 to £7,500, which I received legitimately through my contract.

After a swift private signing ceremony and the manager's cautionary words, we stepped on to the hallowed turf for the benefit of Fleet Street's finest and were pictured with the North Bank terraces in the background, me wearing this rather fine cream-coloured French-style mac which I'd bought at Jaeger back home in Princes Street. Within weeks, every stylish young man about town seemed to be wearing that coat or something remarkably similar. The signing was dutifully reported on the BBC television nine o'clock news and one Arsenal director said,

'We've signed the nearest thing in football to the Beatles.' No pressure there, then.

Leno, George and I flew back to Edinburgh late that afternoon with Gordon Clark in tow. The registration went through far too late for me to play in Arsenal's 1–1 home draw the following day against Blackpool in the FA Cup – the qualification period was a fortnight – so I had a few days at home gathering my belongings amid a bout of fond farewells and 'see-you-soons'. I also popped into Easter Road with £50 for the lads to have a good drink on me, as was the custom whenever a player was transferred, and my mum's parting shot was: 'Keep your hands in your pockets, son, and your money in the bank.' I didn't pay much attention to those words, either, as it turned out.

I returned on my own to London, where Arsenal generously paid for me to stay in the Alexander Hotel, near the tube station at Finsbury Park. I had precious little time to settle in or find my bearings before we were on our way north for an overnight stay, and I made my debut against Manchester United at Old Trafford on Saturday 10 January. I had a suspicion I might be playing on the journey in the thirteen-strong party because George Graham was carrying an injury, although I couldn't be 100 per cent sure until we were in the visitors' dressing-room, so there was no chance of organising tickets for a coach-load of Marinellos and Murrays from Scotland to be in attendance. That was disappointing, but maybe Bertie reckoned the less time I had to worry about the match, the better. I thought the manager might keep me for a game at Highbury to blood me in the First Division.

Best was missing, fined £100 by the English FA and starting a twenty-eight-day suspension for knocking the ball out of referee Jack Taylor's hands at the end of a League Cup semi-final tie with neighbours Manchester City. Georgie Boy's absence reduced the hype a fraction, to the disappointment of the media, so there was just the one skinny winger with long dark hair and his shirt flapping defiantly outside his shorts in the spotlight. I walked down the tunnel and up some steps, and the atmosphere generated by an attendance of over 41,000 for this league fixture just blew me away. I had only ever sampled vibes like that once before, when 74,000 watched the Celtic–Hibs Scottish League Cup final. This felt frightening, yet good at the same time, despite the wolf whistles I inevitably attracted from the Stretford End.

Bobby Charlton had a quiet match for United, which surprised me, because I thought he was a terrific player, and it was a pleasure to be on the same park as him. Charlton had some nice things to say about me in Monday's papers, however. He was impressed by the way I had the confidence to take on players and beat them, and by the fact I wasn't overawed by the atmosphere. David Sadler, an England centre-half, was also gracious, and said, 'Peter has a touch of glamour and showed us he has a lot of ability besides with the ball. Considering this was his first game in English football, he made an impact that augurs well.' Sadler even went as far as to claim I had a sound appreciation of the game and what it demanded. I wouldn't have gone quite that far myself, but new team-mate John Radford went still further, confidently predicting, 'We've signed a world-beater.'

In 2004, I watched on telly as another nineteen-year-old forward scored a hat-trick on his first appearance at Old Trafford, as United beat Fenerbahce 6–2 in the Champions League. I'd like to think Wayne Rooney will enjoy a longer, more productive career than I managed.

My first couple of touches against United were distinctly promising, and then I scored in the fourteenth minute. Our goalkeeper, Bob Wilson, banged a clearance downfield, and I challenged for it near the halfway line, without getting a touch. The ball bounced and both I and a United player missed it. I was first to recover and shimmied a couple of times, leaving Sadler and another defender trailing in my wake. The keeper, Alec Stepney, came out, and I just sidefooted the ball low and wide of him. The instant the ball hit the net it seemed like the best thing in the world that could have happened to me, but that goal became a rod for my back, a bloody millstone. After that, I was expected to score every time I pulled on a pair of boots, and the great expectation weighed me down.

The headline writers with 'Peter the Great' up their sleeves were doubtless as upset as me when United retaliated with two goals to take the points. By an odd coincidence, it was another youngster of Italian descent, Carlo Sartori, who equalised in first-half injury time. Willie Morgan, a fellow Scot, scored the winner three minutes into the second period when Terry Neill was pressured into an unwise back pass. It dawned on me that Arsenal weren't the greatest team in the world. In fact, I would have taken Hibs to have beaten either team that day.

I had another extremely important date the day after my debut – with Joyce at Heathrow. They do say it's a woman's prerogative to keep a man waiting, but I thought Joyce was pushing it when her flight from Edinburgh was held up for nearly six hours because of fog. Joyce was joining me in London, the idea being that we would announce our official engagement a fortnight later. Our airport meeting was captured exclusively by a *Daily Express* photographer. Nearly everything I did in the papers was exclusive to the *Express* because Joyce's uncle, Jim Murray, was their assistant features editor in Fleet Street, and he also swiftly became my agent. It was agreed that she would move in with his family in Orpington, Kent. There was no suggestion of us shacking up together before we got married because the Murray clan would not have stood for it and, besides, I was in club digs.

On Monday I introduced Joyce to the delights and variety of shopping in the King's Road, Chelsea, where I treated her to a leather jacket and grey trousers, topped off by a tasty tam-o'-shanter, while I splashed out on a very fetching little number in Donegal check from Just Men, just one of three additions to my wardrobe of suits that week.

Tuesday found me making by first appearance at Highbury, against Rouen in the European Fairs Cup. The first leg of this third-round tie had ended 0–0 in France before Christmas, and now we scraped through with a solitary goal from Jon Sammels in injury time after I had come within a whisker of scoring again. The Rouen keeper, Pierre Rigoni, a French Under-23 international, defied us virtually on his own. I felt certain I had beaten him fifteen minutes from time with a bullet of a shot, only for Rigoni to materialise out of thin air, catapulting himself across goal to make a magnificent one-handed save.

The matches were coming thick and fast, but I was ineligible for the next trip to Lancashire two nights later, left to fret about whether I'd fit in despite my dream debut at Old Trafford and coming so close to bagging another goal against Rouen, while Arsenal were just plain worried when a 2–0 lead in the FA Cup replay at Blackpool ended in a 3–2 defeat by a club a division below us.

My second league match was against Chelsea, and I thought: 'This is easy,' as I twice sped past Eddie McCreadie, a very talented full-back. But the third time I tried it, Eddie matched me step for step and was right there on my toes and in my face, looking menacing and threatening retribution. It was an early indication that life in the big league would be no bed of roses, or poses come to that, although Eddie said graciously afterwards, 'Peter's got everything there already, though Arsenal fans perhaps may not appreciate it all until next season. But once he fully settles in to the increased tempo of football in England – always a bit of an early problem for young Scots, as I've found myself – I'm sure they'll agree manager Bertie Mee didn't pay Hibs a penny too much.'

Chelsea were an exciting team of emerging talents and murdered us 3–0, with goals from John Hollins, Ian Hutchinson and Tommy Baldwin, but there was an unexpected silver lining to the cloud of a depressing defeat. A combination of my home league debut, a midweek European victory and the attraction of having the boys from Stamford Bridge over for a London derby swelled the crowd to a bumper 51,000. It was also my introduction to a complicated bonus system. My basic pay was £55 a week with a straight £55 extra for an away win, but, on top of that, the first-team squad also shared half the gate money on any home crowd over 26,000. David Court hadn't played against Chelsea, but he was still rubbing his hands with anticipation in the dressing-room afterwards at the prospect of what he calculated would be an extra £120 in his pay packet that week because of the monster gate. We all got that £120 bonus, and I celebrated by taking Joyce into the West End for a slap-up dinner and a show.

Within weeks of arriving at Arsenal, I had been booked to appear on *Top of the Pops* – and that kickstarted a feeding frenzy for my services. The idea was for me to present a silver disc to Sandie Shaw for her smash-hit 'Puppet on a String', and this was a major honour for me because I was a big fan of hers. I was knocked out to be invited down to BBC Television Centre at Shepherds Bush with Joyce, who made sure I didn't get too carried away by the sight of so many mini-skirted girls. It was certainly a little bit different to my only previous occasion in a television studio appearing with Jimmy Hill on *Match of the Day*. I was extremely nervous before that national TV exposure on Saturday night with Jimmy in my first month at Highbury, and the make-up girls worked extra time on me to cover up the sweat on my face – and a nasty little outbreak of acne. I must have looked OK to Jimmy, though, because after the show he offered to act as my agent. But I felt loyalty to Jim Murray and declined the kind offer.

However, if I was shaking in my boots at the prospect of appearing on *Top of the Pops* in front of the many millions who tuned in devotedly every Thursday night, Joyce and myself included, then Sandie's nerves were evidently in an even worse state. I never did meet her. I don't know whether she didn't want publicity with a footballer or if she was just too shy, but she threw a wobbly at the last moment and refused point-blank to emerge from her dressing-room. Now that threw a spanner in the works, even though the programme was recorded on a Wednesday. The producer, Stanley Dorfman, was reluctant to do too much back-tracking and the disc jockey Tony Blackburn had already introduced the show by revealing I was a guest. There had already been loads of publicity about my forthcoming appearance in any case. Some quick thinking behind the scenes rustled up a batch of singles for me to present to the best young dancer in the audience and a similar package to the best-dressed girl, a lovely lass called Celia Hunter with outrageously long eyelashes. Ben Elton, the comedian, captured my moment with Celia for posterity on one of his Christmas videos on telly, in which he took great delight in taking the piss out of footballers.

My disappointment at being snubbed by Sandie was softened to some extent by meeting Billy Preston, who sang his hit 'All That I've Got, I'm Gonna Give to You'. I rated him one of the best artists of the era, a man who really felt every word he sang. And as for Tony Blackburn, he took the mickey out of my Scots accent but turned out to be another consummate professional. He never once flapped or lost his temper with people who worked under him when things didn't go according to plan that day. I respected that.

The world of pop music was central to my generation, and I thought it was the ultimate accolade when I was soon serenaded from the Highbury terraces, where the fans adapted the chorus from 'Nah, Nah, Hey, Hey, Kiss Him Goodbye' by Steam into 'Marinello, Marinello, Hey, Hey, Marinello' as well as converting The Sandpipers' 'Guantanamera' into 'One Marinello . . . there's only one Marinello', while Donovan's huge hit 'Mellow Yellow' was another favourite which lent itself perfectly to a chorus of 'They call him Marinello'.

My little stint on *Top of the Pops* led, in turn, to offers of more 'work', if you can call it that. That brush with Miss Hunter's eyelashes brought a bizarre approach from two brothers, who claimed to be millionaires and boasted of being extremely well connected in the film world. They wanted to train me as an international make-up artist in my spare time outside Highbury. Jim Murray asked me if

I was interested in meeting them, but I already had more than enough on my plate, and I shudder to think what Peter Storey and Bob McNab would have made of my second career. I wonder now whether I'd have been wiser taking up the offer, mind you. Of course, the brothers only fancied me for the publicity and prestige the name Peter Marinello would have brought to their business and they weren't proposing to pay me a bean, just provide me with a skill. But that skill would certainly have come in useful when the time came to hang up my boots and I experienced some lean years. That's the problem of being a teenager with the world at your feet and money to burn. You think you are immortal, you think this is the way it's always going to be . . . like the line from *Fame*: 'I'm gonna live for ever, I'm gonna learn how to fly.' Only you wake up one day, and it's all gone, flown out of the window. I'd left school with meagre qualifications, taken two O-levels at night school in English and maths and failed them both. I could have done with something to fall back on when the bubble burst and my football went flat.

And all too often I struggled to live up to the image other people created of me. Record executives were soon beating a path to my door, and beating a hasty retreat when they discovered that, while I might have looked like an angel in their eyes, I certainly couldn't sing like one. Pye were extremely interested in commissioning Tony Hatch and Jackie Trent to make things work for me. I was suitably impressed because the couple were eminent composers, arrangers and producers in the pop world – a bit like the Stock, Aitken and Waterman of their day. Tony and Jackie did the first TV theme tune for *Crossroads* and lots of great stuff with the likes of Petula Clark and the Searchers. Into the studio I went to cut a demo tape and I duly treated, if that's the right word, the Pye executives to a rendition to Herman's Hermits' 'I'm into Something Good' and the Beatles' 'Ticket to Ride'. The reaction was devastating: the silence when I finished was almost deafening. I tried to make light of it and joked: 'I usually sing much better after a drink,' but I knew that 'Peter Marinello – Pop Star' was never going to happen in a million years when a Pye man asked, 'Err, do you think you could recite some poetry for us instead, Peter?' We went our separate ways, both sides heaving a sigh of relief.

Another brush with the pop world came at a party at Peter Simpson's house. Our central defender was a high-quality, cultured defender in the style of Alan Hansen, although you wouldn't always think so, given his propensity to stick away double brandies, accompanied by large Havana cigars. Peter was a gregarious sort, and it was to one of his bashes that Bob McNab brought the very beautiful, and young, Olivia Newton-John. She had just made it big with 'If Not for You', but became extremely embarrassed when the despicable duo of Eddie Kelly and myself serenaded her with our version. Cue the exit of one Olivia Newton-John, swiftly followed by a glowering McNab.

Melody Maker were keen to follow up my trend-setting image and introduced me to their readership in such glowing terms: 'Peter Marinello is typical of the younger generation of professional footballers. Bought by Arsenal for £100,000 from the Scottish club Hibernian a few weeks ago, Peter has taken to the London life like a duck to water and the scene has taken to him. Long-haired and deceptively fragile-looking, he shares with George Best a liking for visiting clubs and discotheques after the big match on Saturdays. He writes a column for the *Daily Express* and is keen and knowledgeable about pop.' I spent an entertaining morning in the *Melody Maker* offices, listening to eleven new singles in a section entitled 'Blind Date' and here were my immediate verdicts:

Plastic Ono Band: Instant Karma (Apple) 'That's John and Yoko – I heard it when I went to *Top of the Pops* last week. That's a fine sound, and it's a lot better than their last one – "Cold Turkey" wasn't it? I usually like what Lennon does, and this is a good party record. John and Yoko are all right – it's up to them to do what they want to do. Perhaps it's always not what I'd do, but they are certainly honest.'

Peter Sarstedt: Without Darkness, There's No Light (United Artists) 'It's not Peter Sarstedt, is it? That's not nearly as good as "Frozen Orange Juice". He's not a bad singer, but this won't be a hit – it's too ordinary, all on one level. But his first two records were so good that they must be very hard to follow up.'

Harry J & The All Stars: The Big Three (Trojan) 'It's got a fairground sort of backing. It's pleasant enough, but I don't really like it and I can't see it being a hit. I'm a big Georgie Fame fan really – he's making some great records now, much better than when he was doing all that jazz stuff.'

Love Sculpture: In the Land of the Few (Parlophone) 'Is it the Who? It's quite like them. It could get in your mind if it got enough plays, but it doesn't get you the first time. Hey, that sounds like "Zorba the Greek"! It's OK – good for discos but not just for listening.'

Cuff Links: When Julie Comes Around (MCA) 'No. It's a bit childish, and they seem to be in such a hurry to get it over, don't they? Oh, it's the Cuff Links, is it? That's not half as good as "Tracy" which I liked, and it won't get anywhere.'

Jimmy Ruffin: Farewell Is a Lonely Sound (Tamla Motown) 'Is it the Miracles? Jimmy Ruffin, eh? It's quite good, but it would have had a better chance if they'd released it before Christmas. I like Tamla stuff, especially the Miracles and the Temptations, and I got a couple of their old LPs today. But this is not too strong.'

Edwin Hawkins Singers: I Believe (Buddah) 'That's a good start – oh, it's the Edwin Hawkins Singers. I saw them doing this song on the *David Frost Show*. It's a good record, but too many artists have done this song. It's got a very good beat, but it's been done so often before that I don't think it'll make it. What a strange follow up to their last one – that was really great.'

John Rowles: Save the Last Dance for Me (MCA) 'It's the old Drifters number. It's Engelbert is it not? Ah, John

Rowles. It's a good song, and he does it just like the Drifters, so maybe it could be a hit again. This is a very good LP track, but a bit dodgy as a single.'

Billy Preston: All That I've Got (Apple) 'Aaaaaahhh it's Billy Preston, and it's brilliant. It's very much like Georgie, and what a great beat. He used to do instrumental numbers, didn't he?'

Byrds: Jesus Is Just Alright with Me (CBS) 'They're all going in for this religious bit now! Who is it? Oh, the Byrds. They've made a lot of good records, but they haven't had a big one for a long time, and I don't think this is going to do it for them. But it'll probably do very well in the States.'

Van Der Graaf Generator: Darkness (from LP, *The Least We Can Do Is Wave to Each Other*) (Charisma) 'Is it the Moody Blues? Oh . . . who? Is this their first album? It's certainly very dramatic, and very good for their first attempt. I like some progressive music – Moody Blues and Spooky Tooth I've liked, and Cream too, especially "Sunshine of Your Love".'

I was extremely flattered, at such a tender age, to be asked to give my considered opinion on the sounds of the fledgling seventies.

I always liked Peter Sarstedt, who had already enjoyed a No. 1 hit with 'Where Do You Go to My Lovely?' Given the sentiments, he could have dedicated that to me, as well as Marie Claire.

'Instant Karma' was probably the pick of the bunch

which I reviewed, peaking at number five in the UK charts and number three in the States. Never for one instant was my life about to become any calmer, though.

Then it was the turn of the *Daily Mirror*, whose renowned photographer Kent Gavin snapped me and a gorgeous model, Gail Allen, in no more than our underwear, for a picture printed beneath a headline screaming 'Mr Perfect!' A company manufacturing jeans had conducted a survey, asking 300 girls what qualities they wanted in their ideal guy. The overall response was a thirty-inch waist, nicely rounded bum and thighs and well-muscled calves. Apparently, I fitted the bill. And Gail's role in this shameless stunt? She had to hold a tape measure around my middle and gaze adoringly into my eyes. It was a tough job, but somebody had to do it.

I was fair game for all and sundry, and the length of my flowing locks attracted plenty of attention. Fears that the hair might get in my eyes and impair my vision were swiftly met by an artist's impression of what I would look like encased in a sort of hairnet which made me look like Ena Sharples on *Coronation Street*. It was all good, harmless, knockabout fun.

Back in London, my residence at the Alexander Hotel made me extremely popular with team-mates such as McNab, George Graham and Frank McLintock, a trio who thought nothing of motoring round for a free feed. I protested the first time we sat down in the restaurant when their orders went in for prawn cocktail, followed by steak Diane, lobster and a good few bottles of

Liebfraumilch. 'I'm not going to be able to afford this sort of spread very often, lads,' I confided nervously, but Bob instantly put my mind at rest when he roared, bold as brass, 'You can sign for the lot on expenses, you know, Peter!' As I might have mentioned, everything was five-star at Arsenal, and a day or two later, when I mentioned to Bertie that a few of the boys had been round for dinner with me, he just smiled and said knowingly, 'Oh, they have, have they?' The manager knew the score. All that restaurant food was a bit rich for my taste, to be honest, and it wasn't long before I was crying out for a humble plate of egg and beans on toast.

My less than refined upbringing was cause for some amusement within the team. I had a broad Scots drawl on me and, if I thought I wasn't making my point of view clear in a conversation, I was prone to asking, 'D'ya ken?' I'm sure McNab, born and raised in Huddersfield, could understand well enough, even if he did eventually pull me up to complain: 'You do know that none of the lads are called Ken, don't you Peter? So why do you keep calling one of us that?'

George and Frank sometimes took me out for a drink, but I was a bit stranded and lonely whenever I didn't have Joyce in tow. I often used to take the tube on my own to the West End, see a show, have a meal or a drink on my own, and no one batted an eyelid as long as I was safely tucked up inside the hotel by midnight.

Living the life of Riley there couldn't last for ever, and Arsenal found me digs for the princely sum of £12 a week with Mrs Jones in Winchmore Hill. She was a widow in her sixties, fussed over me like a grandma and was a bit of a snob – she would only take in first-team players, strictly no reserves. Ian Ure had moved out – sold to Manchester United for £80,000 – and I took his place in a house that was not without its temptations. Apart from Mrs Jones' fabulous roast dinners, steak and kidney pie and hearty fish dishes, my abiding memory of those digs is her daughter, Julie, who could be an outrageous flirt. She was in her late thirties, going through a messy divorce and had a disarming habit of sunbathing topless (virtually naked at that) in the garden. Both Joyce and I struck up a friendship with Julie, although I never did uncover whether Joyce's interest was to keep an eye on her. You can never be certain what a woman's thinking, can you?

Joyce often stayed the night in a spare room, but there was strictly no hanky-panky. My landlady saw to that. Most of the first team lived further out, in Southgate and Potters Bar, but the digs were handy for the tube into work – and also the West End, which funnily enough suited me just fine. Mrs Jones worried about me arriving back at all hours as I started to spread my wings socially. 'Your life is a bit erratic, Peter,' she warned me. 'You've no time to sit down and relax.' Word reached the manager that I was not keeping appropriate hours, and he pulled me up sharply because he thought I was gadding about too much. Mrs Jones had put the boot in; she wasn't best pleased that I was missing the meals she had lovingly prepared, and when the club inquired how I was settling in, she told them something to the effect: 'I'm not sure, I never see him. Every night he seems to be out, doing this, that and the other.'

I had only been in London for a matter of weeks when I was made to feel a little more at home. I received a telephone call from England's World Cup-winning skipper and West Ham United captain, Bobby Moore. I don't know what I'd done to deserve that honour, but what a gentleman. He explained he merely wanted to welcome me to London and wished me all the very best. Bobby said he'd heard that I liked gear and that I might care to visit him at this clothing factory with which he was associated. I jumped at the chance of meeting him, and Bobby asked if there was anything in particular which caught my fancy. There was: a beautiful, big, black leather coat. 'It's yours, son,' smiled Bobby, brushing off all protestations that I should pay for the item. Bobby Moore, a class act both on and off the pitch.

A few days later, however, I wore my distinctive French-style mac to a show in the West End starring Danny La Rue and must have been spotted buying a ticket because during the performance Danny asked the audience: 'Do you think I'm better looking than Peter Marinello?' and I felt as if hundreds of pairs of burning eyes were swivelling round in my direction. Enormously embarrassed, I left that theatre as quickly as I could without drawing even more attention to myself. Not an easy feat.

Nevertheless, it was an exciting existence as I began to

find my feet around the capital's diverse streets. I went up to the top of the Post Office Tower once to eat in the restaurant that winter, looked out over the never-ending London sprawl at what seemed like a million lights and felt on top of the world. The look, the smell ... just everything about London was thrilling. Carnaby Street was alive and buzzing, with music blaring out of every boutique, while beautiful girls wore mini-skirts, White Musk and Chanel No. 5. You could hardly move in Soho for Italian and Chinese restaurants. Soho was amazing, nothing like anything I'd been used to in Edinburgh. I liked my food, especially Italian, and became a regular at a little restaurant on the corner of Frith Street where they served great rigatoni. Joyce and I would share a nice bottle of red wine, my heavy drinking confined to nights out with the players. There were autograph-hunters wherever I went, and I almost dropped my forkful of spaghetti when one chap – definitely not Marcia Williams – came up to me in a fashionable dining-room, introduced himself as Prime Minister Harold Wilson's 'personal private secretary' and wished me a long and happy career with Arsenal. And Soho had plenty of other diversions. I went to a strip joint with a handful of the lads and paid a fiver to get in, only to be shown to another door for another fiver, and then another in a side-street alleyway. After shelling out £15 without seeing an inch of illicit female flesh, I ended up where I'd started, ripped my ticket up in disgust in front of two big bouncers and put the episode down to experience.

Edinburgh was not the multi-cultural city it is today, and all the black faces in London took me a little aback, but purely because I wasn't used to them. The Marinellos were very friendly with the Camerons, one of the few black families around our way, and they had a son, Eric. A big, big lad he was too, even as a twelve-year-old, and once, when we were playing football, he fouled me. I gave him some shocking abuse, and he chased me all over the field before we ended up in a fit of laughter, rolling around in the grass together. The only prejudice I've ever held has been against full-backs.

There was some football, too, only Arsenal had to wait a fortnight after the Chelsea defeat for our next slice of action as a consequence of that premature FA Cup exit in Blackpool. I encountered another very tough and mobile defender in Chris Cattlin when we travelled to Coventry on 31 January. Full credit to the Sky Blues' manager Noel Cantwell, who had had me watched before the match and compiled a dossier for Cattlin on what to expect. The Coventry left-back was under orders to keep tight and give me as little room for manoeuvre as possible. Cattlin's post-match assessment that I was destined be 'one of the greatest players in the game' was as misguided as his performance was spot-on that afternoon at Highfield Road. My arrival at Highbury did not herald an upturn in fortunes for the team, and it wasn't long before the critics started having a go at Arsenal in general, and me in particular.

Meanwhile, Joyce's accommodation was proving to be

extremely unsatisfactory because Orpington to north London was one hell of a trek, neither of us could drive and consequently we didn't see each other as often as we would have liked. Help eventually arrived in the generous form of Jim Murray's boss at the *Express*, Bill Allison, who owned a large house in Highgate, and he happily accepted Joyce as a lodger. This was a bit more like it. Joyce was now living six miles away from me – although the journey still meant two bus rides or, preferably, a taxi, and she swiftly got a job working on computers at London University. That didn't last long, however, after a few of her colleagues asked rather uncharitably, 'What have you got a job for when your boyfriend's playing for Arsenal?' Joyce soon organised a transfer of her own and was snapped up by the famous Lucy Clayton modelling agency. We were like kids in a sweetie shop. Theatres, the West End, Soho, clothes . . . London really came alive for two teenage sweethearts from Edinburgh in the first couple of months of 1970. It was like Disneyland to us. I was daft and thought nothing of spending £200 a month on taxis with Joyce. That was my greatest extravagance, apart from the clothes, of course. I liked a gamble as well, and wouldn't think twice about sticking £30 on a horse, quite a sum when you consider that represented more than half my weekly basic wage.

An Italian television company arrived at Highbury to make a documentary about me because of my family roots, but they were out of luck when they asked me to speak the lingo. Spaghetti Bolognese and Chianti was about the extent of my knowledge of the language. Still, they filmed me arriving for work, during a match and relaxing at Joyce's digs at Highgate and seemed happy enough with the footage. That led to some speculation about me becoming a 'film star', but the reality is that it would only have been a cameo role, and I found the whole proposal rather vague, so I never really bothered with it.

I had joined Arsenal expecting to become a leading man, not an extra, but was beginning to wonder whether I was ever going to step into the limelight.

CHAPTER 6

Cavalier Among Roundheads

Three weeks after that 50,000-plus gate against Chelsea, the crowd had plunged to under 27,000 for the visit of Stoke City and a 0–0 draw, so our bonus was out of the window for that one. Then it was off to Goodison Park for a 2–2 draw against Everton and a meeting with another tough customer in England left-back Keith Newton. I didn't get much change out of Newton, very few wingers ever did.

There was tension in the air at Highbury, you could almost reach out and touch it. Things were not going right, least of all for me, although I had always stressed, from the moment I was signed, that it would take time for me to settle and adjust to the pace and demands of the English game. The First Division in England was a different world, especially the tighter, fiercer marking. The passing was quicker and there was considerably more thought and attention paid to tactics and training than I had ever encountered in Scotland. But I'd cost £100,000, scored in my first match at Manchester United and everyone expected me to simply continue in that rich vein.

Although I was experiencing difficulty in harnessing my style to an Arsenal side searching for greatness, I suspected there was so much talent and power running through the senior squad that a team to be respected and feared would emerge. The mistake I made was to think I'd be part of it. Yes, I had only played a handful of matches, but there were plenty of people – especially in the media – who had built me up as the second George Best and who expected great things of me immediately. There was so much early nonsense spoken about me getting the cold shoulder from the lads. Only one person was to blame for my failure to settle quickly into the pattern of things – Peter Marinello. In my eagerness to please on the football pitch I wandered inside when I should have been on the wing, and stayed wide when I should have come inside.

Personally, I wasn't doing myself any favours. I wasn't getting enough sleep, I was invariably out in the evenings on matters unrelated to football, I was too accommodating to everyone who wanted a piece of me. Joyce was living in Highgate while I was in Winchmore Hill, and my life was a social whirlwind. I was drinking too much, too often, and afternoon training sessions all added to the draining of my powers. A combination of rest, relaxation, sensible fluid intake and two extra hours in bed every night might have worked wonders.

There were undoubtedly some cruel souls who believed I needed a bomb under me, and it was somewhat unnerving later that February when we were getting stripped at Manchester City and the bomb squad burst in. Some malicious prankster had phoned Maine Road that night, claiming an explosive device had been planted in our dressing-room. The police made a thorough search of all our bags and every nook and cranny of that room while we carried on getting changed for the match amid a barrage of nervous quips and jokes. Sure, we had a good laugh over that bomb scare, but I'm sure it set a few knees knocking.

After drawing 1–1 with City, we went straight out on the town in Manchester, and I ended up in a club chatting to one of George Best's ex-girlfriends, who made it clear she wanted to see rather more of me the next time Arsenal were up north. She got her wish the following month. Like George, I received a stack of abusive letters and was accused, among more disturbing things, of having a swollen head and being incapable of playing football. One crack that tickled me was that I should stick to selling ice cream . . . although I was always at pains to point out that I wasn't going to be sidetracked away from football by the lure of outside interests. I knew the pitfalls, at least I thought I did, and I was also aware how many jealous people were waiting for me to blow it all big time.

Meanwhile, commercial offers flooded in from here, there and everywhere, either to me in person or through the *Daily Express*, until Jim Murray cried, 'Enough! This is getting a bit too much, Peter. You should get yourself a proper personal manager.' Bestie's agent Ken Stanley approached me and proposed I should write a book and open a string of boutiques with George, but I was quite happy with Jim and content to give him 10 to 15 per cent of the money I made outside football.

George himself was good enough to give me some advice and a little inkling of what I had let myself in for. 'Peter Marinello certainly has my sympathy,' said Bestie in one article.

Soon his head will be humming with advice, invitations, pleas and persuasions. There are times when I feel like hiding behind the nearest wall in search of a little privacy. But no, you've become public property, and everyone, it seems, has the right to take you to task on almost any issue. You've a diary that runs out of pages. Correspondents who never seem to run out of abuse and so many thousands of letters that you employ a full-time staff to deal with them. Then you need a person to sift through the filthy letters with all their obscenities, before the young girls dealing with your mail are offended by them. I'm still learning to live with all this. I hope Peter will do the same. The best of luck, mate. You'll need it.

George was spot on about the abusive mail, but wrong about needing a censor. Joyce willingly opened all my letters, sometimes as many as 400 a week, 80 per cent of them from teenage girls. She told me, sniffily, 'Some of them are such drivel – I don't know how they can write such slop.'

Back in the First Division, we travelled up the M1 to take on Brian Clough's Derby County, who had revenge in mind. The previous November, when I was still playing for Hibs, Arsenal had hammered Dave Mackay and co. 4–0, but it was a different story at the compact Baseball Ground, where we went down 3–2. I had been eagerly awaiting this opportunity to play against Mackay, the legend I had cheered as a schoolboy from the Tynecastle terraces as a Hearts supporter, but this was not an occasion on which I could reflect with any great fondness because the match largely passed me by. But losing at Derby was as low as things got before the team forged a winning mentality.

Struggling Sunderland arrived on 28 February, and there was considerable relief all round thanks to a 3–1 home victory which gave me my first experience of winning two league points with Arsenal at the eighth attempt. Barely 22,000 fans braved a cutting wind and, quite frankly, I had a performance to forget. I never had Best's genius: I couldn't turn it on like a tap whenever the mood took me. There were times, too many for sure, when the crowd were desperate for me to succeed, and I failed to rise to the occasion, running into trouble, misrouting that final pass and hesitating around the opponents' penalty area. This was one of those disappointments. What made it worse was that this was a truly awful, relegation-bound

Sunderland side, there for the taking after arriving with just three away points all season, having mustered only ten goals in their previous seventeen away matches. I hoped Peter Storey's penalty and goals from Ray Kennedy and Eddie Kelly might camouflage my contribution, or rather lack of it. But deep down I just knew Bertie Mee and Don Howe, the first-team coach, were sitting there and shaking their heads.

Still, the Sunderland result meant I could walk to work to Highbury with my head held high for once on Monday morning. Several times a week we would train undercover at 'The College', a three-quarter size pitch of brown sand behind the Clock End. Otherwise, it was off to London Colney, near St Albans, on a bus for me with the ground-staff, youth team and apprentices, while more seasoned members of the first team drove their own cars out to our training headquarters in leafy Hertfordshire.

The amount of training Don put me through was a bit of a shock to the system to begin with. It made the training regime at Hibs seem about as strenuous as musical chairs. Tuesdays and Thursdays I hated because that meant weights, and I loathed them. Don was a tremendous influence and took a special personal interest in me. I lifted so many weights I felt like Louis Martin. I could run like the wind, but my upper-body strength left a lot to be desired, and Don forced me to drink half a coffee cup of his revolting yellow concoction of raw eggs and glucose, plus some sort of protein supplement, which was designed to build up my strength. I really had to force it down in one gulp, otherwise my breakfast was in danger of making a rapid reappearance. Don's training methods were very different to what I had been used to at Hibs, where we concentrated on the ball. We employed that many traffic cones at London Colney, George Graham brought the house down when he gazed up to the heavens, shielded his eyes and asked mischievously, 'Is there a plane coming in to land, Don?' We worked a lot more on tactics than in Scotland, where you could get away with off-the-cuff stuff. It was simply altogether more professional at Arsenal.

Don also had me in on Sunday mornings for extra training with Eddie Kelly and Charlie George – 'the future of Arsenal Football Club', he called us – yet, perversely, he would often drive right past me at the bus stop with a wave, rather than stop and give me a lift. (I was more fortunate if Geoff Barnett or George Graham passed in their cars.) Then, after I had got changed and asked Don, 'What are we going to do, then?' he might simply fix me with a firm stare and reply, 'Nothing!' before turning smartly on his heels and leaving the dressing-room. Nothing meant exactly that, and I would change back into my everyday clothes and depart. It was Don's way of showing me who was in control and, undoubtedly, a form of punishment for my lifestyle, of which he disapproved. I'm sure he wanted to know that I could be bright-eyed and sober on a Sunday morning.

Don worked me hard and could be relentless in his search for improvement. We had a particular training exercise featuring half a dozen grids measuring ten yards square with an apprentice in each one. I had to go from one grid to another and if a youngster took the ball off me, it was literally back to square one. It was like football's equivalent of snakes and ladders. I was frequently on the slippery slope. I was at my best when it came to Thursday's 'doggies' – short, sharp sprints to the uninitiated. We ran four times between poles set 30–40 yards apart, rested for 15–20 seconds then repeated the exercise. Three sets of four was the norm, and Don made sure every player's time was carefully logged, so there could be no cheating, and woe betide anyone whose time was slower than the previous week. It was high-tempo stuff, which I enjoyed because it mirrored the sort of effort I might put in during a match. I quickly learned to keep my drinking to reasonable proportions on a Wednesday night at least, because attempting 'doggies' with a hangover frequently ended with players being as sick as a proverbial dog.

It was a mortal sin in Don's eyes to give the ball away, so I didn't endear myself to him with my high-risk approach to the game. If something didn't come off, I sometimes 'did the teapot' – that is to say, stand stock-still with my hands on my hips – and that was another little trait which made Don's blood boil.

I had a nagging fear that I wouldn't fit in. Hibs had attacked with loads of flair in all areas, but the way Arsenal set about things was altogether more scientific, thoughtful and tactical. It lacked creativity to my mind. With my cavalier style, I was like a fish out of water. Don was a fabulous defensive coach, and Arsenal were used to playing a rigid system with a pair of twin strikers plus Geordie Armstrong working like a Trojan on the wing. His level of effort and commitment was awesome. One minute he'd be clearing the ball off his own goal-line, the next he'd be tackling in midfield and before you knew what was happening there would be wee Geordie curling in a cross for Radford or Kennedy. Everything seemed very studied, almost laborious, in the build-up, and if the ball reached me out on the right, more often than not the opposition had been able to assemble a couple of banks of defenders with which to confront me. Wide men had not been flavour of the month since before July 1966, when Alf Ramsey's wingless wonders won the World Cup. My arrival heralded the departure from Arsenal of winger Jimmy Robertson down the road to Tottenham. He scored more often than me, and that no doubt softened any blow felt by Spurs fans that I had snubbed them to join their arch-rivals.

As well as Jimmy leaving, I think Geordie was very close to going back to a club in his native North-east for something like £20,000 until I resuscitated his career. We were different in our approach – for one thing, I didn't work hard or chase back. He saw me as a challenge, although we became great friends and often joked how I put three more years on his Arsenal career. That's true, as well, and in those three years Geordie became one of the most influential players the club has had in maybe the last half-century. Each Thursday, Geordie and I had our own *Chariots of Fire* battle, racing each other over 100 yards at

London Colney with side bets. I generally won, but on one infamous occasion the boys conned me rotten and pretended Geordie was ill at home. I'd already raced eight or nine of the others when Geordie popped up, fresh as a daisy, to hurl down the gauntlet. I accepted like a sportsman, of course, but he left me standing. I felt sure I could improve the team and certainly give Arsenal more attacking options, but I was lazy and slack when it came to retracing my steps and defending. The management knew that with Geordie, however, what you saw was what you got – a 100 per cent committed shift for the full ninety minutes.

Appearances can often be deceptive, and that was most certainly true in the case of full-backs Bob McNab and Pat Rice. I thought I possessed sufficient skill and pace to make them look stupid. They were powerful defenders, although not the greatest going forward. I had this neat little trick of dipping my left shoulder, then dodging away to my right. That was often enough to leave defenders for dead and give me enough time and space to hit the line and put in a cross, but Bob and Pat were having none of it from this cocky little Scottish so-and-so – and certainly let me know it in training.

Yet it all seemed to be happening for me in early 1970. After a handful of First Division matches, the possibility of an international future came tantalisingly into view. I remained in the thoughts of Scotland manager Bobby Brown, who called me up for the Under-23 team to tackle England at Roker Park. I was back in Edinburgh for all of fifteen minutes, the time it took to change trains at Waverley Station, on our way to Sunderland. What a joke my second Under-23 appearance turned out to be on 4 March, all two minutes of it. That was how long I'd been on the Wearside pitch as a substitute for Celtic's George Connelly – not long enough to run the icicles out of my blood – before the referee abandoned the match because of a snow blizzard. I'd seen enough from my place on the bench, however, to know that England, leading 3–1, were very well blessed for talent in the shape of Brian Kidd and the Chelsea pair, Peter Osgood and Alan Hudson.

The evening wasn't a complete waste of time, though, because Bestie's former flame from Manchester had booked into our hotel. She was gorgeous with long blonde hair. There had been a doubt about the match even kicking off, and she was there, hanging about in the bar before the team left. A few of my more perceptive team-mates clocked that she was giving me the eye, and one of them said, 'You're well in there tonight, Peter, if you play your cards right.' I thought: 'Too true, son,' not mentioning that the deck was already well stacked in my favour. She got a taxi to the game, where I'd left a ticket for her on the gate at Roker Park. Later that evening, when she knocked on the door of my room and entered, we weren't about to discuss the intricacies of the 4–4–2 system. I did feel a little guilty, I must admit, because I always intended to marry Joyce – but the ring wasn't on her finger yet. And what red-blooded male would turn down an opportunity like this, offered on a plate? I would estimate that 95 per cent of heterosexual men would have loved to be in my position. By way of a trophy, she ran off home with my Scotland strip. I didn't mind about the kit going AWOL back to Manchester with my one-night stand because I thought there would be a stack of future honours in store. Today it's a different story, and I confess it would be nice to have that shirt at home, framed and hanging on the wall. A lasting memory of when I was good enough to represent Scotland.

I signed a contract with Freemans, the mail order clothing catalogue, for £400 a shoot three times a year and all the clothes I wanted for free in the first twelve months. You wouldn't look too out of place today walking around London in a couple of the suits in which I posed, but maybe not that antique, cherry-coloured velour two-piece effort, a snip at £23.20. It was within easy reach of most pockets on the never-never, that's to say it would be all yours after thirty-five weeks paying 65p and one week at 45p. When the first year was up, Freemans said apologetically they had to start charging me for their clobber, and asked whether £2 an item was OK. I said I could probably afford that much.

In a good week I might see £55 from Arsenal in wages, maybe a hefty crowd bonus and £100 from the *Daily Express* to talk to Norman Giller, who ghosted my column in the sports pages. I did one particular *Express* fashion shoot in poncy clobber, designed by Nino Cerruti, the high priest of unisex, which earned me a whole set of new fans . . . among London's gay community. Looking back,

I'm hardly surprised! Judging by the fan mail which reached me in the following weeks, it wasn't just the ladies who were keen to get me into the sack. There was a cotton velvet play suit like a posh tracksuit, a bold patterned silk shirt with a giant-sized silk scarf and a belted, stretch jersey sweater. All very upmarket and 'now' for then, if more than a touch effeminate for my taste.

Back in the real world, Arsenal were in a transitional stage: they had quite a strong side but were mid-table and had no chance of winning the league. Glory in Europe was another matter, however. The quarter-finals of the Fairs Cup pitted us against Dinamo Bacau of Romania, and I was looking forward on two scores to this little European adventure to the Romanian foothills of the Carpathian mountains. One, I knew I was playing for definite, and, two, it afforded me some precious time out of the public glare to concentrate purely and simply on football as our party flew out on two Russian Ilyushins. After the Munich Disaster of 1958, when seven Manchester United players were among the twenty-one who died, the club always flew in two planes.

We were taking no risks either of going down with gyppy tummy, and our baggage included 18 beef steaks, 18 gammon steaks, dozens of eggs, cornflakes, honey and tea. Bertie and Don had been unable to do a proper spying job on Bacau because they'd been on their mid-season break, so we were relying on a dossier from Walter McCrae, of Kilmarnock, who had been beaten 3–1 on aggregate by the Romanians in the previous round.

We had to run the gauntlet of a fair-sized crowd thronging round our hotel, and there were more than a few pretty girls eager to get their hands on me. Security just about kept them at arm's length.

Bacau were nothing to write home about, and, in truth, there was more chance of us being knocked out of our stride by the crowd at the August Twenty-third Stadium. I liked a bit of history and discovered that 23 August 1944 was the date Romania switched sides in the Second World War and joined the Allies, sensible people. Arsenal's visit, we were led to believe, was the greatest day in Bacau's footballing history, and the city declared the day a public holiday. There were hundreds locked out of a ground jam-packed to its 20,000 capacity and scores of others clinging to trees and standing on the roofs of tin sheds, straining for a view of the action. The noise was such in the first half you might have been forgiven for thinking World War Three had broken out, especially when the giant firecrackers exploded. But Arsenal, being Arsenal, did a competent professional job in giving the home supporters little to get worked up about on the pitch.

I managed a couple of useful early touches, and from one cross Charlie George should have scored with a header. We would have been happy with a draw, but two goals after an hour from Jon Sammels and John Radford silenced the klaxon-hooters and bell-ringers and, rather more significantly, meant our job was as good as done, and the second leg had the word 'formality' stamped all over it.

Before that, there was the little matter of a league match against Liverpool at Highbury in March, and we sent the bulk of a 32,000 crowd home happy with a 2–1 win, which flattered the Merseysiders. Both sides were in the process of easing out their older players and giving youth its head, and on the evidence of this match Eddie Kelly, Charlie George – who hit the bar twice with headers – and I were making sure Bertie Mee kept his nose in front of Bill Shankly. Raddy's winner was one of the best goals I have ever witnessed, a mid-air bicycle kick over his shoulder which left Ray Clemence gasping. I was also introduced to Emlyn Hughes for the first time, or rather, the future England captain marched over to me before the kick-off and stated quite brazenly, 'If you come anywhere near me, you little Scottish bastard, I shall break both your fucking legs!' That pointed threat from Crazy Horse was just that, a threat. I'd heard it all before from hardman defenders. If you let it get to you, then you were definitely in the wrong profession. To Emlyn's eternal credit, he approached me again after the final whistle with an outstretched hand, looked me straight in the face and said, 'Well done, son.' Emlyn was a big man who hated losing almost as much as he hated tricky Scottish wingers. Like Bobby Moore and George Best, he is a great loss to football.

I was such a pain to the Liverpool defence that eventually Tommy Smith was sent over to sort me out in his uncomplicated fashion. That was the ultimate accolade. I'm sure Tommy was never the sort of guy to enrol in my fan club, but I did collect another forty adoring fans that day because a party of Plymouth schoolgirls were turned away from the England–Australia women's hockey international when the 'house full' signs went up at White City and ended up at Highbury instead, where our director, the Reverend N. F. Bone, insisted they should be VIP guests for the day. Inevitably, I suppose, they all wanted my autograph afterwards, although I was more interested in getting treatment for an ankle injury. Liverpool's England winger Peter Thompson had a laugh when he saw me surrounded by a mob of schoolgirls, but was gracious in defeat and told the press, 'I was impressed by Marinello's wing play. He hits a good ball on the run and looks good going forward.'

Sure enough, Fairs Cup duty the following week was a piece of cake, and we walloped Bacau 7–1 with Eddie Kelly, Charlie George and myself receiving rave notices. The Romanians had no stomach for a fight after the opening twenty-five minutes, by which time I had laid on the first two goals for Raddy, with a neat lob to the far post, and Charlie. Both strikers scored again while Sammels helped himself to a couple of goals and George Graham also got on the scoresheet.

Bob Wilson had taught at Holloway School when Charlie was a pupil there and our goalkeeper struggled to contain his enthusiasm for the new brigade. He said:

The last few weeks have been quite a revelation, especially for the young lads. They've had a great boost from this good spell. I saw Charlie in practice sessions at Holloway and I thought then that he was the most natural schoolboy footballer I'd ever laid eyes on, while it's no exaggeration to say that Eddie Kelly, at eighteen, makes us tick the same way as that eighteen-year-old Alan Hudson makes Chelsea tick. Marinello? I think he had a rude awakening coming here from Scotland, but look how he played against Bacau – tremendous. He's getting the hum of things.

I thought I'd overcome my shaky start too and started to put down a few tentative roots in the team as our encouraging league form continued with victories over Southampton 2–0, Crystal Palace 2–0 and West Ham 2–1, a draw against Wolves 2–2 and a narrow 2–1 defeat at Ipswich. I should have been thrilled when we wiped the floor with Ajax 3–0 in the first leg of the Fairs Cup semi-final in April, and I would have been, if only I'd been on the pitch at the final whistle. But you can't keep a good man down, apparently, and they didn't come any better than Geordie Armstrong, who had worked his way back into favour with the management and came on as substitute to replace me. I was very disappointed to be taken off. Geordie kept his place for the return leg in Amsterdam, a harmless 1–0 defeat against the bulk of a side that would go on to win a hat-trick of European Cups.

The little feller from Hebburn also featured in the Fairs Cup final against Anderlecht, where it seemed we had finally met our match in Europe after a potentially catastrophic 3–1 defeat in the away leg. Frank McLintock went into the bath in Belgium convinced he was going to be collecting his fifth loser's medal in a cup final, but something happened to him in there. He came out and verbally tore the opposition to shreds. Their defence was poor and we'd tear through the middle at Highbury. Their midfield had no legs and would be overrun. Their attack had just got lucky and wouldn't get a sniff in the return. By the time he'd finished Arsenal had no doubt that the return would be won; indeed Bob Wilson always says the tie was won at that point.

Stick or twist, that was the dilemma now facing Bertie and his henchman Don. We had a set pattern, 4–4–2, and it worked well because of Geordie's unflagging contribution, yet there was a feeling in the corridors of power that the time had come to go for bust and gamble on my additional pace and flair if we were to turn around the two-goal deficit the following week. I later learned from my mate Eddie that I was selected to play, only for the 'Kray Twins' – Frank McLintock and George Graham – to lead a deputation to the management, telling them the team didn't want me to play and preferred Geordie. Maybe they were right, Geordie played, but that issue was to become a major bone of contention with me.

I wept on that magical night when goals from Eddie Kelly, Radford and Sammels brought the Gunners their first trophy since 1953, and they were tears of joy and frustration. Frank had the players waving the silver pot through our dressing-room window towards the delirious hordes in the street down below in Avenell·Road, and I burst out crying when he handed the trophy to me. I was certainly part of the squad and appreciated by the lads for what I did, but sometimes I felt too much like a spare part. There's no substitute for pulling your boots on, hearing the roar of the crowd when the teams emerge from the tunnel and playing ninety minutes. I was thrilled for the lads, of course: it had been a magnificent effort overturning Anderlecht's first-leg lead, and no man could wish for better comrades. You knew if you had been in the trenches with this Arsenal team that each and every one of them would have minded your back. That bond, team spirit and closeness was their overriding strength.

Then it was all back to the White Hart pub in Southgate, where the first of numerous large brandies awaited the attention of Peter Simpson. That was just for starters, and it was one hell of a long session, one in which I indulged to the full. I paid for it the following morning because Don had ordered in all the reserves, or 'stiffs' as we were known, to pound the running track. The only resentment on my part was not playing, but that was softened a few days later when I picked up a bonus of over £1,000. There was one final league match to fit in, at Tottenham, and Geordie got the nod for a 1–0 defeat which left Arsenal in twelfth place in the First Division. Bertie was utterly convinced the groundwork had been done for the club to progress and win one of the major prizes in England. I was left wondering if I could ever truly be accepted.

There was no end to the trouble to which some people were prepared to go to try to force me to sign contracts to endorse this, that and the other – just about everything you care to think of. One publisher wanted me to cooperate on a book project and kept on and on worrying me, like a dog with a bone. They thought I was going to be the star of the century but they weren't interested in me as a human being in the slightest, only in making money for themselves. They never stopped pestering me – until they realised I wasn't going to be an instant success, that is.

I did one promotion for the Milk Marketing Board, who produced a poster of me urging the nation to 'Drinka Pinta Milka Day' which went up on billboards throughout Britain. One wag with a can of black paint and a brush climbed up the wall of the Gunners pub outside Highbury and transformed the pint of milk I was holding into a pint of Guinness. To be fair, that was a more accurate reflection of my drinking habits, but it went down like a lead balloon with the management. Bertie urged me to cut down on my off-the-pitch activities, and even my trusted business advisor Jim Murray told me straight that things were getting out of hand and suggested we cooled things on the commercial front. I wasn't like David Beckham – I didn't court publicity – but I always made myself available and opened more than my fair share of shops and fêtes, willingly visited loads of sick children in hospitals and healthier specimens in schools, while my affiliation to the club, with its big Jewish following, ensured I never went short of invitations to bar mitzvahs with Eddie Kelly and Geoff Barnett, our reserve goalkeeper, in tow.

Arsenal were a tight-knit squad socially, and it wasn't

unusual for all the players to go out en masse to enjoy such acts as Tom Jones, Shirley Bassey and Matt Monro, although I tended to feel more comfortable in the company of the younger lads such as Eddie, Charlie and Ray Kennedy. Most of the first team were married with children. Frank McLintock more or less ran the side with George Graham. If anything needed sorting out in the dressing-room they were the men to do it, while Raddy was another real character, a big Yorkshireman who liked a drink and enjoyed scoring goals even more. He was grossly underrated, as was Peter Simpson at the back. Storey held court in the White Hart, where we were always guaranteed a late-night lock-in, often in the company of players from other London clubs such as Tottenham's Joe Kinnear and Chelsea's Tommy Baldwin, although the main Spurs pub was a couple of tube stops further out. There you might very well find Alan Gilzean with Dave Mackay, who was now playing for Derby but kept a house in north London. When life at the White Hart got a bit tame and routine we branched out and discovered a drinking den in Finchley called the Purple Pussycat and took up residence there for a spell until the management got wind of it. I was about to settle down, just a little, because my own Match of the Day was on the horizon – marriage.

Joyce and I paid a deposit on a lovely little maisonette with all mod cons, one of a dozen in a brand new development in a cul-de-sac in Winchmore Hill. It was going to cost £8,500, and, very late one evening, after we'd been out on the town, I got carried away with excitement and said to Joyce, 'We've got to go and see it.' We had finally got wheels to call our own after I bought Joyce a yellow soft-top Triumph Spitfire for £1,400 cash for her nineteenth birthday on 23 March. When we arrived about 1.30 a.m., I was dying for a pee and told Joyce to reverse the car while I nipped around the back of our new home-to-be to relieve myself. I was just getting comfortable when I heard this horrendous crunching sound of metal on stone and dashed back to the front to discover Joyce had reversed the Spitfire right, slap, bang into the middle of an ornamental rockery, and the car was stuck fast, wheels spinning furiously but going nowhere. Only about half the maisonettes were so far occupied, but lights immediately flashed on all over the shop and curtains were pulled apart. I ran up the road to telephone for a 24-hour breakdown service, which arrived within half an hour, but there was no immediate peace for the residents, who continued to suffer while the Triumph was slowly cranked up out of the flowerbeds and rockery.

Two days later, Ken Friar, the club secretary, summoned me into his office to deliver the information that, unfortunately, we would not be starting married life in our dream home because the potential neighbours had got up a petition saying they didn't want us living there. They had delivered the petition to the development builders, all fervent Tottenham fans, who had taken great delight in returning our cheque for the deposit to Highbury. Fortunately, this little episode never made the papers.

Marriage was on the horizon but, at heart, I was always just one the lads and there was to be no escape from birds and booze on tour with Arsenal.

CHAPTER 7

Rebel Without a Pause

Hundreds of well-wishers turned up outside St Mary's Roman Catholic Cathedral, in York Place, Edinburgh, on 7 July 1970, when Joyce and I were married. For all our fame and instant fortune, the glamour and trappings of London life, Joyce looked suitably radiant in a plain white dress she picked up for £12 down the King's Road. I wore a double-breasted navy suit and looked like death warmed up, having only just about survived my old-fashioned stag night the previous evening. In fact, I can still recall Joyce's first words to me that day: 'Jesus Christ, what do you look like?'

The stag do had started at full tilt with all the usual local suspects in the frame – Peter Cormack, Sandy Jardine, Jim Steele, Ian Cruikshank, John Murphy, David Ross and my best man, Peter Whitten. After trawling bar after bar, we ended up in Romano's, a disco-pub in the west end of

Edinburgh. It also had the dubious attraction of being a notorious poser's pick-up joint, and we danced with a selection of women, but there was no chance of any of the lads going home with one of them because we were all virtually paralytic through drink. Sandy told me later I'd downed half a dozen pints of lager and ten vodkas throughout the course of the evening. It wasn't ideal preparation for taking my holy marriage vows.

We arrived at Ross's house on the other side of the city at four in the morning before Peter and I eventually made it back to Logie Green for five. I must have been absolutely crazy. Despite the hangover from hell, I managed to put on a brave face and congratulated all the ladies on looking lovely. My sisters Anna and Theresa were bridesmaids, while Jim Murray came up from London and gave his niece away in the absence of Joyce's father, Jackie, who was by now settled down under in Australia with the rest of her family. Also conspicuous by their absence were any of the Arsenal lads, but they could be excused because we were all due to go off on tour to Sweden the following weekend, and I knew that time with the family was important to professional sportsmen.

When Joyce and I emerged from the service and walked down the steps of the cathedral, we were mobbed by a crowd of teenage girls jostling for my autograph and surrounded by photographers. After the wedding, we treated thirty guests to a meal in a hotel in Princes Street before flying back to Heathrow. We flipped a coin to decide our honeymoon destination and headed east for deepest Essex in Joyce's Triumph Spitfire, which had, happily, survived that ordeal with a rockery in Winchmore Hill.

There was no escape from life in the goldfish bowl, even on honeymoon amid the jellied eels, cockles and whelks of romantic Southend-on-Sea. Mr and Mrs Marinello were strolling hand in hand along the promenade when an open-air bingo caller interrupted his game to announce, 'Well, I do declare, if that's not Peter Marinello,' and we had to make a run for it back to our scruffy bed-and-breakfast. We enjoyed three days on our own, trying to be as inconspicuous as we could in that little guesthouse in Southend, and after a few days back in London we kissed goodbye. I teamed up with the Arsenal lads for some blood, sweat and beers at our summer camp, some fifteen miles outside Gothenburg, where the seeds of the Gunners' fantastic Double-winning season of 1970–71 were sown.

The training was intense in the mornings and after-noons, but we were left to our own devices in the evenings. This ploy was excellent for bonding and morale, even if most of the water taken on board for rehydration purposes came mixed with whisky. Eddie Kelly, Frank McLintock, George Graham, Peter Storey, Charlie George and I were thoroughly at home at Harry's Bar, an English theme pub in the centre of Gothenburg, a fifteen-mile taxi-drive away. There was an absolute stack of gorgeous Swedish crumpet on offer in Harry's, and we were in our element, chatting them up and having a laugh as the drinks flowed freely. We must have graced Harry's on eight of the ten nights we spent in Sweden. However much booze we got through it didn't matter because this was pre-season and we knew we'd be training hard and sweating it all out of our system the following day. One night, inevitably, we arrived back late, missing the curfew imposed by Don Howe, who also caught one member of our party in an extremely compromising position with a local village girl he had arranged to meet back at base camp. We escaped a fine, but not a total hammering on the training ground the following morning.

Eddie and I formed a good relationship with Charlie. Maybe the three of us were just a bit too cocky and confident about our own ability, but we were young and rebellious. Our antics on a trip to Germany, the year after the Gothenburg expedition, were hushed up and never became public knowledge. Arsenal had a big squad on duty for a friendly match that day, maybe eighteen or nineteen in total, and the three of us were told that, while we weren't required to play, we had to attend. By half-time, we'd seen more than enough and, frustrated to bursting point, we repaired to the hotel bar and proceeded to hit the bottle with a vengeance. We took out our bitterness on the poor barman, who had to duck suddenly when an empty bottle from our table flew through the air and smashed into the optics behind him. There was a nasty mess of broken glass, pools of sticky spirits and bits of mirror, and the police were called, but the hotel valued Arsenal's custom and weren't inclined to press charges once the club vowed to pay for all the damage. We got a severe dressing down from Bertie after the hotel fracas and he threatened to put us on the transfer list, but we didn't take it seriously because everyone knew the three of us could walk into another First Division club, and Arsenal would be left looking foolish. We were considerably more frightened of Don's training methods and how he would make us pay physically and suffer for our misdemeanours.

Young and rebellious? That's probably a generous way of looking at things. If you boil it all down, we behaved like spoiled brats on more than one occasion. If we were told not to do anything, the three of us took it as a direct challenge – we had to do it. The funny thing is we always respected Don and knew he was doing the best for us. There was never any arguing when he caught us stepping out of line, we simply held our hands up. We were strictly forbidden to ride motorbikes or go skiing, for example, but that didn't prevent us hiring some proper top-of-the-range speedboats at Famagusta on one trip to Cyprus and driving them at each other in a ludicrous game of chicken, just swerving away from head-on collisions at the very last minute with inches to spare.

On tour, with the main business of winning matches out of the way, some of us could be rude, crude and dangerous to know. Arsenal were extremely conscious of their good reputation within football and took their public image seriously, and we were always expected to try and win every match, but those in charge rather turned a blind eye to our antics. If we won, especially, we could get away with murder. Mind you, the management weren't too impressed to discover Eddie and me sitting on the veranda outside our hotel room in Famagusta one afternoon, getting stuck into several huge pitchers of wine with a crate of beer by our side for good measure. The tour had been sponsored by the local Keo brewery, and we were just endorsing their products, we argued. It would have been rude not to.

That same tour also found us staying in the fabulous hotel which featured the film star Paul Newman in the opening scenes of *Exodus*, and which was later blown to bits during an all-too-real war. The bedrooms were huge, featuring massive walk-in wardrobes where you could almost lose yourself. Eddie and I stumbled across a couple of dead rats round by the dustbins one evening and crept into the room being shared by Sammy Nelson and Bob Wilson and stuck a deceased rodent in each corner of their wardrobe. Now Sammy and Bob had no need to use that wardrobe because their clothes fitted easily enough into their bedside cabinets, and at breakfast a couple of days later, they were complaining to anyone who would listen about the terrible smell in their room and how it must be situated over a broken drain. Eddie and I could contain ourselves no longer and burst out giggling: 'Why don't you look in your wardrobe?' Bob was distinctly unimpressed, but Sammy had the last laugh . . . depositing a couple of 'equalisers' in our beds which, fortunately, Eddie and I just discovered in time before turning in late at night.

While we were in Sweden, Joyce was busy finding a first home for the newly married Marinellos. We had already looked at a couple of flats, a particularly nice one in Islington, but the asking prices were decidedly on the steep side compared to what we'd been accustomed to in Edinburgh. Ideally, we were looking to buy, but they were asking for astronomical deposits. Joyce suddenly telephoned me on tour to break the good news that she'd hit the jackpot and found somewhere for us to set up home, an attic flat to rent in Winchmore Hill for £12 a week, through an Arsenal fan who was an estate agent and who had contacted her. It sounded too good to be true, and it was. She gave me the address and said she'd see me there on my return from Sweden. I was excited in the club car bringing me back through north London from Heathrow with Frank, George Graham and Geordie Armstrong in tow. I was excited, that is, until we pulled up in front of this five-storey-high monstrosity that looked like the house next to the Bates motel in Alfred Hitchcock's horror film *Psycho*. Predictably, my three team-mates took the piss unmercifully as I unloaded my bags from the boot and went through the jungle of an unmown front garden and down some steps. It took about half an hour to climb all the stairs to our flat – at least it seemed that long – where Joyce and I were kept awake at night by the noisy combination of cockroaches scuttling around the floorboards and pigeons nesting underneath the eaves of the roof.

Our temporary, miserable, soul-destroying stay at

Psycho Towers came to an end one Sunday afternoon as a result of Joyce's cooking. My beloved put a sultana steam pudding in the gas cooker before we went out for a walk, and we forgot all about it on our return, watching TV before tumbling into bed to make love and fall asleep. In the morning we found a hole in the roof where the pudding had quite literally exploded and I decided there and then that this was a clear sign from above that it was time to call it a day. So I paid for the repairs and we moved after six weeks, from the ridiculous to the sublime – a detached, three-bedroomed house just around the corner in Winchmore Hill Road for £9,500, and ideally situated, as far as I was concerned, between the White Hart and the Chaseside Tavern.

Arsenal were extremely generous when it came to sorting out their players with houses and loaned them as much as they needed to get settled. The more senior members of the squad had beautiful homes in Potters Bar, Brookmans Park and Southgate, but when I approached secretary Ken Friar for a loan, I discovered the club had so much money tied up in those players' houses, a new loan limit of £5,000 had just come into play. I was flush with the first instalment of my signing-on fee, scraped together £4,500 in cash, and the house was ours, although I had stretched us financially to such a limit that Joyce and I found ourselves sitting on deckchairs and beanbags for the first few months until we could afford a few decent sticks of furniture. That's where we had some help from the football agent Dennis Roach, although in the early 1970s he and his brother ran a big furniture store in north London. Dennis was great friends with Bob Wilson and certainly did me a good turn, too.

We got on well with the couple next door, Roy and Jean. He was a builder and did a very tidy job of putting up an extension for us that featured a garage, utility room and extra bedroom. The work enhanced the look of the property, which had already been quite imposing.

There was, however, no immediate improvement to Joyce's expertise in the kitchen! The sorry saga of the exploding sultana pudding was followed by her roasting a chicken without first removing the giblets, baking potatoes without first removing the mud and her tipping a plate of spaghetti over my lovely long hair when I casually mentioned it wasn't a patch on the pasta my dad rustled up. I had that one coming and thoroughly deserved it. Things improved after Joyce took cookery lessons, and I particularly looked forward to Thursday evenings, when she would bring home a lovely meal from her class.

Sundays might find us eating dinner in the home of a wonderful Italian/Jewish couple, Micky Tianno and his wife. Micky was an ex-bookie, a great character and a Jack the Lad in his sixties as well as being a huge Arsenal fan. Despite our age difference, we just seemed to click as friends. I think, maybe, I saw him as a bit of a father figure, and he reminded me of one of my uncles in particular. I frequently sorted out match tickets to be left on the gate at Highbury for Micky.

The non-football-related business was still in overdrive,

and I was asked to judge Miss Great Britain on several occasions, where I met Tony Blackburn again. There would be maybe five of us judging and, on one occasion, three of us certainly agreed one girl should be crowned Miss GB, yet she didn't even figure in the top three. God knows how the winner was eventually decided, but it was all great fun. Joyce got in on the act briefly, too, when she was asked to be a judge on *Come Dancing*.

But back on the football field, one of the greatest seasons in Arsenal's long and illustrious history was on the horizon, and I was to experience more than my fair share of drama . . . including a brush with a friendly gangster, who casually offered to shoot one of my team-mates!

CHAPTER 8

A Stiff Double

The sum total of my contribution to Arsenal's historic Double-winning season of 1970–71 was subbing for Charlie George in the first game of the season at Everton, ninety minutes in the second match of the season, a 0–0 draw at West Ham on Monday 17 August, followed by a solitary appearance as a substitute five days later in a thumping 4–0 win over Manchester United. I replaced John Radford, who went off to a well-earned rest and riotous applause after scoring a hat-trick against United. For me, it was the sound of silence for nine months.

I never doubted my own ability and I felt a bit sick I wasn't really part of it – especially when the big games rolled round. Mind you, Arsenal's party line was always that they bought me as an investment for the future. I was prepared to wait, but I didn't think it would take so long. I had to play for the reserves in the Football Combination away at places like Elm Park, Reading. It was terrible, really. I'd get sorely frustrated and couldn't build up any enthusiasm for the game, especially when the crowd was about 1,500. In the first team, you live the game. In the 'stiffs', you can't help your mind wandering off and thinking about totally unrelated matters.

Still, we had a good reserve team, with the infectious, bubbly Bobby Gould at centre-forward. It was as easy as shooting fish in a barrel for Bobby, and it felt as if he scored ninety-odd goals with me delivering seventy or eighty of the crosses. Charlie George, Eddie Kelly, Jon Sammels, Brian Hornsby, John Roberts and the reserve keeper Geoff Barnett all did their bit, among others, and we couldn't complain too much because we were on a reserve-team win bonus and also 50–60 per cent of the first-team bonuses for good measure.

The reserve-team coach, Steve Burtenshaw, had me on weightlifting and cross-country running. My stamina and physique definitely improved, and Steve also worked hard on me freeing myself from my marker, and that improved the quality of my crossing, which some critics thought was weak and inaccurate when I arrived at Highbury.

Granted, I was still a very young man, but that didn't lessen the sense of deflation. I played well in the reserves, doubled the gates and earned myself my own fan club in the Football Combination, but the first team were enjoying such a wonderful run I knew there was no chance of making the league side. If I hadn't played well in the reserves, I suppose I would have pushed for a move, but I was convinced that all I needed was a good run to justify myself. At my best, I had a glorious natural swerve and the courage to continuously take on opponents, however often I was fouled, however much I was frustrated. I think when I came down from Scotland I tried to fit in and compromise, and that's where I went wrong. Arsenal bought me for my individual ability, and I seemed to get brainwashed.

My first year at Highbury was a bit too much for me, what with the red carpet treatment and being virtually engulfed by the media. Bertie hated all the publicity and called it 'this terrible exploitation'. And, remember, I hadn't been much more than a talented novice at Hibs, and going straight to Highbury was more than I could cope with at the start. The fans, I think, took me to their hearts, but Bertie and Don treated me rather like an ornament. My trouble was that the team was beginning to do well in their particular style, which relied heavily on teamwork rather than individual flair.

We needed nine matches including, famously, extra-time in the 2–1 final triumph against Liverpool to win the FA Cup . . . and I got no nearer the action than a seat in the stands. Arsenal won the Cup the hard way after being handed four successive away ties. Yeovil were seen off 3–0 in the third round and Manchester City squeezed out 2–1 in the fifth, while Portsmouth and Leicester both required Highbury replays before they were eliminated 3–2 and 1–0 respectively in the fourth round and quarter-final. The semi-final was, inevitably, another close-run thing, a 2–2 draw with Stoke at Hillsborough being followed by a 2–0 victory at Villa Park.

Another appearance on *Top of the Pops* beckoned for me, this time with the entire first-team squad to sing our special FA Cup final single, 'Good Old Arsenal', which reached number nine in the charts and earned us about £60 each once the money was divvied up. After the recording, Eddie and I were invited back to a party in a private flat with some of the others who'd appeared on the show. It was quite an eye-opener, with cannabis, loads of booze and sexual shenanigans all quite out in the open. I walked into one bedroom and saw plenty of activity underneath a mountain of coats on the bed. If we'd stayed, we would have stayed all night. But I was a happily married man, there were important games in the pipeline, so we made our apologies and left after a drink or two.

Arsenal clinched the Double over six days in May. There were officially 51,992 at White Hart Lane, home of the traditional enemy, Tottenham, and at least as many fans locked out on the Monday night when a 0–0 draw would be good enough to win the championship, while any other form of draw would send the title to Leeds. It may sound odd, I know, but it was all to do with how the goal average, as it was then, was calculated. I didn't understand it then and I still don't. Just minutes from the end, the ball was disappearing for an Arsenal corner when Geordie Armstrong, the only outfield player to start every game that season, summoned up the energy from somewhere to keep it in play and send over a cross which Ray Kennedy thumped in with his head for a dramatic winner.

Now the Double was really on and it was down to Dorset to prepare for the FA Cup final in the luxurious surrounds of the Dormy Hotel next door to the Ferndown Golf Club, where Peter Alliss learned his trade. Eight of us were more interested in 'sport' of a less disciplined nature on the Wednesday night, and so it was that Frank McLintock, George Graham, John Radford, Peter Storey, Peter Simpson, Eddie Kelly, Charlie George and I piled into a couple of taxis and hit the pubs and clubs less than ten miles away in Bournemouth. The curfew was 11 p.m., but we were just warming up by then, and it must have been well after two in the morning when our party rattled back into the Dormy, to be confronted by a very stern Don Howe. George Graham might have been the self-styled 'Head of the Escape Committee' but he wasn't too good at getting us back inside undetected. The five senior players were all heavily fined, while Don hammered Eddie, Charlie and me so badly in training the following morning, we were physically sick. The coach merely came over and said, 'That will teach you!'

In fact, the lesson had such a profound effect on the three of us that we went out into Bournemouth again the following evening for a good few drinks – despite Eddie and Charlie knowing they were in the team for Wembley. The funny thing is, I thought I might be playing as well. Maybe not in the starting line-up, but perhaps coming on from the bench. It was just the vibes I'd got in training at London Colney beforehand, a feeling that was enhanced when we went through special preparation designed to stop danger man Steve Heighway, the Liverpool left-winger. I was playing for the reserves against the first team and twice dropped my shoulder, like Heighway, cut inside Pat Rice and stuck the ball in the back of the net to leave Bob Wilson floundering. The second time I scored, an exasperated Howe simply glared and barked, 'Fuck me, Peter, can you not do that on a Saturday?' If I could, regularly, under pressure when it mattered most, I might have fulfilled my potential.

Saturday 8 May, the day of the 1971 FA Cup final, dawned bright and sunny. By nightfall, Eddie Kelly and Charlie George, two of the three members of Arsenal's so-called Team of the Future, had come of age as goal-scoring heroes. I was the third man . . . and I might just as well have been the Invisible Man. Only Tottenham in 1961 had done the Double previously in the twentieth century, but I had contributed next to nothing to this slice of history. I watched the Cup final and Charlie's memorable winner, consistently thinking, 'I could have been out there. That could have been me.' While I was again delighted for the team, just like when we won the European Fairs Cup, and the financial implications were also good for me, that was no compensation whatsoever for missing out on a rare chance to play on the most famous pitch in the world and being seen by a worldwide television audience. I always thought Wembley was built for a player such as myself, someone who could take advantage of those big, wide-open inviting spaces behind the full-back. It was strange, really, watching the match unfold, kicking every ball.

Before the game I popped into Highbury and drained a few pints of lager with Geoff Barnett, the reserve keeper, before joining the staff coach to Wembley. Nobody batted an eyelid. Why would they? We were just two of the professionals not required to go to work that day. I didn't even make the bench, and, not unreasonably, the focus of attention was totally on Bertie Mee's select eleven. Geoff and I headed straight for a hospitality bar on arriving at Wembley for two more pints and, in my case, a vodka. I wanted the drink to numb the pain and bitter disappointment of missing out, but my tactic was never guaranteed to be a total success.

By a strange quirk, we were also drawn away in every round of the League Cup, beating Ipswich 4–0 in a Highbury replay and edging past Luton 1–0 before being held 0–0 by Crystal Palace in a fourth-round stalemate at Selhurst Park, only to lose 2–0 back home. You might have thought Bertie would have found a place for me for one of those cup-ties, but you would be wrong. Whatever changes were made to the team, they never included me.

As the campaign approached its glorious climax, I felt just like the spectator I had become. It was, frankly, a diabolical season for me, the worst I had ever known, even if my detractors somewhat unkindly pointed out that I'd only been in the game five minutes.

Fairs Cup time rolled around with Arsenal

understandably determined to defend the trophy with honour and, equally predictably, able to cope without me as the team beat the Italian giants Lazio, Sturm Graz (Austria) and Beveren Waas (Belgium), before falling to Cologne in Germany on the away goals rule in the quarter-final.

The clash with Lazio can never be recalled without a dishonourable mention of the fight that broke out that night at the official post-match dinner in Rome. Giorgio Chinaglia and John Radford had both scored twice in a 2–2 draw in front of a 60,000 crowd, and it had been a physical, nasty, fiddling game with tempers flaring on both sides and the Italians up to their usual tricks – spitting, and squeezing our fallen players between the armpits on the pretence of picking them up and behaving like sportsmen. Raddy and Kennedy were the main targets for the intimidation. The atmosphere was quite charged, although hospitality in the restaurant that evening was first class as we got stuck into the pasta, well lubricated by wine and a few beers to celebrate a very good result. You always wanted a draw at least in Europe if the first leg was away, and now we felt comfortably in control of our own destiny. Lazio, by contrast, could only feel bitter at failing to establish a lead of any sort to try and protect in London. It was a combustible atmosphere, and the spark came when Ray and I went for a pee. In the gents we bumped into four or five Lazio players washing their hands and preening themselves in front of the mirror. An insult was hurled at Ray, a big lad who had been prominent during the match and the subject of a lot of unwelcome attention. I advised him to let it go, which he did.

As we went out of the door and back towards our table, everything boiled over, and tempers erupted. Ray and I found ourselves bundled through the foyer and out into this long, narrow street where one Lazio heavyweight picked me up and threw me on to the bonnet of a taxi. Fortunately it was parked at the time. Ray took a few punches then the Arsenal cavalry burst on to the scene, led by the Kray Twins, of course, and both sets of players went at it hammer and tongs. I bounced up off the street, fuelled by drink and eager for revenge. Although I'd won an Under-10s boxing competition at Butlin's, I hadn't used my fists in anger for years and, on sober reflection, I was relieved I couldn't find my aggressor to have a pop at him because he was a bull of a man, and I might have suffered a serious pounding.

Raddy, Eddie and wee Geordie Armstrong were also in the thick of it, defending the honour of Arsenal, before our gaffer Bertie Mee and his Lazio counterpart put an end to all the nonsense. I was amazed at how quickly they brought the situation under control and even more amazed when both sets of players returned to their respective tables and finished off their dinners. Nobody was interested in pressing charges as far as I could see, and UEFA never batted an eyelid, although today I'm sure there would have been a police wagon, or two, to have carted us all off into custody. A semblance of normality returned, although several rival players looked at each other daggers drawn. The English press boys had been with us in the restaurant, so there was no escape from the inevitable 'Battle of Rome' headlines plastered all over the front pages of the tabloids when we landed at Heathrow.

If looks could kill in the Eternal City, Arsenal would have been in for a torrid second leg at Highbury, but when the time came for action to speak louder than words and Italian threats of revenge to become a reality, Lazio's wildcats had been transformed into pussycats. They virtually lay down and bottled the match, losing 2–0.

Something strange happened on 16 December 1970 – Bertie actually required me to kick a ball in anger. Mind you, given the circumstances, he wasn't exactly taking a risk. We were 4–0 up against Beveren, the Belgian part-timers, from the first leg and drawing 0–0 at the interval in Antwerp when the manager decided to give Geordie a rest and me a run in the second half. 'Marinello's magic perks up Arsenal,' proclaimed the *Daily Sketch* the following morning on the evidence of one weaving ninety-yard run through the Beveren defence which ended with me grazing the post with a shot. That was as close as anyone came to breaking the stalemate, and I resumed my customary position on the bench, in danger of becoming a stale mate!

The record books show that sixteen players had a hand in Arsenal's Double triumph. Fourteen is much nearer the mark in reality because, apart from my 'now-you-see-me, now-you-don't' moments in August, Sammy Nelson started just twice in the First Division and made another couple of appearances as a sub.

Step into the Marinello time machine for a moment and let me introduce you to the squad.

The pints of lager are flowing, just halves for Bob Wilson and Jon Sammels, while John Roberts has a dash of lime in his. Geordie Armstrong and Ray Kennedy have bottles of Newcastle Brown on the go, Pat Rice sips a Guinness, George Graham enjoys a Bacardi and Coke, and Peter Simpson is enveloped in a cloud of cigar smoke as he nurses his large brandy and Coke. It might have been a pint of lager or a vodka and Coke for Frank McLintock. Me? I was never fussed . . . just so long as it was wet.

Goalkeeper Wilson, or 'Willo' as we knew him, came late into the profession from teaching and for two or three years at least Bob was absolutely brilliant at his job. The highlight for me watching him was the manner in which he once fronted up to George Best, clean through at Highbury, and refused to be conned by Bestie's swaying and attempts to sell him a dummy before calmly plucking the ball off the toes of the dumbfounded Manchester United winger. 'Willo' was the butt of many of our pranks and frequently discovered bills on away-days had been signed in his name, but he took it all in good heart.

Pat, alias Mr Dependable, was everything you wanted in a right-back: strong and a good tackler. We had a real character at left-back in dapper McNab, who considered himself a bit of a ladies' man. That was a source of some amusement, but a smartly dressed 'Nabbers' had the last laugh when he was squiring the stunning young Olivia Newton-John about town. Bob also knew some rather less fragrant people and was told off in no uncertain terms by Bertie after inviting the infamous south London gangsters, the Richardson brothers, into the players' lounge. Mind you, that was one occasion when Arsenal's own 'Krays' and the Richardsons weren't at each other's throats.

Sammy made just a handful of appearances in defence. He was the joker in the pack and specialised in sending bogus letters to his colleagues. On one memorable occasion, he decided to wind up both Peter Simpson and George Graham, who were a touch sensitive about their thinning thatches. Sammy pretended to be the manufacturer of hair and grooming accessories with a new wonder product which Peter and George might care to sample, because, as Sammy wrote, 'I cannot help noticing your tendency to baldness under the harsh, unforgiving glare of the Highbury floodlights!'

My room-mate on most trips and godfather to our eldest son, Eddie 'Ted' Kelly, was similar to me in some respects – we were probably bad for each other. We bonded beautifully, despite me hailing from Edinburgh and Eddie being a Glaswegian. Strong in the tackle and a good passer, he was a midfield player who should have achieved a lot more in his career. Don promised him he would skipper Arsenal one day, but that day never dawned.

Number five McLintock was a truly great captain and a good lad. If you had any problems, you'd take them to our centre-half and if you were in trouble on the park, Frank would always be there first to sort it. Enjoyed a good post-match lager or two, as well. Frank's sidekick at number six until November was Welshman John Roberts, dubbed 'Garth' – after the comic strip hero whose adventures we followed in the *Daily Mirror*. He was a giant, a nice lad and dedicated with it. Garth fell out briefly with the lads on one occasion, though. We lived by the code 'What happens away, stays away', and too many stories were getting back to the management of our touring exploits. The culprit was narrowed down to either my wife, Joyce, or Garth's missus. George Graham set a trap, and Garth was caught spilling the beans over the phone to his beloved. The mole was out, but there was no lasting animosity or anything silly like that because this was basically a tremendous, tight-knit squad.

Peter Simpson was simply 'Stan' to us after someone remarked he bore a passing resemblance to Stan Laurel. He was a good sweeper, and there was a great togetherness about 'Stan' and Frank. A quiet man from Gorleston, Norfolk, he liked nothing better than to relax after a victory and another clean sheet with a large Remy Martin and a Havana.

The number seven shirt belonged to Geordie Armstrong, a great pal despite the fact his amazing fitness levels, tenacity, tackling, defensive qualities and ability to send over a stream of high-quality crosses kept me outside the team and resembling a poor little orphan with his nose pressed up against the sweet shop window. Geordie had most of the qualities I lacked. I never worked as hard as him, although I was probably capable of doing so. It just wasn't in my nature. Having Geordie in the side was like having two men on the right. Towards the end of the season, I found myself at a party in Finchley with some less than savoury characters. One of them took a shine to me and was upset when he discovered I couldn't get in the Arsenal team because Geordie was playing so well. The villain asked me in all seriousness if I would like him to shoot Geordie, and I must have recoiled in horror at the very idea. My would-be hitman swiftly reassured me that 'shoot' in this particular instance did not mean 'murder', just a 'leg job'. I almost said, 'Oh, that's all right then!' but thought better of it. Geordie was also an unbelievably generous soul, and his home in Southgate was virtually open house. A constant stream of relatives from the North-east visited, and he also took in the outrageous Ron Tilsed when I asked him to pack his bags.

Ron and I hit it off immediately when he arrived at Highbury. He was still in his teens, and I knew what it felt like to suddenly join a big London club. He was in digs but hated them because they were so restrictive. When he mentioned this to me, I offered him a spare room – but I soon wished I hadn't. He was a ladies' man, and Joyce and I became familiar with waking up in the morning and finding different blondes, brunettes and redheads walking about in next to nothing. Ron had been understudy in the England youth team to Peter Shilton and had joined us as reserve keeper from Bournemouth for £10,000, but you would have thought he was an England international World Cup player with a few hundred First Division matches under his belt from the way he carried on. Ron was probably on £40 a week and doing his level best to spend £100 a week. We were good pals, but I had to throw him out for the sake of my sanity, and Geordie took him in.

Peter Storey was plain 'Snout' on account of his big nose. A very underrated holding midfield player and also extremely volatile, he was deputed to do the man-marking job on the opposing danger man and frequently took his job literally while also finding time to snap and snarl at the referee for ninety minutes. Hard, bordering on dirty, 'Snout' also took a mean penalty and looked forward to a deserved drink after the match. He had the ability to mark George Best out of a match, and there might even have been more to Peter's game, but we never found out because Don slagged him off unmercifully whenever he dared to cross the halfway line and ventured into opposition territory. Every successful team needs its 'Snout', and he was second to none as an enforcer.

Number nine all season long was John Radford, our big Yorkshireman from Pontefract. Raddy was a terrific centre-forward, strong in the air and with a decent shot in both feet, who deserved more than two England caps. He had a droll sense of humour and was good fun. The lads were always amused when we were out on a jolly, the drinks were flowing, and Raddy would focus on me and inquire gently with mock concern, 'Where did it all go wrong, Peter? We thought we were signing a world-beater.' I never did have an answer.

Raddy's strike partner at number ten, Ray Kennedy, was very strong and quick for a big man, but had a tendency to put on weight and was regularly forced on to the scales by the management. Like Geordie Armstrong, Ray hailed from Northumberland – Seaton Delaval, in his case – and was another loyal Newcastle supporter, of the Brown variety, I mean. There was often quite a deal of 'creative friction' between the two proud forwards which made for a strained relationship, particularly as Ray and Raddy lived next door to each other in a pair of capacious semi-detached houses. Don worked them like dogs in training, making diagonal runs. It was deadly serious stuff when it came to tactics and would sometimes end in a bout of fisticuffs as they argued over who should make the first run.

Charlie George possessed an abundance of natural ability and could deliver cannonball shots from either foot with minimal backlift. Just witness his FA Cup final winner against Liverpool. I joked he also invented the forty-yard one-two. Charlie would smash these long, raking passes and control the returns however awkwardly they arrived, at any height, pace or angle. He was a typical rebellious, know-it-all Cockney and bonded with Eddie and me. Everyone got on in the squad, though. There was no room for cliques.

'Stroller', aka George Graham, was an elegant player with an aversion to training. He knew all the dodges, and that's probably what helped him to become such a successful manager. Don was a great influence on him, preaching that if you get your defence set up correctly everything else will follow. An immaculate dresser in his Italian designer suits and carrying a briefcase, 'Gorgeous George', as we also called him, stood out from the crowd. He had a particular aversion to our cross-country races at London Colney and always trailed home among the last half-dozen over the two-and-a-half-mile course until he stumbled across a cunning little short cut along the path through the woods, and let Charlie in on the secret. Charlie was another with no great fondness for running, unless there was a ball at the end of his feet, and he needed little encouragement to join 'Stroller' in taking the diversion, which lopped three-quarters of a mile off their ordeal. The two dodgers overplayed their hand, however, and when they started finishing higher up the field, Don suspected something fishy was going on and hid in the bushes to catch them. 'Bang to rights' was the phrase, I believe, Charlie used to describe their capture.

Jon Sammels won all those cross-country races, and Don loved him for that, but I never could understand why the Highbury crowd took such a dislike to 'Sammy'. If I was playing and Arsenal were winning it seemed like sometimes all I had to do to win a standing ovation from the fans was wiggle my hips and pose like a matador, but poor 'Sammy' could work his bollocks off and still get booed. He was a hard worker who possessed amazing stamina and was good for the team – quite apart from weighing in with half a dozen goals in the successful 1969–70 European Fairs Cup mission, including the winner in the final against Anderlecht on that memorable night at Highbury when Arsenal overturned a 3–1 deficit in Brussels. Last and least, I suppose, there was me: 'The Cat', as I was nicknamed by Charlie. I quite liked that tag because I thought it conjured up images of a sleek tiger ready to pounce. I had long hair, wore my shirt untucked and socks down around my ankles – despite the club rule about shinpads – but then Charlie let the cat out of the bag, so to speak, when he revealed: 'It's Cat as in Catweazle, the tramp on kids' telly, because you are one scruffy bastard, Marinello!'

The Double-winners were going to celebrate in style, that much was certain, but the planned week in Torremolinos with our wives and girlfriends, followed by a lads-only week in Portugal's Algarve, turned into a damp squib . . . and left me feeling like a party-pooper.

We were just a few days from packing our bags when Ray Kennedy, temporarily without a regular girlfriend, sidled up to me and produced a photograph of this absolute stunner. She had written to him from his native North-east, including her telephone number, and Ray asked, 'What do you think?' I told him he was one lucky sod, just providing it was a genuine photograph, not a picture of her mate, and that she didn't resemble the back of a bus in the flesh. I don't know why, but I also strongly suspected she was the sort of woman drawn to Ray because of his fame.

'No, no,' said Ray. 'I'm sure she's the real deal,' and with that he was off to phone Geordieland. Ray collected this twenty-year-old vision of loveliness off the train at King's Cross and brought her to our house in Winchmore Hill, where it had been agreed they could stay because Ray was in digs, and we were flying abroad the following day. The headboard in the spare bedroom that night took some fearful punishment against the wall, which left Joyce giggling in my ear, 'Just what do you think they're doing in there?'

I don't know how often it pisses down solidly with rain for seven days in Torremolinos, but I do know I've been there when it did. Our first week away was spent largely in hotel bars, peeking up at the grey skies and wondering if the sun would ever deign to put in an appearance. It had all turned a touch stormy, too, for Ray and the Lovely One. They only had one thing in common and, when the novelty of that wore off after three or four days, they fell out spectacularly. Ray went off to do his own thing while the Lovely One latched on to Joyce and Eddie Kelly's wife, Sylvia. There were no complaints about our marvellous five-star hotel, however. It was sumptuous, and the six-course dinners took about three hours from starters to coffee.

I didn't know Torremolinos was famous as a gay haunt, but had my card marked in no uncertain terms when I got up to dance at one disco and was joined by this fruity fellow who insisted on trying to hold my hand. Thanks, pal, I managed to smile, but no thanks.

I wasn't thanked either when Joyce put her Women's Lib hat on and, with Charlie's wife, Sue, decided to get militant over the second leg of the jolly. The girls decided that the Algarve should not be off-limits to the wives and girlfriends. If the players were going, then they were going to accompany them, sure as hell. The dispute ended with all the players – apart from Bob McNab and Geoff Barnett – sheepishly flying directly back to London with the girls, and I copped a fair bit of grief from the lads over Joyce's stand.

My drinks kept flowing – with a thirsty royal princess in Chelsea – and there were champagne moments around the corner when I became a racehorse owner. Then I shot myself in the foot by missing a goal in a European Cup tie which might have cemented my place as an Arsenal legend. But that was sport, not life and death. Worse, far worse, was the sudden discovery of manic depression in the family. This was real life, and there was no hiding place.

CHAPTER 9

No Go Gunner

Although I had been virtually a spectator throughout the Double-winning campaign, I was convinced 1971–72 would be my breakthrough season, and at the end of July, when we flew off to Lisbon for a prestigious pre-season friendly against Benfica, I felt coiled and ready to spring. My pal Geordie Armstrong may have been crowned Highbury player of the year, but he knew he couldn't afford to rest on his laurels and that I was breathing down his neck. My confident mood was enhanced when I replaced Geordie in the second half and turned on the style in Portugal, even though we lost 2–0. Three nights later back at Highbury, I replaced Geordie again as we murdered Benfica 6–2.

I was feeling fitter, stronger and better than ever thanks to all the muscle-strengthening and stamina-building exercises Don Howe had supervised. How I cursed him at the time, under my breath, but I knew deep down it had all been for my own benefit. As for pace, I felt I was faster than the 10.3 seconds I clocked with the Powderhall sprinters in Edinburgh. All the nonsense, the razzmatazz and showbiz stuff had largely faded away by now, apart from a wee spot of modelling. That was a relief, a blessing, and I felt I could concentrate on my football, pure and simple. If only it had always been that way.

Don was gone now. He'd left that July for what turned out to be an unhappy spell as manager of West Bromwich Albion, a loss that weakened Arsenal considerably in my view. Frank McLintock had stressed, 'Don mustn't leave Arsenal. I shall be very, very disappointed if Don leaves us and I know I speak for the rest of the players,' while Bertie Mee was similarly upset, saying, 'There is no need for me to repeat how highly I rate Don as a coach, and how sorry I am to see him leaving Highbury.' However, Don was eager to test himself, to see if he could cut it as a number one in his own right and, when the club he used to play for came calling, you couldn't blame him for going home to the West Midlands. Changes were in the air, and we also parted company with Jon Sammels, sold to Leicester City for £100,000, before starting the season with a thumping 3–0 home win over Chelsea.

Steve Burtenshaw was promoted to first-team coach, a move which I felt sure would strengthen my chances because Steve had seen a lot of me in the reserves. Still, I had to wait for Geordie to suffer a knock in September before I got back in the team for the first time in a year in a nondescript 1–0 home win over Third Division Barnsley in the League Cup. I reminded the crowd of my dribbling skills and won my fair share of applause that night, but the team were treated to the slow handclap and booed off. Highbury expected more, much more from their Double-winners. Victories were taken as a given; the supporters wanted to see Arsenal win with style and substance – which meant goals, plenty of them.

Next up was the club's first European Cup tie, and, with Geordie still injured, allied most probably to the fact we were facing amateur opponents in Stromgodset, Bertie decided to 'risk' me in the opening leg. I wasn't about to start complaining, though. Far from it. I relished this rare opportunity to demonstrate my skills, and we were 1–0 up in Oslo inside ninety seconds when I set off down the right and crossed for Ray Kennedy to turn the ball back for Peter Simpson to score. Not bad for starters, I thought, but the main course was something to savour. My pace and ball control exposed the Norwegian side's assortment of commercial travellers, bank clerks, railwaymen and plumbers, and I didn't need the encouragement of my team-mates shouting 'take 'em all on, son' when the ball reached me, out on the left this time. I put in a sprint, their keeper came out, and it was a straightforward matter of chipping the ball over him for a 2–0 lead which eventually became a 3–1 victory thanks to a twenty-yarder from Eddie Kelly, although I had to go off because of cramp near the end.

After the match Eddie and myself were invited out on

the town by a locally-based businessman who was a supporter of the club. We visited Oslo's top restaurant, went through the card, and our table was awash with champagne plus a selection of highly attractive escort girls for 'afters'. The businessman grinned to Eddie and me and said, 'Tonight you are my guests, and when I tell you everything is on me, I do mean everything,' before nodding at the girls. It was all there for us on a plate. I won't pretend we weren't tempted, but Eddie and I polished off another glass of fizz before making our apologies and leaving, to the evident disappointment of the girls (at least I like to think they were disappointed) and disbelief of our genial host.

I wasn't holding my breath after the Stromgodset jaunt because I knew Geordie would be fit to tackle Everton at Goodison Park the following Saturday, and I would be back in the reserves, although Bertie was sufficiently encouraged by my contribution in Norway to say, 'Without doubt, Marinello is a far better player than he was twelve months ago. Stromgodset had to use two players to mark him.' I think the overriding feeling in the team, however, was that I had over-indulged the solo dribbling in the second half and kept the rest of the team waiting. And that, in a side built on the one-for-all, all-for-one principle of hard work, would always be difficult to swallow. Arsenal duly completed a 7–1 aggregate demolition job on Stromgodset a fortnight later without my services.

I wasn't happy and got a gee-up from our chief scout,

Gordon Clark, one of the major players instrumental in bringing me to the club. Gordon enjoyed popping into training sessions at London Colney when he wasn't busy scouring Britain for fresh talent and made it plain he felt I should buck up my ideas. 'What the fuck's wrong with you, Peter?' he demanded bluntly. 'They want me to go and look at Leighton James, but Burnley want £300,000 for him, and, frankly, I don't think he could lace your boots.'

Then Joyce went in to see Bertie, confessing she was worried about my gambling. Joyce knew we weren't saving as much as we should have been, but that was an overreaction on her part. I think it was a manifestation of her illness to come. Little problems used to escalate into major issues in her mind. She did have a point, though: I probably was gambling too much, but it never impacted on our lives to the extent that we ever needed to economise or go without anything. It seemed like a small fortune was coming in every week with my wages topped up by bonuses, plus my modelling money, and I would be a regular in the bookies, George Basham at Southgate, as well as having a telephone account with them. I could happily study the racing papers before training in the morning and spend a couple of hours in the bookies on free afternoons. It was just horses at this stage – I went to the dogs later! The funny thing is, gambling in a casino held no appeal whatsoever. Neither did one-armed bandits or cards. I liked speed, and there was simply no adrenalin rush or excitement attached to watching a little ball spinning round a roulette wheel. I thought nothing of losing £100 in an unlucky week, but it wasn't all gloom and doom. I used to tease Ron Tilsed cruelly that I was going to double his rent, and, of course, there were my winning streaks. I wasn't a mug punter, just fairly addicted.

The buzz from winning was great. One of the London evening papers labelled me 'Poor Little Rich Boy', and I couldn't argue with that – it was quite apt. I still like an occasional flutter, but my finances have taken such a massive hammering that I have to be very careful. I may only win £2 compared to the hundreds I gambled when money was no object, but I still get a buzz out of it. I didn't look at it as money; those notes were more like fun tickets. I'd been bitten by the gambling bug at the tender age of ten at Stenhouse Cross in Edinburgh, where I used to run my dad's bets to this wee guy in an alleyway leading to a dodgy-looking flat, and every so often run home again from the illegal bookie with dad's winnings inside a small plain brown envelope. By the age of fifteen, I liked a bet myself, and the habit was encouraged at Hibs alongside regular punters such as Peter Cormack and Jimmy O'Rourke. I think the Arsenal players all used the same bank, where we enjoyed certain concessions, and I'm pretty certain that Bertie was aware of our financial situations. I was pushing it a bit on the horses, and he advised me to tone things down.

The costliest punt I ever had was £2,000 on Warning, a colt out of Dancing Brave, in a big Group One race in France in 1988. Pat Eddery, Warning's jockey, couldn't believe it when he lost at Deauville. He thought he was on a dead cert, and so did I – but we all got stuffed by a fabulous filly called Miesque. I've had a couple of tasty tickles, too, to balance the books: £1,800 on Reference Point to do the business at 7–4 under Steve Cauthen in the 1987 King George VI and Queen Elizabeth Diamond Stakes at Ascot and £1,200 on Grundy at 5–1 when Eddery won the Derby in 1975.

I still enjoyed occasionally brushing shoulders with the rich and famous, including royalty. *Playboy* magazine organised one celebrity bash in a restaurant off the King's Road in Chelsea with Bob McNab, Geoff Hurst and me booked for a modelling engagement. After a lunchtime fitting, I was bowled over to be invited by Adam Faith to while away the afternoon over drinks in his flat nearby. Adam was a pop idol, a particular hero of mine, and a TV star in the cult series *Budgie*, in which he played an ex-convict, and here I was downing Bacardis in his penthouse. I had to pinch myself it was real and not some sort of dream. I needed those drinks, too. Dutch courage turned me into a cross between an Edwardian cricketer and a character out of *The Great Gatsby* because I was obliged to don long white flared flannels, a white frilly blouse and a black-and-white tank top with matching black-and-white shoes. That was bad enough, but then I had to strut my stuff on the catwalk. Bob was fine in a cream jerkin while Geoff resembled James Bond in his immaculate double-breasted suit. They were thoroughly at home.

I needed another stiff drink to recover from my ordeal and found a willing companion – Princess Margaret. For a member of the royal family, she was totally unaffected, just friendly and interested in my life, although she found my broad accent a bit of a handful. I appreciated her kindness because her husband, Lord Snowdon, took the piss out of me quite unmercifully. The Princess had her own personal waiter lurking in the background to ensure her glass of white wine never got empty, and he was a busy man that evening.

Bertie was busy, too, shortly before Christmas 1971, when he swooped to sign Alan Ball in a blaze of publicity for a club record £220,000 from Everton – a champion buy for a team of champions. Bally may have been a World Cup winner and a terrific player in his famous white boots, but his arrival in the Highbury dressing-room caused immediate friction, not because we didn't like him but because we didn't like the idea he was coming in on massive £300-a-week wages, £200 more than the rest of us, at best, were receiving. Inevitably, the Kray Twins were in like a shot on behalf of the players to lean on Bertie and Ken Friar, who were told in no uncertain terms that 'something had to be done'. It was, and a loyalty bonus system was introduced which rewarded players for how long they had been at the club. Geordie was rolling in it, having turned professional at Arsenal in 1961, while I was pleased with the outcome as well, despite being a relative newcomer. To get a player of Alan Ball's stature and experience was fantastic. He was an even better player than I thought, a clever, fearless midfield man and particularly adept at playing little one-twos in confined spaces to get out of trouble or create a shooting opportunity. A Paul Scholes of his day.

It took Bally time to settle at Arsenal, which came as no great surprise to anybody. It's most odd, and I can't put my finger on it, but a whole host of big-money players – not to mention myself – struggled at first at Highbury almost as if there was a jinx at work. Bobby Gould had cost £90,000 from Coventry in 1968, yet never really made it with Arsenal, while Jeff Blockley followed Bobby from Highfield Road for £200,000 four years later and had a torturous time. Our Welsh international John Roberts and, much later, fellow Scot Charlie Nicholas from Celtic also suffered a similar fate.

Bally's arrival upset the applecart, and the players were wary of him at first. He and I hit it off immediately, however, after discovering a mutual love of racing, and one of his pals in the sport of kings was Newmarket trainer Ian Walker, who asked us in the run-up to the sales there if we had ever considered buying a racehorse. It seemed like a great idea at the time and team-mates Frank McLintock, Eddie, Raddy, George Graham, Peter Storey and Charlie all said they fancied a piece of the action, and that they were prepared to chip in £400–500 apiece. So off Bally and I trotted to Newmarket Sales with Ian, and after a few drinks led to a few more drinks, we ended up paying £6,000 for a two-year-old out of Firestreak, which we decided to christen Go Go Gunner. There was another horse there we liked the look of, but at £8,000, he was a little too rich for us, so that's why we never came to own the 1974 Derby winner Snow Knight.

I got home late that night and relayed the wonderful information to Joyce that she was now married to a racehorse owner. She wasn't too happy to say the least. She had an Italian background, like me, which made her volatile, and the combination of my late, drunken arrival home, the news about the horse and the fact that the nice supper she'd made for me had dried to a crisp in the oven led to a plate of congealed spaghetti Bolognese winging its way towards my head in the kitchen. It was the fastest I'd moved all day.

With VAT and Weatherbys' cut, the final tally came to roughly £6,500 – but that was no problem. Two more players and there would be ten of us in the syndicate at £650 a man. One by one, Frank and the others started to bail out until Bally and myself were left alone with the bill plus the running costs of our trainer. To my mind we were in deep shit, up the creek without a paddle so to speak, and some serious, sober thinking, brains and initiative were required to get us out of the soft and smelly. This may surprise some people, given the apparently chaotic nature of much of my life, but I am quite a sound organiser when I put my mind to it and I created a motley six-man consortium. Along with me and Bally, there was Stan Flashman, the ticket tout on first-name terms with each and every Arsenal player; Nick the Greek, a great Gunners fan and owner of a restaurant where he regularly encouraged us to smash the crockery in the style of his home nation; Bob Merrydale (aka Bob the Mechanic, who looked after the players' cars) and North London Bookie, a chap whose name escapes me more easily than the memory of his extremely good-looking wife. We were up and ready for the off at just over £1,000 apiece.

Go Go Gunner would be running in Arsenal colours, of course, red with white sleeves, and for the jockey we chose a tartan cap, 'Marinello tartan' Bally jokingly dubbed it. Walker was fairly comfortably off and for several seasons had been top trainer at Haydock Park on Merseyside, where Bally, then with Everton, had got to know him. Top trainer he might have been but he soon lived up, or down if you like, to the old adage that trainers are the worst tipsters of all.

Go Go Gunner's first outing was at Newbury in the Kennett Maiden Stakes, but his debut was nothing to write home about. Unplaced: I knew how he felt. Second time out, three weeks later at Newmarket, Walker confidently informed us he had no chance. Consequently, Bally, myself and the rest of the syndicate decided to keep our powder dry and didn't bother having anything on our 20–1 long shot who finished second and would have netted us a handsome profit had we only backed him each-way. Armed with the knowledge that our horse was anything but a no-hoper, the syndicate plunged in big time a few races later at Lingfield, where our combined outlay of £4,000 brought the price crashing down to 3–1 favourite. Then the starting stalls sprang open and our jockey, Peter

Madden, resembled that guy in the advert on TV smoking a Hamlet cigar, without a care in the world. Once it dawned on Peter there was a race on, he belatedly kicked Go Go Gunner into gear ten lengths behind the rest of the field and they came through to be narrowly pipped in a thrilling finish. Peter was subjected to more than a few harsh words from Bally and Stan Flashman. Stan was not a man to cross, or a character who enjoyed losing money, and Madden was summarily jocked off, never to ride for us again.

Then we had a disaster – because Go Go Gunner won a race. It was a foul night at Windsor, lashing down with rain. Bally's wife was out for the evening in their Mercedes, so he reluctantly had to slum it with me in my bashed-up white £300 Mini (the Spitfire was Joyce's pride and joy). Eddie Kelly was almost too embarrassed to be seen out in it with me and would always duck down on the floor whenever I gave him a lift to training or Highbury. Bally was mightily relieved no one spotted him arriving at Windsor, but disappointed when our trusted trainer informed us Go Go Gunner wouldn't like the soft going and that we'd be throwing our money away backing him, even though the services of Pat Eddery had been secured for the mount. All of Windsor seemed to have taken the hint, and we watched the odds on our pride and joy slide out to 9–2, before jumping on with a big bet on 4–1 chance Moor Lane, the second favourite. Our faces must have been an absolute picture as we watched Go Go Gunner get up to snatch victory by half a length from

Moor Lane. Bally must have done a good fifty quid on the favourite, yet when the press badgered us afterwards for a quote and asked if we'd backed our horse, there was no option for us but to stick on a sickly false smile and lie through gritted teeth: 'Yeah, of course. We've had a bob or two.' The remainder of the meeting was a similar tale of woe, and come the end of the night, we had to borrow £20 off a bookmaker to fill the car with petrol and buy a fish and chip supper on the way home. World Cup-winner Alan Ball, Arsenal's club-record £200,000 signing, and £100,000 whizkid Peter Marinello reduced to tapping up a friendly bookie for twenty quid to get home and eat: I wonder what the press would have made of that story?

Give Go Go Gunner his due, however, he did prove to be a model of consistency in his following four races, finishing sixth on each occasion at Kempton, Brighton, Newmarket and Leicester as Walker scoured the country for another lucky track.

Big Stan splashed out to hire Lester Piggott for a race at Newmarket. Lester assessed form and the rest of the field before telling us quietly, but with absolute conviction, 'This horse will win by four or five lengths,' and the syndicate duly plunged in to make a killing. Unfortunately, Lester's presence aboard Go Go Gunner set alarm bells ringing among the bookies, and, instead of going off at maybe 7–2 or 4–1, our fancy was 6–4 favourite on arriving first past the post in the Snailwell Maiden Stakes, Division 2. And Lester was wrong, the winning margin was three lengths.

We also scored in a Listed race at Newmarket, and were beaten by just half a length on another occasion by Angels Too, a classy number who was sold to Italy for £30,000. When our horse could finish no better than fifth at Leicester again, despite going off 4–1 favourite under Eddery, we decided to cut our losses. We had broken even on Go Go Gunner to begin with when his prize money covered costs, but as a three-year-old he was miserable and not much better at four. When Lester's wife, Susan, offered us the chance to sell the horse and double our money, the syndicate decided it was an offer we couldn't afford to refuse. Bally and I had enjoyed a good run for our money and a lot of laughs with a right motley crew. Under a new trainer, I noted the horse managed three more races, finishing third each time. Go Go Gunner's racing career finally ended in my home city of Edinburgh, where he was sent off at 12–1 for the Lothians Handicap and trailed home ninth in the nine-runner field. Played 25; Won 2; Lost 23. I could only sympathise. Go Go Gunner showed great promise, but never really trained on. A bit like me, I suppose.

Meanwhile, March 1972 arrived with me still confined to the stiffs while the first team were competing seriously on three fronts – the First Division, FA Cup and European Cup. The month began with the lads unbeaten in a dozen league matches and having won four on the trot against Huddersfield, Sheffield United, Derby and Ipswich without conceding a goal, while the FA Cup had seen Swindon and Reading eliminated. As for Europe, after the stuffing of Stromsgodset, we had beaten Grasshoppers 5–0 on aggregate, but were drawn against the mighty Ajax. Bertie returned from a spying mission in Holland to see the holders in a domestic cup-tie with a warning that they had improved since the Gunners beat them in the Fairs Cup in 1970. The Dutch masters, with genius Johan Cruyff pulling the strings and weaving his unique brand of magic all over the park, threatened to be very awkward opponents in the quarter-final.

Suddenly, it all went wrong. From looking impregnable in defence, the team suffered a severe case of the jitters and lost three successive league matches without scoring a goal, at Manchester City, Newcastle and Leeds, shipping seven goals in the process, and during this fall from grace came a 2–1 defeat in Amsterdam. It was a hectic period, and our resources were stretched by dogged Derby taking the team to two replays in the FA Cup before we put them out, then going on to beat Orient on the road to the semi-finals.

The return leg against Ajax was on everyone's minds, and the omens should have been good for me personally, if not for the team, because Raddy was suspended for three weeks and ineligible, as was Alan Ball. There was one nasty fly in the ointment – three weeks earlier there had been a jaundice scare at the club. Geoff Barnett was laid low, and traces of the virus were detected in his blood. I always feared Geoff might put me out of the game permanently one day and himself, too, for that matter. Why I let him give me a lift to Highbury for so long I don't know – he used to scare me half to death, driving his three-litre Ford Capri like the wind from Southgate to the ground in about twelve minutes flat and managing to smoke about fifteen cigarettes in the process. We called Geoff 'Marty' on account of his big, bulging eyes, which made him a dead ringer for the comedian Marty Feldman. As for my eyes, I kept them tightly shut on those breakneck journeys into work and offered up a silent prayer or two. Because I mixed frequently with Geoff, the club decided I had to go into quarantine when he contracted jaundice. No way could they risk an epidemic sweeping through the dressing-room. That would have spelled disaster. So, just when I might have been integrated back into the first team, I was stuck at home for three weeks twiddling my thumbs until the club doctor gave me the all-clear to resume training. Being removed from the game for so long gave me plenty of time to think about things. I remained convinced I could do well and began to analyse my play – what was lacking and what was required to convince Bertie that I had at last overcome the Scottish failing of hanging on to the ball too long.

The Saturday before the Ajax return leg, I was given an hour for the reserves before being withdrawn. I knew I was being saved for the big one but I was a jumble of emotions. I had been playing well, yet sixty minutes in the stiffs had left me feeling drained. I knew I would be undercooked going in to face Ajax. An expectant crowd of over 56,000 packed inside Highbury on 22 March with everyone buzzing about how we were going to have a real go at the Dutch with two wingers, Geordie Armstrong and myself, something we'd never really tried before.

It was a magnificent 'golden' Ajax team, containing seven or eight Holland internationals, including Johan Neeskens, Ruud Krol, Arnold Muhren and the right-back who would be marking me, Wim Suurbier. I thought we played them off the park that night. Everything was set up for me to be a hero. In the first minute Suurbier had the ball, and I robbed him. I was clean through, albeit at a slight angle, with only the keeper, Heinz Stuy, to beat. I dipped my shoulder, feinting to go left, but Stuy read my thoughts and never bought the dummy. My shot was too close to him and he saved it. The chance had come too early for me. For over thirty years I've been attending Arsenal functions, and all anyone wants to talk about is that miss. I wish I had a pound for every time someone has told me, 'If you had scored that goal, Peter, Arsenal could have won the European Cup in 1972.' Everyone remembers that fucking miss, it's haunted me all my life. They remember it more than me and Geordie playing well, they remember it more than Stuy's long clearance which bounced off the retreating George Graham's head and left Bob Wilson in no man's land for the only goal of the game. There was no consolation afterwards when Cruyff bragged, 'Arsenal didn't really trouble us – only Marinello and Armstrong.'

There was some slight consolation the following week. Two years and seventy-seven days after I scored my first league goal for Arsenal, I managed another on Tuesday 28

March 1972, and it was enough to clinch a 1–0 win against Southampton at Highbury. It was my first league start for nineteen months since I faced West Ham in August 1970. There was relief all round when I rammed the ball left-footed into the roof of the net after my own header from Geordie's corner was blocked.

My emotions must have contrasted with the thoughts running through the mind of an opposing winger. It was the beginning of the end for Saints legend Terry Paine, dropped to the bench for the first time in fifteen years after 720 appearances. His consistency at the very top of his profession was something at which I could only marvel.

One critic was sufficiently impressed to tell his audience that the 'little boy lost' was showing distinct signs of maturity. Truthfully, it felt like being released from prison. I'd hated every single minute being out of the first team, and there had been a million minutes, and more than a few chats with Bertie Mee about my destiny because I had become more than a little bitter playing in the reserves. The goal lifted a lead weight, and suddenly I felt very glad I hadn't made the mistake of asking for a transfer when I felt so sorry for myself. In my heart I always wanted to do well for Arsenal and had I left them without having a real go at proving myself, I would have felt I was a failure. I believed I was a man finally coming in from the cold on April Fool's Day, when relegation-bound Nottingham Forest arrived at Highbury, more in hope than expectation, it must be said. They departed soundly beaten 3–0, and from the first moment I touched the ball that afternoon, the fans were right behind me. With McLintock injured, Bally was appointed captain for the day and revelled in the responsibility, spraying passes out to Geordie on the right and me down the left. I thrived on the service and must have left the Forest right-back, Peter Hindley, with twisted blood. He chopped me down twice, and they were suicidal fouls because we scored from both a free-kick and a penalty. Sadly, I found I was only keeping a shirt warm for someone else, and when Raddy returned from suspension, I returned to the sidelines, a spectator again as he scored the winner in the FA Cup semi-final against Stoke in a replay at Goodison Park. Arsenal were back at Wembley, and I was on the outside again, looking enviously in, although football was soon to become the least of my worries.

When you look back over the course of your life, certain dates, times and events leap out as being particularly significant. My life would never be the same after my first son, Paul Peter Marinello, was safely delivered on 28 April 1972 – and neither would Joyce's.

Her pregnancy wasn't really planned, it just sort of happened . . . although I am led to believe I did have some significant input. Joyce's mum, Laura, was back from Australia on her first visit, and, when the time came, they went together to the world-famous St Mary's Hospital in Paddington. Arsenal were great at providing private health insurance for players and their wives, and so it was that Joyce found herself in the room recently vacated by actress Una Stubbs, who played Alf Garnett's daughter

Rita in the hit TV comedy *Till Death Us Do Part*. It was quite a difficult birth by all accounts, and Joyce required an epidural injection – I was otherwise occupied, out drinking. There weren't many 'new men' in evidence in the early seventies, and the business end of birth didn't hold us as entranced as the prospect of the brandy and cigars to celebrate fatherhood.

Paul weighed in at 8 lb 6 oz, a bonny, bouncing boy, and we were extremely proud of our wee lad. Mind you, thirty or so years later I sometimes wind up Paul by referring to him as an 'Englishman' or 'Cockney', which can provoke a less than civilised response from a lad with a proud Scots accent. Eddie Kelly took me out for the traditional new father's bevvy, but it was very restrained by our standards because of the sensitive nature of Arsenal's season. The title was on its way to Derby, the prospect of European glory had gone, but the FA Cup could yet save our season.

Joyce came out of St Mary's, and the plan was for Laura to stay with her at our home in Winchmore Hill for a week. I would have relished some time off, but everyone was concentrating hard on preparation for our FA Cup final date with Leeds United on 6 May. And to be perfectly honest, I thought I had a chance of playing at Wembley. Our home was besieged by the media wanting photographs of baby Marinello, and the general fuss and hullabaloo very quickly became too much for Laura, who retreated to Edinburgh, leaving Joyce to cope on her own with Paul. I was in our team hotel in north London, dreaming of Cup glory, when an Arsenal director beckoned me over, and I could immediately sense by his gentle, sympathetic manner that something was wrong. 'Peter,' he said. 'I think it would be best if you went home. Joyce needs you.'

George Graham's wife Marie had popped round on a visit and discovered Joyce sitting in a rocking chair totally oblivious to Paul, who was lying naked, crying on the floor. Developments were rapid – they needed to be – and I took Joyce to see a psychiatrist in Harley Street, who admitted her to his clinic, where she underwent electric shock therapy. At first, we thought Joyce was simply suffering from a severe case of post-natal depression, the infamous baby blues, but the consultant concluded that my wife's illness was more deep-rooted. He diagnosed manic depression and warned us it would very probably stay with her for life. And so Joyce began a course of treatment and tablet-taking which persists to this day, designed to keep her on an even keel. There is no cure, we have been told, just containment. We found out that Laura had suffered similar problems when she was younger. It was in the genes, hereditary, and there was nothing we could do about it.

Suddenly, the Cup final became an irrelevance compared to the turmoil in my private affairs, just another match I was going to miss as the club released me on compassionate leave. I watched on television at home as Arsenal went down to a 1–0 defeat thanks to Allan Clarke's diving header.

A mother-and-baby unit catering for psychiatric

patients had just opened at Shenley, Hertfordshire and Joyce was admitted for a couple of months. While the lads went on their end-of-season tour to Barbados, I was left fretting at home, wondering what the future held for Joyce, Paul and myself.

Mother and son were discharged from Shenley, and within days we made a spur-of-the-moment decision late one Friday afternoon to drive up to Scotland in our brand new Mini Clubman, stay with my mum and dad and show off Paul to all the Marinellos and Murrays. Joyce was still fragile, but confident she was fit enough to drive. I hadn't passed my driving test, despite thirty to forty lessons over the previous two years, and we had no L-plates on the car in any case. By 7 p.m. we had only managed about fifteen miles along the A1 on the long trek north when Joyce suddenly announced that she was too tired to drive any more. She pulled over, climbed into the back and fell asleep nestling Paul, while I took the wheel, somewhat apprehensively, in torrential rain. I'd driven maybe twenty-five miles when the windscreen wipers decided to call it a day just as I approached some complicated road-works. Amid the confusion of the diversion, I ended up driving on the wrong side of the A1 – a mistake forcibly brought home to me as I saw a trail of headlights coming straight for us along the dual carriageway. As luck would have it, I spied a little gap in the traffic cones to my left and went for it, bouncing over the grass verge and into the correct line of traffic. The sweat poured off me in buckets. The traffic police would have had a field day. I could imagine them hearing my story and checking the facts: 'Now, let's just see if we've got this right, shall we, Mr Marinello? It's raining and your windscreen wipers don't work; you haven't got a full licence but you're still proposing to drive the best part of 400 miles to Edinburgh, risking your wife and baby son?'

I could see that this whole messy episode needed to be brought to a hasty conclusion, so I stopped at the next village somewhere north of Watford and booked us into a nice hotel. As luck would have it, there was a garage next door with a mechanic working late, and he arranged to fix the wipers first thing the following morning. By 10 a.m. on Saturday, we were on the road again, me at the wheel. I'd got a taste for driving and also drove back to London a fortnight later. In time I duly gained a full driving licence and gave the examiner, an Arsenal fan, a couple of complimentary tickets for Highbury. 'I do hope you're not trying to bribe me, Mr Marinello,' he said with a grin. The very thought!

Paul was seven weeks old when Joyce and I left him with his grandparents in Edinburgh and took ourselves off for a spot of rest and recuperation in Benidorm. That was a very boozy holiday because we were on our own and living it up when we weren't sunbathing with a cocktail or two close to hand.

I had a chance encounter with one of football's controversial outcasts, Tony Kay, the former Sheffield Wednesday and Everton player who was banned for life for match-fixing in 1965 and sentenced to four months in prison. It turned out I was drinking in a bar he now owned, and when Tony discovered my identity, he persuaded me to play in a so-called friendly on a scruffy, sandy bit of a pitch, and I was taken aback when he tried to kick lumps out of me. I wasn't surprised that Kay had become involved in something like that, because I'd heard similar rumours in the past and players weren't on the astronomical wages they enjoy today. The temptation was there. But I thought the life ban was over the top for Kay and told him as much over several ice-cold lagers after the match. I also told him I was fairly pleased he wasn't playing any more if his approach that afternoon was typical of how he dealt with tricky wingers.

Joyce was fairly insistent while we were in Benidorm that I should stick it out at Arsenal, but soon I was getting itchy feet, which came to the attention of one of the world's most famous football clubs in Italy. I was ready for a fresh challenge, but the following summer there would be time for some serious hard drinking on a club tour alongside musicians as diverse as the James Last Orchestra and Isaac Hayes. Not to mention the hookers and hash.

CHAPTER 10

Bye-bye Highbury

Speculation was rife that I might be on my way to Everton at the start of the 1972–73 campaign, and I must have both impressed and depressed my potential new employers on 5 September, when the Merseysiders arrived at Highbury for a League Cup second-round tie. There was plenty at stake, with both clubs so far unbeaten in the league and consequently leading the way at the top of the First Division. Alan Ball's presence in our line-up against his old pals added a touch of spice, and Bally was distraught after an hour, when we won a lucky penalty, and he placed his spot-kick too close to the keeper, David Lawson. With Geordie Armstrong's form affected by a nagging injury, I was in from the start and out to make my mark, which I succeeded in doing by creating the only goal of the game. I remember carrying the ball out on a forty-yard dash from defence, exchanging passes with Pat Rice, before sending over a killer cross for Peter Storey, of all people, to latch on to and score with a swerving shot. Don Howe might have cursed Storey for neglecting his primary defensive duties, but with Steve Burtenshaw now chief coach, the players were encouraged to be more adventurous, take a few more risks and play a little more football. I was happy with my night's work, and one report stated, 'It was a moment of magic,' before predicting, 'Arsenal are going to see a lot more of this Marinello.'

A month later and Rotherham United were battered 5–0 in the third round with me among the scorers, and I also featured in our 2–1 victory at Sheffield United in the following round. I scored my only league goal of the season in a 3–1 win at Wolves, and by the next time Everton were in town, on 18 November for a league fixture, I thought I'd cracked it, and that my Arsenal career was up and running . . . which merely shows what a poor judge I can be. Our results continued to be more impressive than our football, but I was playing well. I wasn't just beating people – I always had the ability to do that – I felt I was making the crosses count, I was producing things. For the first time at Highbury I was satisfied with my game. We beat Everton 1–0 again to consolidate second place.

Now, I sensed, I would finally play a significant role in a trophy-winning Arsenal side, something I had craved from the moment I joined the club. But my dreams were shattered in the space of five days. Not only that, my precious career with the Gunners was blown to pieces.

First, Norwich City came calling in the quarter-final of the League Cup on 21 November and destroyed us 3–0 with a hat-trick from Graham Paddon. Four days later, we were still licking our wounds when we travelled up the M1 to Derby and were absolutely murdered. Bob Wilson returned in goal after seven months out following a cartilage operation, but we couldn't use his rustiness as any sort of excuse. There was only one winger on display worth his salt – Alan Hinton. I might just as well have been a pillar of salt for all the use I was. I would need to watch a video of the first half (through my fingers, mind you) to be sure of my facts, but I believe to this day that I never touched the ball once before the half-time whistle sounded and we went in 4–0 down on the way to losing 5–0. I never kicked another ball for Arsenal in league football.

Talk about unlucky thirteen; the Derby game was my thirteenth league start on the bounce. Bertie Mee replaced me with Geordie for the following fixture, and he retained his place for the remainder of the season. The manager responded to this sudden, shocking slump in form by ordering us in for two days' non-stop training, and we had a long meeting 'to clear the air'. It was a case of so near, but yet so far for me at Arsenal.

Sometimes it felt like I was beating my head against a brick wall, but then I very nearly escaped over that wall in sensational fashion. I had become a bit fed up playing in the reserves and went in with a transfer request. Bertie was less than impressed and told me in no uncertain terms, 'You will go when it is convenient for this club, not when it suits you.' The funny thing is, I loved Arsenal and got on well with everybody, but by now I was just desperate to play regular first-team football. It wasn't long, however, before Bertie called me in to his office and said, 'Juventus are interested in you. They think you would be ideally suited to their style of football and they are not very happy at the moment with their right-winger, Franco Causio. Are you interested?' Was I interested? Was the Pope a Catholic? I could hardly wait for Arsenal to give the go-ahead.

My grandparents had come to Scotland from Florence and Naples, so in some ways it would have been like going home. The Italians still had a self-imposed ban on foreign transfers at the time, put in place several years earlier after Joe Baker and Denis Law were injured in a car crash, but Juve were sure it would be lifted at the end of the season.

Several weeks later I was back in Bertie's office to meet Gigi Peronace, the Italian super agent. He was a Lazio fan who had become the first real agent in England. Way back in 1957, he had negotiated the £65,000 transfer of John Charles from Leeds to Juventus and had since been instrumental in Baker and Law moving to Italy. Gigi confirmed that Juventus had first been alerted by my name and were not put off in any way by the fact I had been playing so much reserve football. 'Do you want to come to Juventus?' he asked, and I replied with a grin, 'Yes, please, Mr Peronace!'

With that, it was down to basics, with Gigi outlining

that, while Arsenal were getting £200,000, my terms were also distinctly big time. Immediately on moving to Turin, I would collect £25,000 as a signing-on fee. If Juventus liked me after the first season, there would be another £25,000 on the table, followed by a further instalment of £25,000 if I stayed for a third term. As for the wages, would £16,000 a year be acceptable? We were talking in telephone numbers, those long international ones with about fourteen bloody figures. And, of course, there would be a free luxury motor for Joyce and myself to swan around in, courtesy of Juventus' links with the influential Agnelli family, who owned the Fiat company. All I had to find for myself was enough lire for an apartment. Given the mountain of money coming my way, I thought I might just be able to handle that relatively modest outlay. 'Are you still interested?' asked Gigi. I replied in the affirmative, and, with that, papers were produced which I signed, expecting to become a Juventus player that April. To all intents and purposes, I put my name to what I considered to be official transfer forms.

Who said I was born unlucky? Gigi was utterly convinced the ban on foreigners would be lifted, but it wasn't, and the deal was off. When he broke the news to me, Joyce and I were extremely deflated and we went out for a quiet drink in an effort to numb our sense of disappointment, but nothing could lift my gloom for several days. The impending transfer had been very hush-hush and kept under wraps, so the collapse spared me huge embarrassment and loss of face, although I had confided to Bally and a few of the other lads that my destiny lay away from Highbury. I was quite correct, too. Only I wasn't leaving for Turin, but Portsmouth.

Meanwhile, I made one more fleeting appearance for Arsenal as a substitute for Charlie George in the fourth round of the FA Cup when we eliminated Bradford City 2–0 at home. Other than that, I watched as Arsenal's double Double dreams went up in smoke at Hillsborough on 7 April when Second Division shock troops Sunderland beat us 2–1 in the semi-final en route to winning the Cup in that famous final against Leeds. As for our league crown, that went to Liverpool, who finished three points better off than us, having led the table since late September.

The move to Fratton Park was initiated by my old pal Ron Tilsed, who had gone down to the south coast when Arsenal decided he wasn't going to make the grade with them. Portsmouth's new chairman, John Deacon, an influential property magnate from Southampton, was soon throwing his money around, promising signings that would take the club up from the Second Division. Ron phoned me to say, 'Deacon's spending money like there's no tomorrow. He's already got Ron Davies from Southampton and now he's looking for a winger. Are you interested?' I indicated that I certainly was, and Ron acted as a go-between.

Back at Highbury I stuck in two or three transfer requests, which Bertie tore up in front of my face and hurled into his wastepaper bin, while Portsmouth went

MAY 28 1968

ALS THAT ED IBROX

● Peter Marinello's great scoring double against Rangers. ABOVE — Peter Cormack congratulates Marinello after Hibs' first goal as disconsolate Ranger John Greig retrieves the ball. BELOW — Marinello turns away triumphantly after scoring his second. Ka? Johansen looks on as John Greig makes a despairing effort to clear

PETER MARINELLO . . . Nigeria-bound.

Hibs fly out on safari

GEORGE ASHTON

Dad, Mum and Joyce's folks, Laura and Jackie, before they head off to Australia.

£100,000 Marinello signs for Arsenal

MUNSC

They look alike . . . they play alike . . . George Best (left) and Peter Marinello.

Arsenal's pin-up wows the girls

PETER MARINELLO, Arsenal
youngster whom Bobby Cha
reckons will be a real good
Marinello impressed Bobby h
he had the confidence to tak
and beat them. And by the
he was not over-awed by the
Trafford atmosphere

That's quick! Just 15 minutes for Marinello (left) to score a debut goal.

Mr Perfect

Peter botto tops the g

IT may ... why yo star Peter N the girl fa every week.

But now come up to it they; abou ing, behind a It's not flowing locks It's ma smile.

He's top with the gi ... his bod

The movie out that a bottom ... girls' ualwe

And Peter fits the bill so to speak.

The sei by a man factnrer, which kin they liked rounded or

And a wh too per cen rounded bo curve of th curved then

Flat botto seat with b of the cuts bottoms ...we rear with cent.

Rounded c clubs from cent. of the

Attr

Slim one anne finger the popula Professio the girls waists knee of a thirty ...ment ... w Peter's.

The sur: by the Fabr ing Compa

Managin Landau s "We want poster wh tre in decided is to sub-ed girls go for for a man waist, a st well-round

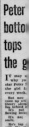

The eyes have it! Peter Marinello is fascinated by Pop dancer Celia Hunter's eyelashes.

PICTURE: HILARIA McCARTHY

Minis—they'd get pinched at home

MARINELLO

Arsenal's £100,000 new boy

THIS has been the most gruelling and hectic week since I came down to London more than a month ago.

It was a week of double training at Highbury, where the lads are determined to break the rotten run we have been having lately.

It was a week of appearing as guest on Top of the Pops and meeting disc jockey Tony Blackburn.

And it was the week of NOT meeting Sandie Shaw and wondering if I'd ever get as choosy as that if I made the grade as a world famous pop star.

I was knocked out when Top of the Pops producer Stanley

girl friend. I don't know what she felt about all those young girls dancing in the studio with mini-skirts up to the middles... one thing is sure, they'd get arrested for that in Scotland.

The only other time I'd been in a TV studio was with Jimmy Hill for a Match of the Day programme. But that was nothing like the scene on Wednesday night.

The bustling, shouting, running about, handwaving, and dancing were so chaotic it almost left you breathless just watching.

It made me realise just what pressures show business people work under. Honestly, I felt out of my depth. I fint I felt

Dorfman asked me to come down to Television Centre to choose the best young dancer in the audience and the best-dressed girl,

A model wife.

MARINELLO

Hey, they want to colour me Pop!

By PETER MARINELLO
Arsenal's £100,000 new boy

'VE been over-
med this week
s from people
nt to turn me
Pop singer,
male model, and
ilm star.

n may be the
Land, but this is
ulous.
o is keeping his feet
rmly to the ground.
paid out £100,000
play football for
it is to this that I
my full, undivided
on.

E PROOF

ws, the singing, the
modelling, and the
may come one day.
t, I must prove
a footballer. That
means helping Arsenal win a major trophy.

Arsenal have not got a game this week, but I have had to train as if preparing for a Wembley Cup Final.

Don Howe, assistant manager and coach at Highbury, has pushed me through a fitness programme that makes the training we used to do at Hibernian seem about as strenuous as musical chairs.

Just this week I have melted away 5lb. and am now down to a slim 10st. 2lb. That's the sort of weight I like to carry for top speed.

Sprinting is an important part of my game. I used to train with a top professional sprinter and was usually able to hold him level until the final run-in over a 100-yard dash.

But Don Howe has really

got through to me this week the fact that there is so much more to football than just speed and ball work.

I have, for instance, much to learn about proper positioning so that Arsenal can get the full benefit of my speed and skill.

You can be the greatest controller of a ball in the world, but you are useless if your team if you cannot manoeuvre into the right place at the right time.

I continued my exploration of London with a visit to the restaurant at the top of the giant Post Office tower.

As I took a panoramic view

of London's skyline I felt, well, on top of the world.

The look, the smell . . . Just everything about London excites me. Yes, for me it really is the Promised Land.

TRAINING

I am off home to Edinburgh this weekend to see my mam and dad, and, perhaps look in at Hibernian's match against Rangers.

But I shall be back on Monday for more torturous training. Musical chairs was never like this!

© *Beaverbrook Newspapers 1970. Interviewer Norman Giller.*

CROWDS FLOCK TO BIG MATCH

N'S EYE OTONEWS

Marinello
(WITH A FAIRS CUP TIE TODAY)
sets the style for Europe

by HARDY CLARKE

RE: Bold patterned silk shirt with a giant-sized silk scarf. Cotton velvet play suit "Like a posh track

THE clothes of Nino Cerruti, the French-Italian darling of the Paris couture scene . . . modelled by Peter Marinello, the Scottish-Italian

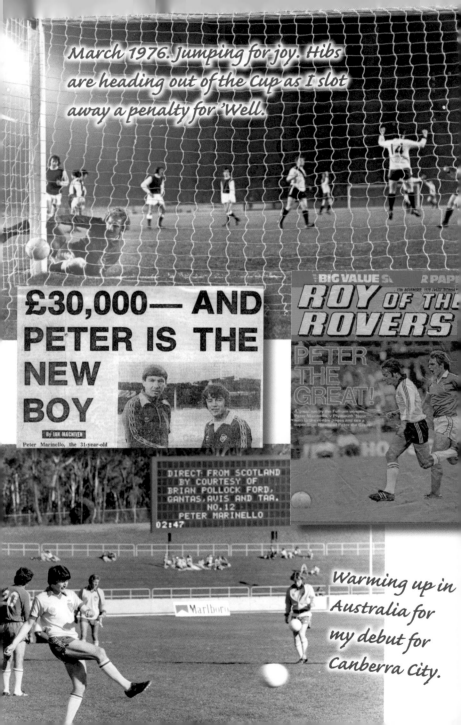

March 1976. Jumping for joy. Hibs are heading out of the Cup as I slot away a penalty for 'Well.

£30,000— AND PETER IS THE NEW BOY

By IAN MACNIVEN

Peter Marinello, the 31-year-old

BIG VALUE S... R PAP...

ROY OF THE ROVERS

PETER THE GREAT!

DIRECT FROM SCOTLAND
BY COURTESY OF
BRIAN POLLOCK FORD,
QANTAS, AVIS AND TAA.
NO. 12
PETER MARINELLO
02:47

Warming up in Australia for my debut for Canberra City.

"I feared my wife wouldn't recover"

SOCCER STAR'S TORMENT

Up Pompey:
Life in the second
division...

HATTIE MILES

through official channels and tabled a bid for me of £100,000. Arsenal disliked news of their transfer business becoming common knowledge, and I could tell they were unimpressed by the press coverage. Thoroughly exasperated, Bertie conceded, 'If you are so desperate to get away, then fine, but first you're coming on tour with us.' No sooner had he agreed in principle to letting me go than he was badgering me to change my mind and he was particularly keen for me to go on tour, no doubt convinced that his concentrated powers of persuasion would change my mind.

I travelled down to Fratton Park to meet Ron Tindall, the manager, and Deacon. It was all done and dusted inside ten minutes after I demanded a £10,000 tax-free signing-on fee plus £100-a-week basic, and they simply agreed before shaking hands. I never actually saw that ten grand. Instead, Portsmouth gave me the deeds to an £18,000 town house, with a garage underneath, which they had purchased in Somerset Road, Southsea, about 100 yards from the beach. Joyce was quite keen on the move and said it would be good for the kids, although at that time we only had Paul. It was spelled out to me that my mortgage would be for just £8,000. I was delighted, and even happier when the club secretary, Jimmy Dickinson, Mr Portsmouth himself, invited me into his office and explained, 'You're still due your five per cent remember, Peter.' When I was looking for that ten grand, I had fully expected it to include my signing-on fee, yet here was Jimmy Dickinson paying me another £5,500 and stressing how much I was entitled to it. Needless to say, my only response was a very broad smile.

It was two days after the Sunderland–Leeds FA Cup final, 7 May 1973, that I promised to sign for Portsmouth, and almost immediately Ron Tindall moved up to become general manager, with John Mortimore appointed team manager, but I wasn't officially transferred until the end of June because Arsenal wanted me for their summer tour of Canada and Bermuda, which turned into my leaving party.

Bertie's sister lived in Toronto, and I reckon that's why we stayed there somewhat over-indulgently for a week after playing one friendly in which I caught the eye of the local press. Not that we were complaining, you understand, far from it. Our luxurious accommodation was in the beautiful five-star Royal York Hotel, complete with ten bars, half a dozen different restaurants and at least three discotheques. It was not altogether a stress-free tour for Bertie, however, constantly hounded by the press, who kept demanding to know why I was being sold when I looked such a good player. He kept asking me to reconsider my move to Portsmouth, but I wasn't having any of it. Things had gone too far, I'd been neglected for too long for me to have a change of heart. Mind you, Bertie had a devil of a job trying to find me and Eddie Kelly during that week.

We hooked up with singers and musicians from the world-famous James Last Orchestra, who were using the

Royal York as their headquarters while they played a string of gigs throughout Canada. We were invited to go and listen to them, but rather than merely attend as guests, Eddie and I declared ourselves unofficial roadies and were happy humping their gear about backstage amid some ferocious bouts of drinking and pot-smoking. Eddie and I both tried to smoke hash but we were drinking as well, weren't very proficient when it came to inhaling and ended up being sick.

Back at the York we encountered musicians of a more soulful nature – Isaac Hayes and his crew, although we found some of the people hanging around quite menacing. I discovered that two of the Arsenal party ended up with a prostitute in their bedroom, but were too plastered to perform. By three in the morning, she was hollering to be paid and released; then a massive minder appeared at the door complaining that the boys had messed her about. By all accounts, it was quite tense for a moment before the guy asked, 'Hey, are you those soccer guys?' Another bottle of Jim Beam was opened, and the three of them became best pals.

From Toronto it was on to Bermuda for a one-match jolly, after which three gorgeous girls turned up at the hotel to escort us around the island's major tourist spots. The match itself was a 4–0 romp against a local side called Devonshire Colts at the National Stadium, where I produced a few tricks and a goal to take the man-of-the-match honours.

My Arsenal career was finally laid to rest at Heathrow,

with Bertie imploring me to think again. I should have listened to him. As we left the plane to board the little bus taking us to the airport terminal, he made one final effort and asked me, as a father might inquire of his son, 'Have you thought any more about what I've said about staying, Peter?' I replied, 'I want to go, Bert' and that was it, really. We went our separate ways.

I had forced the issue and been stupid, headstrong and quite mercenary. 'Fuck it,' I told myself, 'I'll go for the money.' After a whole jumble of emotions and the feeling of being pulled from pillar to post, I was chasing the cash rather than the prospect of a higher grade of football at Highbury. It was a crucial point in my career, and I made a big mistake, a mixture of petulance and pig-headedness on my part and the fact Portsmouth were giving me a lot of money.

There was regret at leaving Arsenal, where I'd had plenty of good times socially and playing when I did, to offset the frustration of never being a first-choice pick. I made lifelong friends at Highbury and, whatever failings and defects of character I may have, I am quite a loyal person. Hibs wanted the money when I left, but Arsenal didn't need the cash and didn't want me to leave either. But had I become a commodity? My mind flashed back to that moment in Bertie's office with Gigi Peronace, and it seemed the club were willing to sell me to Juventus for £200,000. I recalled Bertie telling me, 'We're signing you for the future, Peter,' in January 1970, but here we were almost three-and-a-half years on and I still wasn't a regular – even if I was only twenty-three. You can't put an old head on young shoulders.

I briefly thought it was a relief to be leaving Arsenal, where the expectations on me were so high because of my £100,000 price tag and the association with George Best, but that would always be with me wherever I played. And who was I kidding? I was becoming Portsmouth's record signing as well, and there would be pressure on me there to perform from the very start, although my first appearance in a royal blue shirt was hugely enjoyable. Typically, though, it gave a totally false indication of what was to follow – just like that goal on my Arsenal debut at Old Trafford. It was a testimonial match for loyal servant Albert McCann against West Ham, which pulled in a great crowd of over 20,000. Testimonials were proper matches then, not the slap-and-giggle 6–6 draws you witness all too frequently these days, studded with numerous substitutions. If you pay good money to go to a football match, I believe it entitles you to see two sides trying to win. Anyway, we beat West Ham 4–1, and I must have made a couple of goals at least for Ron Davies, a Welsh international and the best header of a ball I ever saw in the business.

Afterwards, Big Ron and I went for a drink together in a nightclub, and he was clutching a very sizeable brown paper package, which he tucked down between his feet while we sat boozing at a table. 'What the fuck's that, then?' I asked him, and his face just cracked into this wonderful wide grin as he replied, 'It's only my signing-on fee now, Boyo. All part of the contract mind you, but they've gone and paid me in readies.' I thought he was mad carrying that amount of cash around while drinking, but then who was going to be brave enough to take it off Big Ron? I told him he was crazy and he agreed, 'I know, I know. I'll be off down the bank to drop it off tomorrow.' Ron thought he'd done well to get £6,000, which softened the blow felt by a proud centre-forward when Southampton said they were prepared to sell him. He took that decision very badly and felt bitter about it. Ultimately, he regretted going to Portsmouth and he was not alone. Ron also looked a bit sick when I casually informed him about my ten grand. Mind you, after my performance in that friendly against West Ham, I think I could have asked Pompey for the world and got it.

As Joyce and I said goodbye Winchmore Hill, hello Southsea, trouble followed and it didn't take long to find me. We hadn't quite yet moved into Somerset Road and were in a hotel the night friends invited us out to dinner on the outskirts of Portsmouth. I had a few drinks inside me, maybe a vodka or two, plus a few glasses of wine, but considered myself perfectly fit to drive our Mini Clubman back to the hotel. On the return journey, Joyce and I argued, and I thought I would drop her at the hotel and take myself off for another drink. That's what I started to do, before it dawned on me how selfishly I was behaving. I'd only driven about 100 yards when I decided to go back to Joyce. So I swung the car round in a U-turn at a junction and had a motorbike plough into me. The machine went under the car and the rider flew over the bonnet. The guy was screaming blue murder at me, and everyone piled out of an adjacent pub to watch the sideshow. The crowd grew when they discovered the crash involved Pompey's new £100,000 star signing. What a tale they'd all have to tell their mates in the morning, and it hardly helped matters when poor Joyce appeared on the scene, having heard the commotion from outside the hotel.

I stayed with the biker, apologising profusely and trying to calm him down, while the police were duly summoned and I was breathalysed. I was over the odds and taken down to the police station, charged and locked up for the night. At least, I thought, I'd be eating bacon and eggs in my cell the following morning, but Ron Tindall turned up three hours later, and I was released. Ron had every right to give me an almighty bollocking, but he just smiled and said, 'At least you're in good company,' before revealing not only that he had been done for drinking and driving six months previously, but Ron Davies was also serving a ban. What a hat-trick that was. Inevitably, the court case made front-page headlines in the *News*, Portsmouth's evening paper, and I was banned for twelve months and fined £100. There were plenty of whispers that the motorcyclist was preparing to sue me for damages, but I certainly never received a writ. It wouldn't have surprised me if someone at the club had sorted everything out with the biker without my knowledge.

I needed cool heads and calm, sober influences around me to put my career back on track. Instead, I found the two

Rons, who thought nothing of throwing twelve vodkas apiece down their necks for lunch at the Jolly Sailor during pre-season training sessions.

CHAPTER 11

Pompey Crimes

My time at Portsmouth might not have got off to a flying start, but Joyce's did, quite literally. She jetted off with son Paul to visit her family in Australia ... and I settled down to a life of domesticity, cooking myself regular meals and enjoying early nights in preparation for the new season. In your dreams, pal! It was like someone pressing fast forward while I was on the hairiest ride at Southsea funfair.

I'd had no complaints about the camaraderie at Arsenal, and now I soon discovered that Portsmouth were another extremely sociable side. I wonder what attracted me to them? Within a one-mile radius of Somerset Road, there must comfortably have been twenty drinking venues, ranging from the Playboy Club, where we were all honorary members, to Hoddies Bar, a little private drinking den where you tapped on the door to gain entry.

The lads knew Joyce was away, and my house became a very convenient stopping-off place for them to crash after a session. On the very occasional evening I decided to turn in early, you could virtually guarantee the doorbell ringing in the wee small hours. I would silently curse, before getting up to let in one of the lads, who would demand, 'Let's have one for the road and a bed for the night, Peter.' Then we'd have a beer, or get stuck into the vodka or whisky. We always managed to grab a couple of hours' sleep before training, but sometimes Saturday night merged into Sunday morning, and dawn broke to find us still hard at it. I might cook breakfast for three or four of us – I was a dab hand at bacon and eggs with black pudding – then we'd go out for the Sunday papers before reaching the Captain's Table pub, fifty yards away from my front door, for opening time at noon. My life was especially chaotic while Joyce was away, but I retained enough sense to employ a cleaner to ensure the house didn't resemble a tip.

Pompey needed whipping into shape for the nine-month ordeal to come, although a lot of bonding had already been done at the bar, so the club whisked us off to an army training camp out in the wilds of the Brecon Beacons in Wales for a week. Of course, it pissed down with rain for all seven days, despite it being mid-summer. Our temporary home was a barracks, and we were shaken out of our beds at six each morning and, after breakfast, pushed through the door with a packed lunch. The activities ranged from twenty-mile hikes to abseiling and potholing. Ron Tindall got stuck crawling along one hole between Eoin Hand in front and Ron Davies bringing up the rear. Eoin managed to turn round and pull the manager's hands while Ron was pushing his feet, but they were getting nowhere. Eoin half-scared the boss to death when he calmly announced, 'Right, we both want a pay rise or we're leaving you here.' Bobby Kellard took one look at the caverns, refused to join in and simply walked away. No one thought any the worse of him for it.

We were expected to use our initiative in the Brecon Beacons and we did, finding a friendly hotelier in the nearest village prepared to keep the bar open as long as we were still standing. That led to a few sessions when eight or nine of us would stumble back, merry and muddy, to the barracks at three in the morning. I would feel hungover, inevitably, being woken at six in the morning but I'd had plenty of practice at surviving on just a few hours' snatched sleep. It wasn't a disaster because we weren't expected to play a game. I used my initiative when Ron Tilsed and I were expected to provide the evening meal. All the other pairs had done proper kitchen work such as peeling potatoes, preparing sprouts, slicing carrots and cooking mince, but we strolled down for a pint at the hotel and picked up sixteen fish suppers from the local chippy. It cost us a bob or two, but it was well worth it to see the look on the lads' faces.

Pre-season training back in Hampshire took place at Eastleigh, where the management misguidedly allowed us ninety minutes for lunch when we knocked off from the morning session at noon. That was long enough for most of the squad to jump in their cars and hightail it back to the Jolly Sailor at Southsea where the two Rons, Tilsed and Davies, held court over a pile of prawn sandwiches washed down by anything up to half a dozen double vodkas apiece before racing back to Eastleigh in time for the afternoon training session. Now I liked a drink as much as the next man, more in fact, but there was a time and a place for everything, and I dutifully stuck to a Coca-Cola, or perhaps half a lager, while the two Rons brought out the worst in each other.

Pompey were no great shakes, just shaky, having escaped relegation to the Third Division the previous season by a couple of points in a campaign which had seen their crowds dip as low as 5,000. Just before Christmas 1972, in fact, during a run of one win in twelve matches, the visit of Middlesbrough attracted 4,688 diehards – the lowest league attendance ever witnessed at Fratton Park, I believe. The next time Portsmouth played Boro at home, on 25 August 1973, there were nearly 20,000 to see me make my debut for the club in the Second Division in a 1–0 defeat. Jack Charlton's Boro were fancied for promotion before a ball was kicked in anger, while we were second favourites to go up. Boro went on to justify the bookmakers' odds, winning the title with my old pal Graeme Souness in a key midfield role, by a staggering fifteen points – and this, remember, in an era when it was two points for a win.

Portsmouth had only just stayed up the previous

season, but the club had signed a host of big names –
including me. Having paid big money to bring in Ron
Davies that summer, John Deacon recruited another man
who was to represent Wales in right-back Phil Roberts
from Bristol Rovers. In December, two new central
defenders arrived – Malcolm Manley from Leicester for
£45,000 and Paul Went from Fulham for a club record
£155,000.

Optimism was extremely high when the season kicked
off. I suppose I was a major factor in that optimism and I
felt there was no reason why we couldn't have a cracking
season, even if my preparation had been less than perfect.
I'm sorry to say that particular Saturday morning dawned
with me in a fairly wretched state thanks to a heavy night's
partying. Well done, Peter. Not a smart move on your
home debut. I woke up early and went down to the beach
for a swim in the hope a brisk plunge might sober me up.
Southsea was already teeming with Boro fans but,
fortunately, none of them recognised me. Compared to a
previous appearance at Fratton Park in old Albert's
testimonial, I was unrecognisable on the pitch too, beating
one or two defenders but then running into dead-ends and
being tackled by a third Boro man. It was a pretty awful
personal performance, if I'm being honest.

Our early form was poor too. Ron Tilsed was quickly
dropped, and we were six games into the campaign before
we managed a win, 2–0 at Carlisle, though we did win a
League Cup match against Southend United.

One Sunday morning after yet another impromptu

party at my house, the phone rang at eight. At that hour I was expecting to exchange pleasantries with Joyce from the other end of the world, so you can imagine my surprise when the deadpan voice of Ron Tindall barked, 'Get your clothes on, Peter. I'll be round to pick you up in thirty minutes.' I suspected we weren't about to embark on a gentle Sunday morning potter around the Hampshire countryside in his car. Ron arrived precisely half an hour later and must have suspected something was dodgy because I wouldn't let him into the house, where he would have discovered a fair sprinkling of the Portsmouth first team sleeping off the excesses of the previous night.

Ron drove me in near-silence to Heathrow to collect Joyce, who had been informed by the club that I was in danger of going completely off the rails in her absence. I wasn't doing myself any favours and although I was the quickest player at the club, I could obviously have been fitter. In fairness, I didn't miss any training sessions, which was always regarded in the game as the first sign of a player with serious drink problems. The club had got wind that I was operating an open-house policy, and that's why they wanted Joyce back in charge. She was away for the Boro game which launched our campaign and had been due to stay in Australia for six weeks, but was summoned home after less than a month, feeling embarrassment and shame. Her face looked like thunder when I saw her. I wasn't so much in the dog house, as living in Battersea Dogs' Home, and Joyce's mood was not improved by the state of the sheets in our bedroom. But I wasn't guilty. That one was down to one of the other lads and a cracking little blonde. Things did calm down a little bit on the social scene after that. They had to.

We took a little time to find our feet, but the omens were promising in mid-October when Pompey ended Sheffield Wednesday's eighteen-match unbeaten home run and celebrated a 2–1 victory at Hillsborough which took us up to tenth place in the table. I turned in a man-of-the-match display in Sheffield, earning headlines like 'Magic moves by maestro Marinello' as I tormented the Wednesday defence, creating the winner for Norman Piper. John Mortimore was so chuffed, he went on the pitch at the end and congratulated each and every Pompey player as we came off, before declaring, 'We played well and I couldn't fault anybody for effort. Marinello is really coming back into his own.' John was far less complimentary on a couple of long journeys home that followed. Hillsborough should have been the springboard for a concentrated promotion push, but that was as good as it got. We could be wildly inconsistent and succeeded in losing our next two away matches, 4–1 at Hull City and 5–0 at Blackpool, to underline the point.

That marathon haul up to Hull was memorable – but not for the football we played. It coincided with the race in which Lester Piggott was riding Go Go Gunner at Newmarket and came in three lengths clear. There were some big punters at Pompey, including Phil Roberts, Norman Piper and Richie Reynolds, and the team rustled up £400 all told and got it on Go Go Gunner at a bookmakers near the ground on Humberside. Our minds must have been on the outcome of that race, rather than the three o'clock at Boothferry Park, because, as I've said, we were stuffed out of sight. We were sick as pigs, and quiet as mice boarding the coach for the trek back to the south coast until I asked the driver to switch on his radio so we could listen to the racing results. You would have thought we'd just won the FA Cup, judging by the roar that greeted news of our victory on the racecourse. Ron Tindall was far from happy with our response, but it did brighten up the journey going home.

The least said about our League Cup exploits, the better. After beating Southend 2–1, we crashed out 4–0 in the second round at Plymouth, who were a division beneath us. The Southend match gave me my introduction to a young Peter Taylor, who was to become an England inter-national, winning a handful of caps as a Third Division player with Crystal Palace, before going into management successfully and taking charge of the England Under-21 side. The moment I first clapped eyes on Peter, I thought he was going to be a great player and I pulled him aside afterwards and said, 'Keep playing like that and there will be a big team in for you.' There was, after Palace, and he joined Tottenham. Damien Duff today reminds me of Peter in his prime, all twists and turns with his left foot, and I would rate Taylor as one of the most naturally gifted wingers I've seen in the English game alongside Peter Thompson, Peter Barnes and Chris Waddle.

Portsmouth's interest in the FA Cup was a totally different proposition, however, and I was an influential figure in an exciting run. We were staring at humiliation midway through our third-round tie on 5 January when Swindon took a 3–1 lead at Fratton Park, but we forced a replay and won that 1–0. The fourth round pitted us at home against Orient, another club at our level, and the magic of the FA Cup suddenly captured the imagination of the Pompey public. The sleeping giant awoke and started to roar.

The previous month, our gates had dropped to 13,000 for the visits of Bristol City and Preston, but there were almost 33,000 inside the ground to see a 0–0 stalemate with the east Londoners. Extra-time at Brisbane Road, and the two sides were still deadlocked after a 1–1 draw, so it was on to neutral Selhurst Park, the home of Crystal Palace, for a second replay on a really shitty February night with rain pouring down. Our support was magnificent, however. The fans travelled up to south London in their thousands, swelling the gate to over 19,000, and I responded by playing out of my soaked skin. Orient couldn't live with us, and we murdered them 2–0 with goals from Bobby Kellard and Ron Davies in each half as the Pompey Chimes rang out with a vengeance.

The streets of Portsmouth were virtually deserted on the Sunday morning of 17 February as a travelling army estimated at 23,000 strong made its way to Nottingham. I ran out to warm up at the City Ground and remember thinking, 'This is just like a home match,' because the whole place seemed to be awash with blue and white. The following month there was a crowd of 14,000 to see us at Forest, but this fifth-round clash attracted a bumper gate of 38,589. My pal Peter Cormack, a Forest old boy, was in attendance, twenty-four hours after helping Liverpool beat Ipswich 2–0, and I was keen to show him what I could do. Peter was there purely out of interest to see me take on his former club; I'm sure he wasn't overly worried about meeting either of us later in the competition.

I should have been in that crowd too, because I was suffering from flu and there was no way I was fit enough to play. Sometimes I was a bit stupid in my career (all right, maybe more than sometimes), and this was one of those occasions. I should have come clean and told the management how rough I felt, but I was desperate to play and I paid for it, never coming close to doing myself justice. The match was extremely close and tense, decided in Forest's favour by Duncan McKenzie's penalty in the second half, when I was finally put out of my misery and substituted not a minute too soon.

The football fever died instantly in Portsmouth. There were under 9,000 at Fratton three days later to see the team scratch a 1–1 draw with Sheffield Wednesday, while I was on my sickbed at home. As for Cormack, he went back to Merseyside to Bill Shankly's last great team, which won the FA Cup at Wembley a few months later with an emphatic 3–0 victory over Newcastle.

As for my Portsmouth colleagues, they could be mad, bad and dangerous to know. Norman Piper was a good little midfield player, who used his brain and at one stage was believed to be on the fringe of the England team. But playing for such an unfashionable side as Pompey for so long didn't improve his international chances.

Our goalkeeper, Ron Tilsed, with his blond hair and good looks, was a cross between Robert Redford and Bill Clinton. He used to pull all the birds and took a fancy to Joyce. One night we had a row which ended with Joyce threatening, 'I'm going to run off with Ron,' to which I replied, 'Good!' before we both collapsed laughing at the notion. I might not have been a model husband but I was a paragon of virtue compared to Ron, and Joyce knew it from putting up with him briefly as a lodger that time in London. Ron was a pretty nervous, extremely hyper sort of character who could drink double vodkas and Coke like water, but loveable all the same and generous to a fault. Football came second to his social life, although he wasn't a bad keeper, and 1973–74 proved frustrating for him. Ron was dropped after the fifth league match after conceding three goals in a draw at Luton and only made one other appearance all season before clearing off to South Africa. That wasn't the end of our friendship, however, and we were destined to play alongside each other in Australia.

In goal by the end of the season was David Best, a decent keeper, if tubby with it. I was shopping in my local store in Bournemouth just a few years ago and was stopped dead in my tracks by this huge bear of a young man. I couldn't believe how much of a chip off the old block he was on discovering it was David's son.

Our right-back, Phil Roberts, became a good pal of mine, and many an afternoon was spent together in the back office of our friend Hughie the Bookie. Hughie was a youngish chap, a huge Portsmouth supporter, quite well off and an independent bookmaker, as well as owning the 106, a nightclub in Titchfield. One of Hughie's best customers was a big gambler, John Pegley, who would phone Hughie from London, placing bets of anything from £2,000 to £4,000 on horses. Sometimes they won, sometimes they lost – but if Pegley was on a horse, Hughie would always accept his bet and lay it off elsewhere while Phil and I would dive through the door to get some of our own money on at the nearest Ladbroke's. Phil was a serious gambler and once took Hughie for nearly £12,000 when a 20–1 shot came in during the Cheltenham Festival. Hughie offered Phil a quarter share in the business, but the Welshman wasn't having any of it. He wanted cash, and he got it.

Never without a smile, left-back Billy Wilson was another loveable guy. He was quite plump and came from Seaton Delavel, the same Northumberland village as my Arsenal mate Ray Kennedy. On one away trip, I recall John Mortimore leaving Billy's room aghast at discovering the defender relaxing with his traditional four cans of beer, which he did every Friday before a match. Before John could issue a bollocking, Billy had stolen his thunder by calmly announcing, 'Oh, Ron Tindall knows all about my ale. Helps me to relax and get a good night's kip.'

I got on extremely well with our tall, lanky centre-half,

Alan Stephenson, dominant in the air and a man who had played a lot of football in London for Crystal Palace and West Ham before arriving on the south coast. He was another player who liked a few lagers (come to think of it, which of us didn't?), but he was dependable with it and also a good family man. Joyce and I often popped over for dinner with Alan and his wife in their home on Hayling Island.

The much-travelled Bobby Kellard must rank as one of the first football itinerants. He was a little midfield grafter, who always gave 100 per cent. When I pitched up, he was in his second spell at Fratton Park, having already performed for Southend, Palace (twice), Ipswich, Bristol City and Leicester. Bobby was a Londoner from Edmonton, Tottenham territory, living off his wits – and out of a suitcase. If Egon Ronay had needed an expert to provide the lowdown on Portsmouth hotels, then Bobby would have been his man. His arrangement with the club was that they would pay for his hotel accommodation until he found a house to buy in the area. It didn't take Bobby long to figure out the longer he couldn't find anywhere for his family to live, the longer Portsmouth FC would have to keep footing his bills. I accompanied Bobby on some epic trips to see some lovely houses in Hayling Island, available for £40,000, and admired his nerve and cheek when he put in silly offers of £30,000, only to feign hurt and frustration when he was laughed out of the estate agents. The club cottoned on to Bobby's little game, and his level of hotel accommodation steadily declined from five-star, room service with knobs on, to a pretty basic bed-and-breakfast.

Ron Davies was a good lad, although I don't think he ever quite got used to the idea Southampton could cope without his services, and it was inevitable we would become friends after signing at virtually the same time and sharing an interest in the social side of football. The best header of a ball it has ever been my privilege to see, Ron would simply hover in the air waiting for a cross at the far post. That was a problem as far as I was concerned, because after doing my bit, showing off and beating a couple of defenders, I was usually too knackered to get the ball over to the far post, while Ron was never interested in making a run to the near post. It's fair to say we hit it off as a double act over the large vodkas much better than we ever did in the Portsmouth attack. When sober, Ron was like greased lightning over 200 yards but he wasn't in the mood to do much running, only boozing, when Joyce and I went on holiday to Majorca with him and his wife Sylvia. Ron and I would leave the wives and go drinking every afternoon. I was younger than him and could hold my drink quite well, while Ron would usually collapse about 11 p.m. and need a hand putting to bed.

Alan Durban, from Derby County, was staying in the same hotel with his wife and children and he and Ron hated the sight of each other. It was some sort of personality clash from playing in the same Wales team. Truth told, Ron could be an awkward, bitter customer at times, no matter how well we got on with each other.

Alan's wife liked to retire for the night at a reasonable hour, leaving him free to join Sylvia, Joyce and me out on the town. Ron would have been mortified that I was happily drinking with one of his sworn enemies. I had no axe to grind with Durban, though. He was a good guy, and I envied him every morning when I woke up, looked out of my hotel window and saw him running on the golden beach. Mind you, Alan knew what was good for him. Brian Clough would probably have murdered him if he'd gone back to Derby out of shape.

Ron loved Spain and hooked up with a businessman who was building a holiday complex out there. It was £8,000 if I wanted to join a syndicate of backers. I'm glad I turned down Ron's offer to become a business partner, because the deal went pear-shaped and the businessman ran off with Sylvia.

Brian Lewis, our man-marker, was another who enjoyed a drink. Such was his undiluted enthusiasm for their products, Bacardi and Coca-Cola really should have sponsored the man we all knew simply as 'Louie'. It didn't seem to affect his usefulness on a Saturday afternoon, although Louie had a fierce streak in him and was feared for the sort of tackling that would have seen him sent off half a dozen times a season today. His style was liberally sprinkled with culture, however, and Louie could also despatch the sort of wonderful diagonal passes from right to left that made David Beckham famous. An underrated player, Louie had been one of the heroes in 1971 when Fourth Division Colchester rocked the football world by beating then-mighty Leeds 3–2 in the fifth round of the FA Cup. He was back in his second spell at Portsmouth when I got there and we hit it off well. Louie also knew Hughie the Bookie, and one notorious night at the 106 club ended with two willing girls staging a live sex show. On another evening out, I never made it home and had to crash out at Louie's house. That proved a very expensive mistake and not one I was tempted to make again in a hurry, as on returning home I discovered a livid Joyce had taken a pair of her sharpest scissors and slashed the backs of all eight of my suit jackets. Joyce decamped to stay with team-mate Albert McCann and his wife for a few days.

You would have got short odds on finding Richie Reynolds with his nose still deep inside the *Sporting Life* thirty minutes before kick-off. The gambling man was quite a useful inside-forward with Bobby Charlton-style hair, despite being relatively young when I met him. Richie was a big lad, a condition not helped by his unswerving devotion to fish and chips, which even led to him and his wife opening a chippy.

I loved Eoin Hand, a typical Dubliner with a wicked sense of humour. When the Pompey match programme editor did the typical question-and-answer stuff with Eoin, he asked the Irishman, 'Who in the world would you most like to meet?' and Eoin replied, 'A nymphomaniac who owns a pub!' and that actually appeared in print. Larger than life, defender Eoin was big and dependable and spoke his mind.

Our other centre-forward, Ray Hiron, and goalkeeper, John Milkins, were in the minority as quiet family men, while Micky Mellows was a nice lad, who became a born-again Christian. He popped up briefly many years later after he'd been to America, and I'd been through the mill in my private life, but what he was peddling proved far too heavy for me. Religion, to my mind, is a private thing between you and your conscience. I've never been into all that happy-clappy stuff, the feelgood thing.

I was delighted when Paul Went arrived from Fulham in December for two very good reasons. He was a terrific centre-half, and suddenly the pressure was off me to some extent because I was no longer the most expensive player at Fratton Park. I liked Paul. He had already played for Orient and Charlton, and was a strong lad, good in the air, a typical Cockney, up for a laugh and always at the centre of things. I was convinced that he and Malcolm Manley, a Scottish lad bought from Leicester at the same time, would provide the impetus we needed for a promotion push. Their introduction sparked three successive wins – over Bristol City 1–0, West Brom 2–1 and Preston 3–0 – as Alan Stephenson and Eoin Hand were relegated to the sidelines, but almost as soon as the partnership started, it was destroyed by the serious knee injury Malcolm suffered in a 4–0 hammering at Notts County. That was only Malcolm's tenth start for us and effectively the end of his career at the club. He played just once again, the following season, before being pensioned off. It can be a cruel game sometimes. Malcolm could be a bit dour, but I rated his skill as a sweeper and his intelligent distribution of the ball.

I would like Albert McCann to know the watch he gave me for playing in his testimonial match in 1973 is still alive and ticking. What a great servant to Portsmouth Football Club he was before retiring to become a newsagent, making 377 appearances all told. Even in the seventies, bow-legged winger Albert seemed somehow a throwback to an earlier, golden age. 'Born on a horse and never seen a saddle' is the first thing which springs to my mind whenever his name crops up in conversation. The second is that wonderful smile he always wore, particularly at the size of the gate for that testimonial against West Ham.

By the end of the season I was delighted to reflect on having started thirty-nine of our forty-two league matches. If that was a very pleasant change to those lengthy spells of inactivity at Highbury, my shortage of goals wasn't. I managed to find the net just three times all season, and my purple patch came in the space of two matches in March. The first arrived in a 2–1 win at Swindon, and the following Saturday I scored twice in a 3–1 victory over Hull, our first home success since New Year's Day, so little wonder there was a crowd of less than 10,000 to see me do the double. That was a pity as we had a score to settle with the Tigers following our shabby result up there earlier in the season, and I really turned it on. The contest can't have been more than three minutes old when Billy Wilson sent me zooming away down the left wing. Norman Piper was racing into space, screaming for a pass, but I chose to ignore him and scored with a perfectly controlled shot. Goal number two came on the hour and brought the fans to their feet as I took possession inside our half, left my marker gasping and simply accelerated away to drive the ball under the diving body of Hull keeper Jeff Wealands. 'Magnifico Marinello!' screamed that night's local football Green 'Un.

The end of April arrived and the campaign closed with a 2–0 home defeat by Forest, which left Pompey six points away from relegation down in fifteenth place, as far away as ever from reaching the promised land of the First Division and rubbing shoulders with elite clubs such as Arsenal.

If we had been as proficient at football as we were drinking or playing cricket and darts, promotion would have been on the cards. The club encouraged us to form a darts team, insisting it would be good for public relations, which it was. And it proved even better for regular piss-ups. The cricket matches we had were enormous fun, although I barely ever scored a run. I didn't need to because we had four men who weren't far off county standard in Ron Tindall, John Mortimore, Norman Piper and Brian Lewis. The lads stuck me out on the boundary, where I eyed up the talent and proved fairly adept at catching the ball as well.

Wimbledon FC may have laid claim to the Crazy Gang nickname when the likes of Dennis Wise, Vinnie Jones and John Fashanu were in residence at Plough Lane and up to their tricks years later, but we made them look like amateurs. There was another club down the road called the Saints; we were the Sinners. At one stage, two of my team-mates were having affairs with each other's wife, while George Best scored with the other half of another prominent member of the team. Another team-mate proved very successful at getting one young player drunk, just so he could take him home . . . and make love to his colleague's wife. I must confess the temptation was always there, and the opportunity was huge for infidelity in Portsmouth, but shagging other players' wives was bang out of order, as far as I was concerned. And I was a lucky man – married to one of the best-looking women you could ever see.

CHAPTER 12

Saint and Sinners

John Mortimore must have known he needed to hit the ground running when the new season kicked off with an impatient chairman breathing down his neck. In the event, he got just five matches before Mr Deacon's axe fell on Friday 6 September, and, by way of compensation, he was offered a scouting job. By then Portsmouth had been beaten at Bolton and Manchester United (yes, in the Second Division), drawn at Orient, yet seen off Nottingham Forest 2–0 at Fratton Park in the league, while the potential League Cup first-round banana skin at Swindon had been safely negotiated, courtesy of Norman Piper's goal. The United match was the first time I'd been back to Old Trafford since my famous debut for Arsenal four years earlier, and the outcome was identical, although I failed to score. This time a crowd of over 42,000 saw us lose 2–1 to Tommy Docherty's young thrusters, somewhat unluckily in my view.

Ron Tindall took charge as acting manager for seven days, which brought no change of fortune, merely two damaging home defeats as speculation spread like wildfire through the town that former England boss Sir Alf Ramsey was poised to take over. West Brom beat us 3–1 and Derby won 5–1 in the League Cup on the night I registered a rare goal. Bobby Kellard threaded an inch-perfect pass through for me to tuck a neat left-foot shot just inside Colin Boulton's far post from about fifteen yards for a consolation goal which made it 4–1.

The chairman missed my effort and didn't arrive until after the final whistle, so busy had he been trying to convince Sir Alf to relinquish his job with a building firm and return to football management. Deacon apologised to my old idol Dave Mackay, manager of a Derby side heading for the Football League championship, and said, 'Sorry to be so late. I gather I missed something special.' Tasty as my goal had been, I think that was possibly a reference to Derby's display. Deacon was not exactly a happy chap and told the world, 'I was very depressed last season when I read phrases like "straw man of Portsmouth". We feel that we must get a great manager to get a proper return for our investment.' Mind you, we weren't exactly over the moon at the prospect of welcoming the ex-England manager out of retirement. When Deacon said something, he generally went ahead and did it, so there was trepidation among several of the guys, who would have preferred a younger man in charge and thought of Sir Alf as too defensive.

It soon didn't matter because Ramsey couldn't be persuaded by the chairman's silver tongue and riches, so

Motherwell were duly compensated, and Ian St John became manager on 13 September. That came as a bit of a surprise, but I wasn't complaining because Ian brought Billy Hunter, or 'Willie' as he was known, with him from Scotland as his assistant; Pompey's new No. 2 and I went way back to our playing days together at Hibs. I don't think Ian had a clue what he was walking into. No doubt it must have seemed like a good career move at the time, but the reality is that he had been handed a poisoned chalice. We were little more than a shambles, a million miles away from being a team capable of going up. There was dissent in the ranks, where the old guard resented the fact that the likes of myself, Ron Davies, Phil Roberts and Paul Went had been recruited on huge salaries. I know I was on three times as much as some of my team-mates, and that bred discontent – especially as we were so manifestly unsuccessful.

Ian suffered a baptism of fire immediately after his appointment, for the following day Portsmouth were due to renew hostilities with Southampton at The Dell. Football hooliganism was rampant, and our 2–1 defeat, in which I was guilty of missing a couple of good chances, was overshadowed by the arrest of a trainload of Pompey fans at Southampton Central station and the decision by referee Clive Thomas to take out a summons for common assault against a fan who ran on to the pitch and pushed him. I thought we were the better side that day, but you get nothing for going close. You must stick your chances away.

Two goals from Ron Davies completed the double over

Forest three days later to give Ian his first win, but it proved a false dawn – we were a poor side, for all the money lavished on the club by Mr Deacon – and it was another two months and a dozen matches before we beat Sheffield Wednesday 1–0 after slumping to the very foot of the table. We couldn't buy a goal during that awful, barren spell in which we scored just five times, and it was obvious that we were in for another relegation fight. There was talent in the side but little or no belief, no drive to aspire to anything more than a safe mid-table position. There were some at the club who had got comfortable – older, more established players only interested in rousing themselves for home matches to keep our fans happy.

I don't think I was ever particularly ambitious, otherwise I wouldn't have left Arsenal, although I always tried 100 per cent on the park. And I suppose I was guilty too of slipping into that sloppy mental state where you thought, 'So we haven't won, what the hell? Bollocks, I'll play better next week.' But I never knew what I was going to do from one week to the next. It was all instinctive with me, I was only young, a free spirit. Against a good full-back who kept robbing me I should have laid the ball off but I had a persistent, perverse streak. I'd keep taking him on, again and again, hoping to beat him once, maybe twice, as a badge of honour, to regain a bit of pride and rouse the crowd. I had been built up as this player who took people on and felt I had to do it or the supporters would feel let down. A little voice in the back of my mind cried, 'I'll show Arsenal' – but it never bothered me one way or another whether I played in the First Division again. I was doing OK personally, the fans liked me, and I was playing more good games than bad.

The new boss wasn't found lacking when it came to trying new ideas and took the team to see a self-made millionaire and spiritualist, who was heavily into self-improvement, in his beautiful mansion in the Hampshire countryside. He was to psychoanalyse us in a group and also as individuals. I had my session with him, and he told me I was too gentle to be a professional footballer and would be much more suitably employed in the arts world, maybe as a photographer or a poet. Ian St John didn't know whether to laugh or cry at the verdict, and said simply, 'So what you really mean to tell me, Peter, is that this club has paid £100,000 for someone who should be reciting fucking poetry!' The spiritualist seemed genuine enough and kept reminding me, 'You've got to be honest with yourself, Peter,' so I was somewhat shocked to find out he was later tracked down by police to a remote Scottish island after conning fortunes out of congregations on the pretext of raising money for new church organs. Be honest with yourself, indeed!

Ron Davies was as honest as they come on the field and our top scorer with five goals overall come the end of November, but he was sacrificed because Ian believed we needed more craft and guile in the side. That's how Ron went to Manchester United and my old Arsenal pal George Graham left Old Trafford for Portsmouth in an exchange deal. That swap came as a surprise to many, but the big smile on Ron's face soon disappeared because he only made eight substitute appearances and never started a single league game for Docherty's young Reds as they dominated our division totally, stayed top all season and swept back to the First Division at the first time of asking. The Doc only wanted him as an insurance policy in case something happened to Stuart Pearson or Lou Macari. At one stage, I thought I was bound for United, too. At least, that's what Norman Piper claimed and he did have the ear of a friendly United scout. 'United are looking at you, Peter,' he confided, but it was big Ron who went up to Manchester.

Still, I was happy to see George Graham again and glad to chauffeur him around Hampshire for a few months, looking for houses, until he spied a property he bought in Southsea. George came off the substitutes' bench to make his first appearance in the 1–0 win over Wednesday and he helped to spark a mini-revival which saw us win six out of nine league matches to climb to seventeenth in the table, which is where we finished in April.

I knew how much George hated training and couldn't suppress a laugh the time St John told us he'd hired the services of an athletics coach to improve our stamina. Thirty-odd laps of a local track were on the schedule, and it wasn't long before George and Brian Lewis had been lapped, and lapped again. George was much happier with a briefcase in hand, rather than training shoes on his feet, and pointed out the merits of joining a new local independent bank in Portsmouth, which was offering preferential interest rates, better than those available at the building societies. Several of the lads, including Micky Mellows, transferred their money to the bank in question. But when it became public that it was in trouble, George was the only one of us savvy enough to withdraw all his loot before the bank went defunct, losing poor old Micky about £6,000. No wonder he turned to religion, while I chided George: 'Are you sure you weren't one of the directors at that bank?'

St John started unloading the more experienced players and bringing in kids, who simply weren't adequate replacements in my view. Bobby Kellard's nomadic existence living out of a suitcase came to an end when he was knocked out on loan to Hereford and joined Torquay United before he decided to give it all up and head to South Africa to try his luck with Cape Town City.

Although our interest in the FA Cup was snuffed out immediately in the third round in January with a 3–1 defeat at Notts County, where I managed to score, the goals suddenly started to flow as if someone had turned on a tap, and I popped in another one a fortnight later as we completed the double over the Owls with a 2–0 win at Hillsborough.

St John tried everything he knew to turn our season around. We came back for afternoon training sessions, then received days off when we weren't expecting them, but nothing he did seemed to work. The malaise within the club was too deep-rooted. There was bother within the camp, friction between some players and domestic tension. Gambling had become a big problem at the club. Six or seven of us were heavily into the horses. One player once had £200 on a novice hurdler at 20–1, and we watched it win on television in our hotel on a Saturday lunchtime before an away match. At one point, the gaffer called me into his office and pleaded with me, Scot to Scot: 'Can you nae have a word with them, Peter?' I did try, but it was very difficult. I didn't feel comfortable lecturing older players on their morals. I wasn't a saint and I felt their private lives were none of my business.

I had some sympathy for the boss. He had been in line to take over at Leeds when Don Revie was appointed England manager, but Brian Clough got the job, albeit for only forty-four days, at Elland Road. Instead of having loads of money to play with at Leeds, Ian found himself having to count the pennies at Portsmouth and was left complaining, 'They had no money, so I wasn't able to buy a single player in the three years I was there. BT cut off the telephone line because we couldn't pay for it. I had to find a public phone if I wanted to contact other clubs. We couldn't pay the bus company to get us to games, and had to wash all our own laundry. Talk about running a club on a shoestring.' I liked Ian St John. He had been such a great player himself for Liverpool and Scotland, but he couldn't cope with average players. His next move was richly rewarding, however, as he transferred into television, where he struck up a great relationship with Jimmy Greaves, and the Saint and Greavsie legend was born.

At one stage of the season, the boss thought a nice little

trip to Spain might perk us up, and while we were there we played a friendly in Seville. I turned it on and the next thing I know Ian's telling me, 'There's a club ready to pay £100,000 for you. Do you trust me?' I replied that I did, but nothing more was said. The proposed transfer fizzled out, much as my secret move from Arsenal to Juventus had come to nothing.

Our status was in jeopardy with just four games to go before we went to Blackpool on 5 April, and, by way of an incentive to pull something out of the fire, St John promised us we could stay the whole weekend in our big, posh seafront hotel if we got a positive result. Before I removed my backside from the substitutes' bench, it looked for all the world as if we would be heading back to the south coast pointless that Saturday night. Then the ball reached me inside their area, about ten yards out, and I turned to hit a low shot which crept agonisingly slowly into the corner of the net to earn us a draw, much to the delight of the Pompey faithful present at Bloomfield Road. Our supporters were brilliant throughout my time at Fratton Park. Crowds did dwindle, but never once did they turn against us.

That evening was an absolute belter, what I can remember of it. We kicked off in the hotel with a few drinks, which turned into a pub crawl before ending up in Brian London's nightclub. The old boxer was there himself and proved to be a nice guy, very hospitable, as he regaled us with tales of his one-sided punch-up with Cassius Clay, later to become Muhammad Ali, and how he'd taken a remorseless pounding for three rounds before the fight for the world heavyweight crown was stopped in 1966 at Earls Court. It was time to return to our hotel at three in the morning, but the bar there was still humming with St John and Hunter carousing along with none other than P. J. Proby. Ian fancied himself as a singer. But Willie was certainly good enough to have made a living out of it. As for P. J. Proby, I recall hearing him belt out a few bars of 'Maria' and boldly declaring, 'That guy cannae fucking sing,' before heading up to my room. Sunday was more of the same in terms of alcohol consumption before we sobered up sufficiently to travel back to Portsmouth on the Monday. Win or lose, have some booze . . . get a draw, have some more – that was our motto.

The 1974–75 campaign dwindled away to leave us five points safe of the relegation dragnet, which claimed Wednesday, Cardiff and Millwall. The record books show we had become a marginally worse side, one in which I started 38 of our 42 league games, made one other appearance as a substitute and managed four goals (two in the league and one apiece in the FA Cup and League Cup).

Our season of conspicuous under-achievement ended on a suitably downbeat note – a 3–0 home defeat by Norwich, who went back up with Manchester United and Aston Villa. It wouldn't be long before I was heading back up too: back up to Scotland, driven all the way in the chairman's Rolls Royce. Meanwhile, Joyce decided to do a runner with another man, and I was obliged to turn ugly and threaten violence.

CHAPTER 13

Last Night a DJ Stole My Wife

I was one of the lucky ones: I managed to bale out of the good ship Pompey before the club disappeared beneath the waves to the Davy Jones' locker of the Third Division, where trips to York and Chester awaited. Mind you, I might very well have departed in August 1975, before the season had even started. Ian St John revealed the Norwich manager John Bond had been on the phone to him and they had agreed a deal. I was going to Carrow Road, while Portsmouth were apparently getting Doug Livermore plus £20,000 in exchange. That was the first I'd heard of it, and I felt uncomfortable on several counts: I thoroughly enjoyed living in Southsea, our fans were great, and I didn't want the supporters to think of me as some kind of Judas or a rat for turning my back on the club.

If St John had no use for me, however, Norwich were

promising First Division football again, and when Bond phoned me at home that evening, I agreed terms. He told me to spend whatever I needed on expenses to get myself up to Norwich railway station the following day, and that a car would meet me there. Thirty minutes later St John phoned to ask, 'Are you going in the morning?' and I reassured him that I was. Then everything went haywire when Deacon called to tell me, 'Peter, you aren't going to Norwich. The deal is off.' I felt like piggy in the middle.

A frustrating week passed before I was summoned to the manager's office, where I found St John and Deacon virtually at daggers drawn. Talk about tension. Deacon said, 'Right, Peter. We've decided to accept Norwich's offer. I'm sorry you're leaving, but we're getting some money – as well as Doug Livermore.' That was most certainly news to St John, who casually announced, 'You do know, Mr Chairman, that Doug Livermore was sold two days ago to Cardiff for £18,000?' I just turned on my heels and walked out of the door, there and then. The two most important men running a professional football club were in the same room as me and the effect was like watching a Punch and Judy show.

The club was lurching towards a fully-fledged crisis, with rumblings in the press about our financial problems growing steadily louder. Paul Went and I, as the highest wage-earners, seemed to be singled out for criticism, despite the first-team squad accepting a £10-a-week pay cut. Our wonderful supporters coughed up some money, the chairman had put in more than his fair share, and there was even speculation that Portsmouth Football Club would have to be sold. Every player was made available for transfer, and George Graham quipped, 'We should be running out with price tags on our backs, not numbers,' although our plight was far from a laughing matter. St John was suspended, and that faithful old retainer Ron Tindall became caretaker manager once more.

My rate of finishing must have been improving because by early December I had scored against Bristol Rovers, Aldershot in the League Cup and West Brom in a 3–1 defeat, although there was no cause for celebrations at The Hawthorns as that result made it nine league beatings in a row for poor old Pompey. Soon after the West Brom match, Deacon informed me that he had accepted an offer from Motherwell manager Willie McLean, apparently after Ayr rejected Willie's £60,000 bid for their Scotland Under-23 right-winger, John Doyle. I flew up to Scotland early the following week to play in a practice match, but McLean offered me a pittance, and I told him in no uncertain terms that I wouldn't be signing.

The next thing I recall is Deacon driving me in his black Rolls Royce to Glasgow to oversee the move personally. On the long journey up from the south coast, the chairman revealed he had sunk £400,000 of his own cash into Pompey and had guarantees amounting to £378,000 outstanding at the bank. He clearly felt a little bit of payback was due. I agreed. I liked Deacon, and three-quarters of a million pounds was a very substantial amount of money to lavish on chasing a dream that had become his worst nightmare. It was almost as if Deacon had spent fortunes grooming a pedigree dog to win best of breed at Crufts, only for it to turn into a Rottweiler which had turned round and taken a big chunk out of his arse.

The wages at Fir Park weren't great. I eventually agreed to take a drop, but I did get £8,000 to sign on. McLean said he'd been looking at me for some time and was of the opinion I had a bad reputation but had received only good vibes from people within the game he had sounded out about me.

Driving back, Deacon asked me not to disclose the exact amount of the transfer fee and, in all honesty, I didn't even know then that it was as much as £35,000. Sure enough, St John was on the phone that night, eagerly asking, 'How much did you go for, Peter?' I told him I was in the dark, and he just sighed, 'Fuck me, all I've been given is a poxy £6,000 to replace you.'

I trusted the chairman, however, in all our dealings. Portsmouth still owed me money, and Deacon asked me to sign a piece of paper. I couldn't remember what it said at the time, but later I recall it related to a pension. The club were supposed to have been paying into a scheme on my behalf, but had let things slide for a couple of years. My signature was my bond not to come haunting Fratton Park for more money in the future. Deacon simply shook my hand for the last time, looked me straight in the eye and said, 'That's it now, Peter.' I knew I wouldn't be conned out of anything due to me. Yet it was all rather desperate, and I still felt a bit guilty, almost as if I was leaving Pompey in the lurch.

The 1975–76 season probably ranks somewhere among the worst in Portsmouth's history because they were never out of the bottom three from August to April, finishing last – a dozen points, or six victories, shy of salvation.

I made a profit on our home in Southsea, selling for £26,000, and paid £27,000 for a two-bedroomed flat in Fettes Row, a quiet and dignified cul-de-sac in Edinburgh's Georgian 'New Town' and a stone's throw from Princes Street. We still had our house in north London, which we rented out. Money was the least of my worries.

Motherwell was a tough little steel town, with a team to match, and were already enjoying a storming season in the Scottish Premier Division, lying in second place when I made my debut for them on 13 December 1975 against my old club Hibs at Easter Road in a 1–0 defeat – precisely one week after playing my last game for Pompey. I was excited and thought Motherwell were a better side than Hibs, despite the result. I had a good game, and we were unlucky not to win, let alone draw. It was a fresh start, and if somebody was prepared to buy me I knew I must have something. All in all, Motherwell were a great bunch of lads, who gave me a warm reception. When I came home to Scotland I thought it would be for the rest of my career and for a while I never dreamed I'd ever leave again.

I had a month to wait for my first goal, against Dundee United in a 4–1 home win on 17 January, and life on the pitch, at least, looked decidedly encouraging. The Scottish

Cup brought us our finest hour during the campaign, and we so nearly pulled off Mission Impossible by eliminating both Celtic and Rangers. Marching boldly into the semi-finals looked as plausible as scaling Ben Nevis in a pair of carpet slippers, mind you, when Celtic came calling on 24 January in the third round and they were sitting pretty at the interval with a 2–0 lead under their belts, with Kenny Dalglish scoring one of the goals. I don't remember what McLean slipped into our half-time tea, but it had a miraculous effect, and we fought back to delight the bulk of a 25,000 Fir Park crowd, winning 3–2 with goals from Bobby Graham, Ian Taylor and Willie Pettigrew.

Bobby was a smashing little player and marvellous partner for Willie. When I hit form, we could be one hell of a threesome in attack. Bobby could turn on a sixpence, much like Dalglish, and was a great drinker. Without a shadow of a doubt the title of fastest player in the Scottish Premier Division belonged to Pettigrew. He was pace personified, quicker than me – and I was fast. Nearly sold to a German club, Willie was a good striker, but we came to rely too heavily on him for goals. Pettigrew was mustard in the box that first season, blasting twenty-nine goals in the three competitions. We used to kid on that the perfect summer job for him would be standing in for the Loch Ness Monster. He wasn't blessed with good looks. He and Iain Dowie together really would have been a pair to frighten the life out of the opposition!

Suddenly, I had something fairly horrible to confront on the home front. It might have seemed as if I was in my element to outsiders, but on a personal level I had problems as big as Pompey's . . . because Joyce had run away with a disc jockey. It would be an understatement to suggest she wasn't keen on returning to Scotland. Joyce loved living in Southsea, so close to the beach, and she had deservedly earned a lucrative, fulfilling career for herself, modelling in London and all over the south coast. She had an enviable lifestyle, a nice deal with the Castrol Oil company among other contracts and had recently enjoyed some high-profile work at the Earls Court Boat Show.

One weekend, just as I was getting my feet under the table at Fir Park, she phoned from a modelling assignment to tell me, 'I'm not coming back,' and I knew from the tone of her voice that something was wrong, very wrong. My transfer had been the trigger for domestic friction. Sudden change and upheaval always had a very detrimental effect on Joyce, and still does to this day. I swear there was nothing wrong with our marriage, but it was all too much for my poor wife, and she became extremely vulnerable. This nasty little creep of a DJ in Portsmouth, who Joyce had met through her agency work, had wormed his way into her affections while he was doing the background music to her catwalks. He befriended her while she was vulnerable. I don't think anything had been planned. The relationship certainly hadn't been going on for long, and I'd had no reason to be suspicious. Joyce was heading for a nervous breakdown and this smooth-talking, friendly man seemed like someone to cling on to. When this chancer promised to give her the opportunity to stay in the south, she couldn't have been thinking clearly.

I wasn't there, and it was a nasty mess, which needed sorting out at the first available opportunity. I told the boss, 'I've got problems, the wife's having a breakdown, and I've got the kid to consider.' McLean was sympathetic and asked me if I wanted time off. I refused his kind offer, told him my mum would take care of Paul and that I'd sort it all out in my own time. I hired a private detective from the west of Scotland on £100 a day, plus expenses, to get evidence of the affair, but my super sleuth was so idle and incompetent he made Inspector Clouseau look like Sherlock Holmes. He spent three or four days in one of Portsmouth's top hotels at my expense after I'd even told him the address at which he could find Joyce and her DJ lover.

Finally, I put the matter to bed myself. Two hefty pals were positioned outside the address when I phoned the DJ to tell him, 'Look out of your window, pal. If you don't leave Joyce alone, there are people ready to break your fucking legs.' My threat had the desired effect. The music man was as shallow as they come and he suddenly told her he couldn't hack it any more. In my view he'd taken advantage of Joyce, and the whole sordid episode ended, almost inevitably, with Joyce having a breakdown. She was very sensitive to anything that upset the norm and disrupted her routine.

As soon as we'd beaten Celtic in the Scottish Cup, I jumped in a car that Saturday night and drove all the way down to Southsea with my brother-in-law Martin, reaching my old empty home at three in the morning. I'd phoned a few pals, and they arrived for a few drinks. It might seem a bit insensitive, given the fact I was back on serious personal business, but the Celtic result was worth celebrating, and there was nothing I could do about Joyce until the following day.

Friends had been good enough to tend to Joyce after the DJ hastily showed her the door, and I met her in a church later that Sunday. She refused to come back to Scotland with me then, but she was ready a fortnight later – and it wasn't a moment too soon. I brought Joyce back to Edinburgh, where she was admitted to the renowned Andrew Duncan Clinic, which specialises in psychiatric illnesses. I had my mother to thank, not for the first time and certainly not for the last, for being there to pick up the pieces and look after our son Paul while Joyce underwent treatment.

We were reconciled, and there were no recriminations on my part because I was never an angel. There were plenty of tears, though, mostly from Joyce because she felt guilty about Paul and felt she had abandoned him. Angry scenes were out of the question, although Joyce used to blame me for her illness. I didn't help, but she had an hereditary chemical imbalance in her brain. If you don't act to treat the condition it becomes bigger and bigger, like a snowball going downhill. The main thing was for Joyce to get better, and it was impossible to hold a logical conversation with her then: I just had to wait between six and eight weeks. The treatment involved lithium, supposed to keep her on an even keel with no highs or lows. Famous personalities such as Sir Winston Churchill, Mike Tyson and Stephen Fry were all prescribed lithium, I understand. It's reckoned to be the best drug for manic depressive and bipolar personalities.

Once Joyce began to return to a sense of normality, it wasn't a case of us apportioning blame for what had occurred. She'd gabble and worry, while I'd just stroke her hair, give her a hug and say, 'Look, Joyce, we'll get you better and take it from there.' That was the humdrum reality of the situation we found ourselves in. I knew I was never going to be able to wrap her in cotton wool for the rest of our lives, and Joyce has always believed she could fight her condition without medication. Sadly, that's not the case. A specialist told me only 20 per cent of patients make a full recovery; problems recur for the other 80 per cent. Any undue excitement – a lively night out, or worrying about my gambling – could carry her over the top. She's a very sensitive, caring person, and the lithium has produced some cruel side-effects, such as causing her to pile on weight while still being obliged to drink at least six pints of water each day to counter-balance the fact that it is a lead-based drug which can damage the kidneys.

Trauma over, I went back to work and scored a goal in the second half in the Scottish Cup to wrap up a routine 2–0 win in the fourth round at Cowdenbeath after Graham had hit the target. That brought us nicely into a three-game epic with Hibs. We drew 2–2 at our place, with me slotting in a penalty, and the tie remained deadlocked after extra-time at Easter Road. Ibrox was selected for the second replay, and Hibs led at the break thanks to a goal from Harper, but then I enhanced my reputation as a penalty king by equalising from the spot, and Ian Taylor, a clever schemer, grabbed the winner.

So the scene was set for Motherwell's journey to Hampden Park to face Rangers in the semi-final on 31 March. In a total reverse of the Celtic scenario, we found ourselves leading by two goals at half-time that Wednesday night in front of a 50,000 crowd through Stewart McLaren and Pettigrew before Jock Wallace's men came storming back to win 3–2 with a penalty and two goals from their leading scorer, Derek Johnstone. So near, but yet so far. We were absolutely heartbroken, while Rangers went on to beat Hearts 3–1 in the final and complete the treble.

The memories of that night are still vivid. We murdered Rangers for a long time, and it would have been no injustice had we taken a 4–0 lead. I was getting a bit tired and McLean decided to replace me with Vic Davidson, a midfield player. Then Rangers were handed a lifeline that prompts arguments in Motherwell bars to this day. Johnstone was in our box, but facing away from goal, and the ball was heading out of play when our keeper Stuart Rennie went down at the striker's feet, and Johnstone collapsed like a dying swan. Talk about a con job, it was the sort of dive that made Brian Phelps famous. But the referee awarded Rangers a penalty, Alex Miller stuck it away, and that was all the encouragement Wallace's men required. As we sat on the team coach heading home later that evening, the radio suddenly blasted out the Eagles' hit 'One of These Nights', and a few of us just looked silently at each other and shook our heads. It should have been our night, definitely, we should have finished off Rangers while we were playing them off the park and we would have fancied our chances very strongly against either Hearts or Dumbarton in the final.

Vic was particularly upset, having come through the ranks at Celtic alongside Lou Macari, David Hay and Kenny Dalglish. A clever inside-forward who could drink like a fish, Vic hated training but loved the treatment table, where he could invariably be located all week before Friday, when he would magically declare himself fit for the weekend's exertions. McLaren bordered on the illegal sometimes when it came to winning possession, hence his nickname 'Chopper' after Chelsea's Ron 'Chopper' Harris. His ball-winning and marking was in the mould of hard men Peter Storey and Nobby Stiles. An unselfish player, he was unconcerned about flair. Rennie was another interesting guy, a civil servant and one of the Edinburgh contingent. He was underrated, mainly because he was a part-timer, but could have been top class had he devoted his life to professional football.

Defeat by Rangers hurt, and, although we put a brave enough face on it by winning our next three matches, losing in that cruel manner had a bad long-term effect, and we only collected a single point from our final five games.

After my first goal in January against Dundee United, I'd popped in a couple more in the league, against St Johnstone from the penalty spot and Dundee, before the curtain came down on the season in May with Motherwell in fourth place, behind the Old Firm – who else? – and Hibs.

That summer found the lads eagerly packing for an exotic tour of Haiti, Mexico and Colombia, which led us into no end of trouble and strife. Motherwell would immediately have been in hot water with the Scottish Football Association had they discovered our two fixtures in Haiti were against the hosts' Under-23 side and then their full national team, because the SFA had decreed we should only be playing local club sides. We beat the Under-23s, but were robbed blind by what I can only assume was a bent referee who ensured the Haitian national team won by the odd goal in front of a crowd of 22,000. Mind you, I don't altogether blame the match officials because Haiti was by now under the dictatorship of Jean-Claude 'Baby Doc' Duvalier, who was almost as tyrannical as his infamous father, Papa Doc, had been.

There were only another three or four guests in our hotel, but we befriended a local beggar called Matthew, who showed us the sights. After a few glasses of the local firewater one night, we joked about going with Matthew into the nearby hills to witness a voodoo ceremony but bottled out in the end. That was a shame because Willie Pettigrew wouldn't have needed a mask to put the wind up those voodoo priests! So, instead, we befriended the hotel barman, who regaled us with a sob story. Apparently, he only earned about £40 a year and passports cost a fortune. He was keen to sample life under a less oppressive regime, and we felt sorry for him, organising a whip-round which produced £60 on the understanding that he could have the rest of the night off. We fancied pouring our own drinks for a change. I took over the running of the bar, to the fury of the hotel manager the following day, when it dawned on everyone that the barman would never be returning. Our £60 was the equivalent of eighteen months' salary to him and was his one-way ticket out of Haiti, but I wasn't allowed to go until half a dozen of us chipped in £140 in cash to cover the cost of the previous night's excessive drinking.

Matthew encouraged us to visit what he colourfully described as a seafront nightclub, which, on closer inspection, turned out to be no more than a ship at the local quayside with girls hanging out of every porthole and an orchestra playing on the jetty. On closer inspection still, after visiting the sirens on this floating brothel, a few of the guys felt it necessary to visit the club doctor we'd brought with us on tour. Two or three of them caught a nasty dose of the clap. You can't hide anything in a football club, and when the symptoms materialised, they had the piss taken out of them unmercifully. I restricted myself to having a laugh with the girls on the quayside. They drifted from table to table and enjoyed sitting on our laps, trying to negotiate a price for their sexual favours. There was huge activity in that lively harbourside, with groups of

Russian sailors, in particular, keen to sample everything which was available on board.

On to Mexico, where we discovered our fixture was another international. Unfortunately, the game was televised and only attracted a derisory gate of 14,000 to the giant Aztec Stadium, but we put on a decent show, losing 3–2.

It was a crazy time in Colombia. One of the youngsters in the squad was forced into a quick submission by this big-breasted South American señorita we fixed him up with as an eighteenth birthday present in a seedy back-street bordello in Bogota. He had been spending all his money on expensive phone calls back home to his child-hood sweetheart, but we, in our wisdom, decreed that it was high time he swapped romance for pure, unadulter-ated sex. It was history repeating itself, and I knew exactly how he felt, having been through a very similar experi-ence, of course, on tour with Hibs as a teenager myself. There were some stunning young girls in that knocking shop, but the rest of the party, somewhat put off by minders packing pistols, were too nervous to perform.

We certainly did the business in Bogota out on the pitch, though, against Santa Fe. They had played Millonarios in front of a frenzied 60,000 crowd hurling firecrackers in a championship decider before they met us, and we knew their two Peruvian wingers, in particular, would be a handful. The venue was something like 2,000 feet above sea level, and poor Pettigrew was so overcome by the con-ditions he required oxygen at half-time. The atmosphere was not improved by our tactics. Motherwell were an extremely tough-tackling team, and the South American side's delicate, fancy-dan touches acted like a red rag to a bull. The friendly degenerated into a brawl with us leading 2–1 and was abandoned while our stopper, big Willie McVie, was chasing their centre-forward around the track. I once made the mistake of squaring up to Willie in a training-ground fight and was rewarded by having my nose spread all over my face. He was a huge, uncompromising fellow. The crowd went potty, while we were forced to make a run for it to the sanctuary of our dressing-room. Even there, we felt far from safe, with fans jumping on the roof and banging on the windows before the police arrived to escort us back to our hotel. There were a few shaking Scottish hands on the lager bottles that night as we counted our blessings at escaping in one piece.

We were greeted the following morning by the revelation that Millonarios were refusing to play us and, more seriously, our tour guide Enzio had done a bunk. No game meant no fee for him. We had a team meeting and decided to cut short our trip because there was nothing to stay for. Under the terms of our visas, we were obliged to stay in Colombia for ten days and had to pay a £30 penalty apiece to get out earlier. After our experiences against Santa Fe, we weren't about to complain.

Motherwell were nobody's fools on home soil, however, as a young manager by the name of Alex Ferguson would discover to his cost when he bad-mouthed me . . . and bit off more than he could chew.

CHAPTER 14

Call the Fire Brigade

Having survived our eventful tour of South America more or less intact, we welcomed my old pal and Easter Road legend Jimmy O'Rourke to Motherwell for the new season. I was particularly pleased because this meant someone to share the journey from Edinburgh, and we took it in turns to drive, one week at a time. The forty-five miles usually took us just over an hour, depending on the traffic. Those journeys gave Jimmy and me plenty of time to discuss what we'd do in the future, when age caught up with us and we had to make a living outside football. The pub business looked to me as if it might be fun, and we made an offer for a bar in the Corstorphine district of Edinburgh. It wasn't quite enough, though, and there were complications concerning the leasehold. Jimmy eventually did make it into the pub business with another partner, leaving me to bid £72,000 for Tamson's, a busy little neighbourhood bar down Easter Road way. My plan was to put my dad in charge, but I was outbid by a couple of thousand quid. It was such a close run thing, I always wondered whether the chap who got Tamson's got a tip off about the size of my offer.

Willie McLean wanted Jimmy to share the goal-scoring burden with Willie Pettigrew, and he obliged at first, scoring a hat-trick in thirteen minutes on 6 November as we came from two down at half-time to beat Kilmarnock 5–4 at home in driving rain. The fans gave both sides a deserved standing ovation after the final whistle. I was particularly pleased with my afternoon's work, which hadn't started until the half-hour, when the manager summoned me off the bench to replace Colin McAdam, a huge boy we nicknamed 'The Horse', with Killie leading 3–0. Three of my shots brought rebounds from which we scored, and I also stuck over a cross for Jimmy to head into the net.

Life was good and it improved in December 1976 when Joyce and I celebrated the birth our second son, Jon. He was just two months old when he made his 'debut' at Fir Park, Joyce being snapped by a photographer with Jon in her arms, watching us beat St Mirren 2–1 on 26 February in a most eventful Scottish Cup fourth-round tie. Our defender Gregor Stevens, a sound lad, needed a police escort to get him to the ground in time because of traffic jams which caused the kick-off to be delayed by ten minutes. Hundreds of fans were locked out of the bumper 26,709 crowd, and there were fourteen arrests as feelings ran high.

This tie always had the makings of a cracker. The St Mirren manager, a young Alex Ferguson, had assembled a very tasty side, which stormed to the First Division title that season, losing just twice, and he had a couple of players capable of operating at the highest level in captain Tony Fitzpatrick and forward Frank McGarvey. In time, Fitzpatrick went to Bristol City for £235,000 while McGarvey headed to Liverpool for £250,000. All week before the match, the papers were full of what St Mirren were going to do to us, with Ferguson describing me as a 'flash in the pan who only plays one match in four' and Willie Pettigrew as 'one-dimensional'.

The criticism got our backs up more than a little. Pettigrew and Bobby Graham, in particular, had storming games as we played them off the park. We had muscle to go with our method, thanks to the effectiveness of defenders such as McAdam, McLaren, Willie Watson and Stevens. Willie was known simply as 'The Whale' on account of his size and drinking ability. An almighty full-back who could kick lumps out of the opposing winger, he would devour anything in his way. There was a grain of truth in Ferguson's whinges afterwards when he complained, 'Motherwell kicked us off the park.' McGarvey was involved in an X-certificate collision with McAdam which still makes me wince today whenever I recall it. McGarvey went down under a challenge, the ball came to rest against his head and McAdam, who might have been trying to clear the ball, caught McGarvey full on with all his considerable force. Poor Frank. He managed to continue playing, but didn't appear to know much about what was happening. We soon got our comeuppance, however. Rangers proved too strong for us in the quarter-finals and won 3–0.

I contributed little to the second half of the season because Joyce fell ill once more, and my services were required at home, looking after baby Jon and his big brother, Paul. Jon's birth had triggered her illness again. Obviously, it was a massive event in her life, and I knew full well how badly Joyce coped with huge change. She was still on and off the lithium tablets, plus a combination of other drugs. Sometimes she would take eight tablets a day, other times she would feel OK and cut her dosage right down. She was treating her condition as a physical illness, feeling better when she took tablets and then stopping. But it was a mental condition, and she really needed to keep taking all her medication regularly. Joyce hated piling on the pounds and drinking all that water. It made her feel so tired. I suppose it's only human nature to believe you're better off without medication – but Joyce wasn't. Now I can see that I really should have been stronger, more persuasive with her about taking the regular dosage that had been prescribed.

I felt despair, wondering, 'Will this ever end?' You can mend a broken arm, but the brain is a very strange organ. I took relief in gambling, drinking, training and playing football, but Joyce's condition was never far away and preyed on my mind. At her manic worst, Joyce couldn't sleep for days on end. She might get out of bed at three in the morning and either phone or visit a friend, driving off in the car into the dead of night. I'd say they wouldn't be up, but Joyce wouldn't have it and was sure friends would be happy to hear from her – or even see her in person. Joyce would turn it round the other way and tell me, 'You're the barmy one. You're the suitable case for treatment, Peter.' There was no reasoning with her when she was like this, she was totally and utterly convinced she was in the right, and I lost sleep worrying.

I remonstrated with one of the Motherwell players, when he joked, 'Why don't you just knock her on the head and lock the door?' This was no laughing matter.

Joyce's health wasn't improved by smoking over forty cigarettes a day. Sometimes she would chain-smoke fifty to sixty. I always feared it would end in disaster – and it nearly did while I was at Motherwell and Joyce almost burned the house down. She was in the kitchen and carelessly discarded an unfinished cigarette in the bin. Fortunately I was at home, got Joyce into the garden and dashed over the road to a neighbour who, by a stroke of good fortune, was a fire station boss, who put in an emergency call to his team. By the time I returned, the kitchen was ablaze, and, although the fire brigade responded very promptly, the room was gutted. Our place reeked for weeks as the smell lingered. We had to redecorate, which was a burden because the house was up for sale and we were in the process of moving into a bungalow. The incident didn't put Joyce off smoking, however. She could go two or three days with no sleep whatsoever, and I was constantly on edge during these dark periods and became extremely worried that, when she did nod off in the lounge, she might go with another lighted cigarette, causing a fire.

When things got out of hand, the only solution was for a doctor to be called in to section her – which must have happened on maybe half a dozen occasions through the years. To be perfectly honest, it often came as a relief when she went into hospital. At least I knew she would come to no harm there and that I could go and visit two or three times a day.

During my Arsenal days, I must have spent almost £3,000 searching for the elusive cure in Harley Street, where a specialist and fellow Scot told me, 'Joyce will always have this problem.' I thanked him and replied, 'Don't be too quick to tell all your patients that, or you'll do yourself out of a job.'

Motherwell were very understanding and sympathetic to my plight, and I repaid them in some small measure by returning for the last match of the season and scoring in a 2–2 home draw with Celtic. Travelling with Motherwell always came with the guarantee of a good laugh, and the lads especially welcomed our Highland tours to the fishing towns of Fraserburgh, Buckie and Keith. On one infamous occasion, a club official caught four of the first team with two local girls in a hotel room and threatened them with dire consequences unless he was allowed to join the party, which featured plenty of vodka. We tried to persuade one of the girls to do us a favour by going to visit him in his room, but she was less than impressed, and her response was, 'I'm not going with that old bugger!' Keith were only a bunch of part-timers, plying their trade in the Highland League, and when the local butcher scored the winner against us it made headlines. McLean went ballistic.

Among the other characters I came to know and love was Joe Wark, our Mr Dependable, and one of the longest-serving Motherwell players ever. Peter 'Doomie' Millar was a good, strong player but a born pessimist. He would have been brilliant in *Dad's Army* as Private Fraser, the character who rushed around proclaiming, 'Doomed, we're all doomed.' Midfield man Bobby Watson was well respected by all as a good, strong tackler. Pat Gardner had reached veteran status by the time I arrived at Fir Park but had been a good player in his day, and everyone still looked forward to his company, especially on Thursdays, when he would arrive with boxes full of smokies... smoked kippers to the uninitiated.

We were a good footballing side on our day, a nice blend of strong defenders, creative players and men with an eye for goal.

CHAPTER 15

Wizard in Oz

Nothing lasts for ever, especially in football, and Willie McLean was replaced as Motherwell manager in December 1977 after we had gone down 2–1 at Hibs on Christmas Eve – a ninth defeat in fourteen league matches, which left us struggling in eighth position in the ten-club Scottish Premier Division. The team were placed in the hands of Roger Hynd for safe-keeping, while Willie was snapped up to manage Raith Rovers and went on to win promotion at Stark's Park.

It wasn't long before I knew what it was to feel wanted again. The George Best/Rodney Marsh revival roadshow had come to an end at Fulham, and I received a phone call from their manager, Bobby Campbell. At first, I thought it was a wind-up, and maybe Peter Millar, Vic Davidson or Jimmy O'Rourke was taking the piss, but the Scouse accent was quite strong, and I was soon happy it really was Campbell on the other end of the line. The gist was simple. He wanted me at Craven Cottage, had watched me a couple of times playing for Motherwell and believed I would be an effective winger as well as adding a touch of colour to a side missing the mercurial talents of Best and Marsh. Bobby wanted me to ask Motherwell for a transfer, but I wasn't interested in a move at the time. I said, 'Thanks, but no thanks, Mr Campbell,' but a seed had most definitely been sown in my mind – and Fulham watered that seed for a long time before it sprouted.

Meanwhile, far away from the temptations, glamour and glitz of west London, Hynd had been brought up in a rock-hard Scottish mining village and made his name as a no-nonsense defender at Birmingham, blowing into Fir Park with claims that he would fashion a side capable of becoming championship material. And there were times when I thought we would win things under him. O'Rourke always compared Roger to Ben Turpin, the actor in black-and-white films whose eyes went in different directions, but I had no complaints with the new manager and liked him. To outsiders, he came across as a very hard man, and anyone who ever saw him play on the park would never have suspected that, in reality, he was just a great big softie. Roger would train us hard, but if you did well for him and got a good result, you could get away with murder. He always backed his men and gave them the benefit of the doubt in any argument, any dispute. Some took advantage of that and didn't always put in 100 per cent effort.

Roger laid great emphasis on defensive solidarity, and we responded immediately to his ideas by winning four games on the trot against Partick Thistle, Celtic, St Mirren and Ayr without conceding a goal. The 3–0 victory over Ayr stands out because I took on the entire visiting defence before lashing a shot into the roof of the net for our second goal and then sent over the free-kick from which Stevens headed our third. A fortnight later we travelled to Gayfield Park to turn over First Division Arbroath 4–0 in the Scottish Cup third round, and I opened the scoring with a penalty and finished it by scoring our fourth goal. Back in the quest for points, a 0–0 draw with Aberdeen meant we had gone six matches without conceding a goal, but suddenly, and inexplicably, it all started to crash down around our ears.

I partially blame the hooligan element among Rangers fans. Everything was going brilliantly on 25 February 1978 when goals from O'Rourke and Davidson put us 2–0 up, but then the visiting fans decided to invade Fir Park en masse. Play was held up for thirty minutes, and the referee threatened to abandon the match. We were badly affected by the untimely pitch invasion and collapsed to a 4–2 defeat. If that was disappointing, it was nothing compared with the morale-sapping defeat we suffered two days later. We cobbled together a shocking display in the fourth round of the Scottish Cup, stumbling to a 3–1 defeat at home to Queen's Park, a side lying tenth in the Second Division. We were hot favourites, naturally, but diabolical on the day and finished a well-beaten side. The Spiders thoroughly deserved their surprise victory. Two games later, Hibs came and helped themselves to four goals at our expense.

It wasn't all disaster after the Rangers game, however. Celtic fancied their chances when they arrived on the night of 22 March, particularly when Joe Craig scored shortly before half-time, but I stole the show with two goals in five minutes as we recovered to win 2–1 in the teeming rain after the boss had switched me from the right to the left wing. That proved a master stroke, and I equalised, sending a retaken free-kick high into the net from just outside the area, before racing past young full-back Alan Sneddon into the area and cutting in sharply to fire a shot past the Hoops keeper, Peter Latchford, for my second. That victory cemented us in fourth place and raised the prospect of qualifying for the UEFA Cup, but losing our last four games of the season to Dundee United, Aberdeen, Clydebank and Rangers put paid to those dreams and dumped us back in sixth.

I was a wanted man that summer. Gordon Clark, the scout responsible for getting me to Arsenal, was now recruiting for Philadelphia Furies in the Northern American Soccer League and had already got my old pal, Alan Ball, and Peter Osgood on the books. Now he wanted me, and I was extremely tempted by wages of £25,000 for the season. There was no question of a permanent transfer because the £60,000 asking price was too steep for the Furies. They still fancied me on loan, but Hynd insisted I had to sever my ties with Motherwell for good if I was going to spend the campaign in the USA because it overlapped with the start of the Scottish season.

When Philadelphia fell through, I got an extremely interesting phone call from Ron Tilsed, my former Arsenal and Portsmouth team-mate, who was now playing down under for Canberra City, and that's how, three weeks after running out in front of 40,000 at Ibrox against Rangers, I found myself doing the business for Canberra for the benefit of 7,400 customers in a 1–1 draw against Marconi, the unbeaten Philips Soccer League leaders. Playing for Marconi that day was an Italian, Roberto Vieri, whose son, Christian, grew up in Sydney and went on to become a legendary striker for Italy.

Motherwell had been good to me, and I was still officially their property. Hynd sensed my disappointment at missing out on the megabucks in Philadelphia and he made it an easy loan for Canberra, where I became a heavily sponsored guest player. Qantas splashed out on airfares for me and the family, while Avis paid my wages and picked up all our accommodation bills. It was good to see Ron again (I knew I'd never be short of a drinking partner), and I also wanted Joyce to sample life in the country where her family had emigrated and spent several years before they returned to Scotland.

Fortunately, Joyce looked forward to the move, and that was a relief for me. It wasn't a disruption to prey on her mind and not as if we were emigrating for good, of course. She viewed it as an all-expenses-paid holiday and was happy Paul and Jon were coming too. Her health was a little more robust, and I know Joyce was happy thinking I wouldn't be gambling as much in Australia. She always worried I would lose far more than I ever did in reality. Our family stayed on the top two floors of a fabulous four-storey hilltop home owned by Canberra coach Johnny Warren, the Bobby Moore of Aussie soccer, who had his own TV show. I was quickly into the swing of things, spreading the soccer gospel in schools and keeping busy with plenty of public relations work. I loved Johnny. He was a wonderful character, a playboy extraordinaire who came home with a different bird every week. He was shrewd, too, with more bank accounts than you could shake a stick at. I was so sad when he lost his battle against cancer in 2004.

We had one little Croatian midfield player called Ivan, who was treated like a king by his fellow countrymen now living in Australia when he arrived to play for City. So much so, they built him and his wife a bungalow. Now, Ivan wasn't the greatest player I'd ever clapped eyes on, and it didn't surprise me when Johnny dropped him. A few days later, I saw Johnny looking unaccountably worried, which was very unlike him. 'What's wrong?' I asked. 'I've had a letter threatening me and my daughter,' he replied. 'It says she's going to be kidnapped – or shot – if I don't put Ivan back in the team. What shall I do?' I told him, 'If you want my advice, I would get Ivan back in the side pretty sharpish!' We both laughed. Passionate when it comes to sport, those Croats, although I don't suppose Ivan would have thanked his 'fans' if he'd got wind of why he regained his place in the side.

The clubs were very ethnic, with Marconi representing the Italian community and another side made up entirely of Croats, but City were a pretty cosmopolitan lot. Apart from those two nations, we also had native Aussie players and guys from Greece, England, Ireland and, of course, Scotland. As for the actual standard of football, it was below the Scottish Premier Division, probably on a par with the Third Division in England. As for me, I was bought to create goals. I was never a prolific goalscorer – and managed just one in the league, the winner in my eleventh and final match against Fitzroy United at Olympic Park, Melbourne, in brilliant sunshine. Still, I just had to get that goal because the boys in the team had been ribbing me something rotten.

They treated me brilliantly in Canberra, although the team was fairly hopeless and bottom of the league after my eleven-week stint. I was very popular, not only with City's home crowds, as a flair player prepared to take risks, but also with those in Adelaide, Sydney, Melbourne and Newcastle. Mind you, Joyce wasn't too happy when the fixture list sent us away because Qantas supplied City with open-ended flights, and it was often Tuesday before we all got home, very much the worse for wear. Hospitality at away games was commonplace: there was always a reception followed by a post-match meal, then some copious drinking and partying to detain us – with Ron Tilsed inevitably to the fore.

The club gave me a rousing send-off in their social club, and City president Doug Holman paid me this tribute: 'Peter is a tremendously professional person, both on and off the field. His behaviour has been exemplary.' Come on now, you didn't seriously expect anything less given my track record, did you? My general play was fine, so much so that Canberra wanted to buy me. Several months later the chairman and one of the directors flew over to try and convince me to sign a permanent deal. But I knew Fulham were waiting in the wings, and I thought football in Australia and America would still be there for me a few years later.

Alex Ferguson might never have rated me, but back home in Scotland there was one manager whose reputation far exceeded Fergie's. Jock Stein was now the national manager, and was about to offer me a sudden, unexpected audition for the Scotland team.

CHAPTER 16

Craven Image

The beginning of the end for me at Motherwell was caused by money, or rather my jealousy for the size of pay packet I discovered Willie Pettigrew was taking home, added, of course, to the knowledge that Bobby Campbell had been on the phone again from Fulham. Willie was beginning to attract some envious glances from clubs in Germany, but when he was offered a new contract and signed it, we all followed suit. I pledged to stay for another three years. Over drinks on a tour of Denmark to prepare us for the 1978–79 season, I found out that our prolific centre-forward was earning £180 a week compared to my £100. No way was Willie worth £80 a week more than me; my pride had been stung, and I immediately stuck in a transfer request, which did not go down at all well with the chairman, Ian Livingstone, a solicitor and a good guy.

That tour did far more harm than good, although we

won all the half dozen or so matches crammed into less than a fortnight. It was an arduous schedule and not altogether compatible with our idea of a summer break. We expected to enjoy the Danish nightlife and give the local brew a rigorous examination. This was not how the Motherwell management had envisaged things, however. Before one match John Haggart, our coach, caught us returning to the hotel at three in the morning after we had been told to stay in our rooms, but rather than take disciplinary action, John and Roger Hynd organised two crates of beer to share on the eve of our next game. It was a generous, mature gesture and one to which the Motherwell team stuck up two derisory fingers. The beer was duly polished off, and then I headed the escape committee, bunked out of a window and into town. There was no escape this time from the management's wrath, however, and we were fined £200 apiece and threatened with being sent home in disgrace.

The problems always kicked off when four of us – Peter Millar, Willie Watson, Vic Davidson and myself – got together. Frankly, we were a dreadful influence on each other, worse than the Wild Bunch with our macho drinking competitions. We'd never settle for one or two drinks if there was time to get nine or ten down our necks.

I got everyone involved in our night-time caper to write out transfer requests, and the dispute became front-page news in Scotland, where our long-suffering wives must have thought we'd taken leave of our senses. I suppose it was out of order, a bit childish and petulant, but in mitigation we did beat all our Danish opponents and trained hard. Livingstone pulled me to one side and said, 'This is getting out of hand, Peter. What can we do to stop it?' I simply replied, 'Give me what Willie Pettigrew is getting.' I didn't want to leave Motherwell, and we agreed to talk again when we returned home. The press hounded us at the airport back in Scotland, but the whole episode blew over. The club agreed to pay me £100 a week plus £80 appearance money, as long as I promised to keep those figures a closely guarded secret. I was quite content.

Although the other lads had never been spoiling for a fight in the first place, a sense of suspicion and resentment crept into a squad that had previously been relatively happy when we were all on similar money. Far from building us up for the rigours of the following nine months, the Denmark trip left us knackered and emotionally drained. The last thing we needed was an immediate date with Ron Atkinson's West Bromwich Albion – even if it was a thoroughly merited testimonial match for Joe Wark. Poor Joe, he was turned inside out and back again for good measure by Albion's dashing young winger Laurie Cunningham, while Bryan Robson, Cyrille Regis and Willie Johnston also handed out lessons everywhere you cared to look. We lost something like 7–0, and it would have been double figures had the visitors really put their minds to it. To add injury to insult, I played the first forty-five minutes with a hamstring injury that did me no favours whatsoever.

So all was far from rosy in the garden at Fir Park when

the 1978–79 campaign kicked off on 12 August with fewer than 4,000 bothering to turn up to watch us go down 1–0 at home to Partick Thistle. Hynd bought Jim Boyd, a young full-back and part-time player from Clyde, whose signing experience tells you what a softie the manager could be. On the morning he arrived for contract negotiations, Jim informed the lads that he'd be happy with a signing-on fee of £2–3,000, and we arranged to meet him later for a welcome-to-Motherwell 'christening' jar or two. It was clear from the size of the smile on his face when the beers started flowing that Jim had 'had a result' in the manager's office, and he blurted out, 'When the boss asked me how eight grand sounded, I almost ripped his hand off!'

Sadly, neither Boyd nor any of the other changes were the answer to our problems, and the malaise that had crept in at the end of the previous term developed into a full-blown losing habit. By the end of November, the club was in freefall. Celtic came calling in the Scottish League Cup, and I scored, but the night turned sour because I also succeeded in missing two penalties as the Hoops ran away with a 4–1 win. A few mornings later, we were running through town on our way to the brown-dirt training ground at Clelland, and it seemed as if every other window shot up, angry voices berating me: 'Marinello, don't you ever dare take another penalty for this club!'

I must have been doing something right, however, because the Scotland manager Jock Stein selected me to play for the Scottish League representative side against the

Irish League from Northern Ireland at Motherwell. Jock pulled me to one side before the game and said, 'You can do yourself a big favour tonight, Peter.' Clearly, I took that to mean I had the chance to play myself into the full Scotland team, and the dice seemed to be loaded in my favour. I was playing on my home park against less-than-demanding Ulstermen, but it turned into something of a humiliation. Scotland could only manage a 1–1 draw against the Irish League players, who were usually cannon-fodder, and cramp forced me off after seventy-five minutes.

To be honest, my preparation for that Scottish League game wasn't the greatest. I had moved home the previous day and Joyce was back in hospital. Sometimes it seems as if the dream of every professional who has ever pulled on a pair of boots is to represent his country. And good luck to each and every one of them. I mean that sincerely. But it simply wasn't ever in my make-up to be that ambitious when it came to the international stuff. If my club football was going OK, the bread-and-butter business was enough for me.

My mind was on other things: Joyce's health and our move from a three-bedroomed terraced house in Corstorphine into a bungalow in Braehead Road, Barnton, a pleasant area of Edinburgh. Joyce knew nothing of the bungalow. I thought it would be a nice surprise for her when she was discharged from hospital.

Eleven defeats in fifteen matches had left Motherwell nailed to the foot of the table, and relegation became a matter of when, rather than if. It was a bad, bad start to the season by any yardstick, a disastrous run of results. Hynd tried everything he knew to turn it around and had my utmost sympathy when he found himself out of a job after twelve months and John Haggart was appointed caretaker manager.

As for me, I was banned by the club and stuck on the transfer list. My crime had been to get myself sent off for a clash with Jim Jefferies after scoring in a 3–2 defeat at Hearts on 25 November 1978. The afternoon began very promisingly when I collected a pass and surprised everybody by clipping a swerving shot past a wall of defenders. The early bath was for retaliation with ten minutes to go and the match neatly poised at 2–2. I had beaten a couple of opponents down the touchline before noticing, out of the very corner of my eye, Jefferies leaving his stomping ground at centre-half to come over and sort me out. As I skipped past him, Jim scythed me down around the thighs. The challenge was so high a world-class hurdler couldn't have cleared it. He absolutely poleaxed me. By the time I got to my feet, the red mist had descended, Jim was still on his knees, and I smashed a fist into the side of his jaw. Had we been standing eyeball to eyeball I wouldn't have had the nerve to whack him because he was a big man, the sort of character who might have me for breakfast. Nothing could have been a clearer sending-off offence, and the Hearts fans lapped up seeing a former Hibee depart in shame. What I did was diabolical, in my own home town against the club I supported as a boy, the first professional team I ever watched. I apologised to all the lads afterwards as well as Bill Samuel, who had become club chairman. I accept I wasn't fully focused on the day. Bad feelings from the pay dispute lingered, and I had a potential move to Fulham lurking in the background, but I'd obviously been sufficiently on the ball to score, and I thought I'd been playing pretty well. Coincidentally, a considerably more famous player was sent off that Saturday – Jimmy Greaves, representing Barnet in the first round of the FA Cup against Woking. How the mighty had fallen!

As fate would have it, when I joined Hearts in October 1981, the first player I met was none other than Jim Jefferies, who greeted me with a big grin and said, 'You little bastard, Marinello. You knocked two of my teeth out that day, and the private dental work cost me a fortune,' to which I could only reply, 'If you had just stood up, Jim, I would never have dared to thump you.'

Meanwhile, I knew I was walking on thin ice at Motherwell because I'd previously been sent off right at the start of the season against St Mirren when we tumbled out of the Anglo-Scottish Cup. In mitigation for the Hearts offence, I would like to call as my defence witness reporter Willie Woodburn of the *News of the World*. Willie is better known, indeed infamous north of the border, as the last professional footballer in Britain to be banned *sine die* for indiscipline. He was a Rangers legend, a centre-half with a temper to match his superb talent, but he overstepped the mark in 1954 for butting an East Stirling opponent. Here's what Willie made of my dust-up against Hearts:

I was genuinely disgusted to see the best player on the park being ordered off for allegedly striking an opponent. For most of the game this skilful exponent had virtually torn Hearts' defence apart, invariably flying in the face of chopping tackles that even made me shudder. But Peter Marinello bravely carried on playing his own game regardless, until one final scything job brought him to the end of his tether. The outcome was a free-kick to Motherwell, a yellow card to the Hearts player and marching orders for poor Peter. I always thought that referees were meant to protect ball-players, but maybe there are so few of the latter around these days that the former don't know the difference. It's time they started thinking about it, before the species becomes extinct. The Marinello affair was a classic example of the original offender getting off scot-free while the bloke who retaliates gets the hammer – a subject near and dear to my own heart! Good players seldom get into trouble playing against good players. It's the fly men – the ones who can't play but want to stop others at all costs – who cause most of the bother.

Bobby Campbell, of Fulham, must have sensed I was ripe for picking and flew up from Heathrow to Glasgow, where we held a clandestine meeting over a few drinks to which I brought Peter Millar for support and guidance. Bobby explained how he had bought big Chris Guthrie, from Swindon, who was beginning to score goals – and would score many more with the sort of service I could provide. I was impressed with what Bobby said and also that he still wanted me after my recent trouble. It was never going to be an easy transfer because Motherwell initially quoted Fulham £60,000 when the London club were only prepared to pay half that amount. I had bought the bungalow in Barnton and signed a lucrative new contract, but the team was beginning to break up at Fir Park, and I thought, 'If I'm not wanted, fuck it. I'm off.' It was a bit spur of the moment, I was headstrong, but I knew Campbell had been after me for about a year, and that there would be a few bob in it for me from Fulham.

Ally MacLeod, the former Scotland manager, had taken over permanently as manager at Motherwell by now, and, although there was no personal animosity between us, he told me in no uncertain terms that he was far from happy with the improved contract which guaranteed me £100 a week, plus £80 for every match I started. 'I can't afford to pay you that,' he told me. 'Fulham are interested in you, and there's a midfield player at Aberdeen I want to sign. Are you interested in leaving?' Ally made it clear he wasn't going to play me, so that was my £80 appearance bonus up in smoke for starters. I was interested in leaving, but on my terms. I knew from talking to Campbell that Fulham would be extremely hard-pressed to pay me £180 a week. Ally sensed he could be lumbered with me and asked, 'Do you want money to leave the club?' Now he was talking my kind of language, and we quickly shook hands on a £3,000 pay-off to quit Fir Park.

Ally's deal had been literally a handshake agreement. No more. Virtually every deal I agreed in football was done on trust. Some time later I became rather agitated because no money had been forthcoming from Motherwell, so I phoned Ally at the pub he ran in Ayrshire and politely asked him to keep his end of the bargain. Ally simply asked me for my bank account details and, when I checked two or three days later, I was £3,000 better off. Better still, although I dropped basic wages to go to London, Fulham gave me an £8,000 signing-on fee.

We'd only been in our new home about four weeks when I broke the news to Joyce that we were on the move again. I didn't give her much choice in the matter, but you learn to be selfish in football and you have to go where you're wanted. You have to be ruthless about it because you're only as good as your last game, and that last game could end at any time with a broken leg, and then your earning potential would be considerably reduced. I reckoned Joyce would be happy to move back to London, and I looked forward to proving a few things to Arsenal while playing under less pressure for a Second Division team.

I returned from suspension to play my last match for Motherwell on 16 December 1978 in a 1–1 home draw against Morton and signed for Fulham for £30,000 a few days later. Joyce stayed with the boys in Edinburgh to sell the bungalow, while Fulham paid for me to stay in a smart hotel in Earls Court for several weeks. That was interesting, to say the least: my temporary accommodation was in the heart of the gay community, and I got plenty of admiring glances. I preferred to make friends with the hotel staff, who looked after me extremely well, and I gave them tickets to come and watch me play.

Fulham were not exactly rolling in money, however, and the indulgent life of taking taxis to go training soon came to an end when they moved me into digs, run by a warm-hearted Cockney couple, Julie and Don, twenty-five yards over the road from Craven Cottage. While Julie was a physically small woman, she was larger than life and liked a drink. Don ran an off-licence and twice a week helped out in a seafood restaurant in the City of London. Thursday night was the highlight of the week as Don would return from work with seventy oysters, which we'd wash down with half a dozen pints of Guinness apiece. It was a very lively place, and I was joined by Gordon Boyd, who had signed from Rangers. 'Have boots, will travel' sums up Gordon Boyd, the young Glaswegian who flattered to deceive. Boyd was a forward who looked great in trial matches and training but suffered dreadfully with nerves when it came to matches that mattered, even for the reserves. He had a tendency to go missing in action and was an enigma – much like me, I suppose. I stayed for three or four months in the digs.

On the playing front, I made a dramatic impact, enjoying an absolutely storming debut at the Cottage on

Boxing Day 1978 as Fulham ripped Cambridge United to shreds. It was just brilliant, and I had a hand in three or four of our goals as we ran out 5–1 winners.

Joyce's family had returned from Australia, and her mother died of cancer a few months later. I have always felt guilty at missing the funeral in Edinburgh. I should have been there for her – and Joyce. But Fulham were going well, and Bobby Campbell really wanted me to concentrate on the next match. I just couldn't say 'no' to him. The club sent a huge bunch of flowers, but that bouquet could never atone for my absence. Never in a million years. I was too accommodating, I've been that way throughout my life. I didn't want to rock the boat. I mentioned the funeral to Bobby, of course, and half-hoped he'd suggest I went, but he had the gift of the gab and talked me out of it.

I thought Campbell had put a tasty little side together with reliable players around a clutch of up-and-coming youngsters. But whatever the mix, it didn't work when I was at Fulham. Attendances were generally poor, around the 10,000 mark, although the fans who did come to watch us were a fantastically loyal bunch, and Fulham are rightfully proud of their reputation as a decent, family club. Money worries were never far from the surface and I think the manager was encouraged to spot a bargain, polish the player a little, then sell him on for a profit.

That winter was bitter, and one Scottish Cup tie between Inverness Thistle and Falkirk was postponed at least twenty times. The weather down south wasn't much kinder, and the pools panel had to work overtime. January 1979 saw Fulham complete just one league fixture in the Second Division – a 2–2 home draw against Sunderland, which left us sitting in sixth place. While the drive for promotion stalled in the snow and ice, our exploits in the FA Cup aroused great excitement. Local rivals QPR were heading for relegation from the First Division and found no respite from the depression when we knocked them out 2–0 to set up a mouth-watering fourth-round tie with Manchester United.

Dave Sexton had taken over from Tommy Docherty and managed a United side that was to go all the way to the FA Cup final, where, in a memorable finish to an otherwise extraordinarily dull match, they lost 3–2 to my old club, Arsenal. I thought United were fortunate to survive two matches against us. Craven Cottage was rocking with over 25,000 packed inside when I gave Stewart Houston the run-around for the benefit of a live TV audience, and John Margerrison earned us a replay with an equaliser to Jimmy Greenhoff's first-half goal. Then Greenhoff poached the only goal of the replay on 12 February, when I understand Denis Law had some very complimentary things to say about me in his radio analysis. 'Marge' was a big, strong inside-forward I worked with well. Selling him to Orient at the end of the season was an ill-conceived move by Fulham.

If we were hot against United, we were almost in seriously hot water the following month against Preston North End. Up we travelled on the Friday in dreadful weather for an overnight stay in a hotel just outside Manchester. It was freezing cold and snowing heavily, with the forecast of more to come. By early evening I looked out of my bedroom window and estimated the snow to be at least five inches deep. The match at nearby Deepdale the following afternoon was a cast-iron certainty to be postponed, and, in those circumstances, there was only one thing to do – get the beers in, unbeknown to Bobby Campbell and Mike Kelly, the assistant manager, of course. One of the rooms became an impromptu bar, and one of our party produced some marijuana. He claimed he enjoyed smoking it to calm his nerves before matches, and a few of the lads nodded sympathetically and joined him in a joint or two.

Very few players I knew smoked dope, but it was common knowledge in the dressing room that one of our players was very partial to a joint. He'd rather have a smoke than a few beers. If it relaxed you, I had no problem with that – each to his own. Smoking dope was common outside football, although not in it, but none of the lads raised an eyebrow. Drinking was a bigger problem. I recalled my time in Scotland at Hibs, where one character regularly used to take valium before the match to calm himself down, while the rest of us preferred a nip of brandy or whisky before the kick-off and another at half-time, usually in our tea, especially on a cold winter's day before venturing out to entertain the public on a frosty pitch.

The night before the Preston match developed into a

right old sing-song, and it was three in the morning before the party broke up. I woke at 8.30 a.m. with a hangover and was delighted to see it was still snowing. We learned the pitch at Preston would be inspected by the referee at 9 a.m. and were all extremely confident of returning to London later that morning after a long and leisurely breakfast. Nine o'clock came and went without a definite decision and another inspection at 10.30 a.m. did nothing to finalise the matter as the snow continued to fall. Word reached us that Preston had called in volunteers to clear the pitch, and we were all absolutely staggered at noon when the surface was declared fit for play.

Campbell greeted us with an icy grin when we got on the coach for the match. He could hardly have failed to smell the stale aroma of the night before cloaking several of the squad and said, 'I know exactly what you lot have been up to, so you had better get a fucking result today – or else!' Things looked grim at half-time when we went in 2–1 down, but I improved as the game wore on: I sobered up, and my befuddled brain cleared. I was delighted to see Guthrie equalise and earn us a point. Campbell greeted us when we came off, saying, 'Lucky bastards!' but he'd mellowed on the trip home that evening and bought us fish and chip suppers.

Preston came near the start of a mediocre run which saw Fulham win just two of their last seventeen matches in the Second Division and slide from sixth place to finish tenth in the table. I featured in just three of those games because of an Achilles injury.

I returned to Edinburgh some weekends to see the family and was taught a painful lesson when I reported back for training a day late on one occasion. I had my Achilles in plaster, but our trainer, George Wright, who I'd known from Arsenal, took no mercy and made me hop the full length of the pitch on my one good leg as a form of punishment. The point was well made. Injured or not, I never took liberties again.

Eventually the sale of the property in Edinburgh went through, and Joyce, Paul and Jon came down to join me in a lovely four-bedroomed house I'd bought for us in Kenyon Street, near my digs, and no more than 200 yards from Craven Cottage. Paul was installed in a private school in Putney, and we settled into a quiet social life, hardly bothering to use the car. Driving in central London was a nightmare, and once you'd lost your precious parking space in Kenyon Street there was no telling when you might get it back. Joyce loved being back in London, as I knew she would, and that was a happy family summer with big, long walks all together in Richmond Park, trips to Madame Tussaud's, London Zoo in Regent's Park and the Natural History Museum to see the dinosaurs, which the boys loved. The fond memory of one particular outing with Jon always makes me laugh. I took him to Harrods to choose a present for being a good boy. His eyes lit up at a bright yellow pedal car and, being so young, he was distraught at the prospect of having to wait for it to be delivered. I could see no harm in allowing him to 'drive' the toy car to where I had parked – and then had to chase after him as he started scattering shoppers along a stretch of pavement on Brompton Road.

Birmingham City away never looked like the easiest option when the 1979–80 campaign opened on 18 August, but the fixture computer sent us to St Andrews, and after forty-five minutes only one result was possible – a handsome home win – with the Blues, relegated the previous season, leading 3–0. We were getting murdered, nothing was going right, and Campbell went into paint-stripping mode with his half-time rant, jabbing a finger at me and spitting, 'And as for you, Marinello, you need a ball to yourself.' I thought to myself, 'It's shit or bust now, Peter,' because I knew I had ten minutes to perform or it would be the hook. I would be the first player hauled off by the manager in the second half unless he witnessed a dramatic improvement. I switched wings from right to left, and suddenly we burst into life with Gordon Davies scoring a hat-trick and Chris Guthrie adding the other goal in a famous 4–3 victory. They were our principal strikers, a Little and Large combo. Wee Welshman Gordon, known as 'Ivor' to all and sundry, was a classic goal-poacher. Rapid over ten to fifteen yards, he enjoyed a couple of seasons in particular at Craven Cottage when he was scoring goals for fun. Gentle giant Guthrie was another handy goalscorer and good in the air with it. Sadly, Chris was another player sold on by the club for a profit.

Birmingham was one of the comebacks of the season, and I enjoyed one of the best forty-five minutes I ever had for Fulham. I was skinning people, getting crosses in, and the team simply sparkled. The momentum after our first goal simply carried us, and long before the end the home crowd were streaming out. I had a hand in two of the goals, and we murdered them. It was one of those very special occasions you look back on and think just about everything you've tried has come off. Obviously, the manager's bollocking at half-time got through to us. I had got absolutely no change out of Mark Dennis, the Blues' left-back, in the first half but succeeded in leading Glaswegian Jimmy Calderwood a merry dance after swapping flanks. Three matches later I registered the solitary goal of my Fulham career to clinch a 1–0 home win over Preston, but we soon came to resemble a relegation side. And believe me, I was familiar with the signs by now.

Any sense of disappointment I felt soon paled into insignificance when poor Joyce became extremely ill in December 1979 and ended up in a hospital cancer ward, where some of the women put the fear of death into her with the things they said. Joyce had had a contraceptive coil fitted and it was a disaster, leaving her bleeding heavily and feeling wretched. She was beside herself with pain and required emergency surgery to remove the device. An infection started to spread through Joyce's abdominal region, and I thought she might die when they moved her on to the cancer ward. In fact, the female consultant steered me gently by the arm to a quiet corner and said, 'Prepare yourself for the worst, Mr Marinello.' I learned that the following forty-eight hours would be critical, and that time ticked past so slowly it might have been forty-eight weeks. Joyce was beside herself with fear that she had cancer, the disease that had killed her mother. If Joyce's mental problems were hereditary, then it followed that cancer would be too, wouldn't it?

While Joyce was in that ward, I was just living day to day, hour to hour, concentrating on the boys and going to visit Joyce twice a day. My mum came down to help me look after Paul and Jon, while Bobby Campbell was very sympathetic and said, 'Take as much time off as you need, Peter.' Thank God, Joyce slowly recovered after ten agonising days in hospital, where extensive tests for cancer came up negative. The sense of relief as Joyce gradually improved and received the all-clear was immense. In the event, her Fallopian tubes had either burst or become seriously infected. And it felt as if a lead weight had been removed from my own body. We were strongly advised to sue for compensation against the coil-fitter, but I wasn't interested. All I wanted was my Joyce fit and well again.

I did my best to keep the story under wraps, but it made front page headlines in the *Daily Star* on Saturday 2 February, with the lads on their way to Burnley without me for a sixth successive league defeat, which kept Fulham nailed to the foot of the table. I woke up to see a picture of Joyce and me next to the words 'Soccer Star's Torment' and 'I feared my wife wouldn't recover'.

I already knew my career at Fulham was in serious doubt because Campbell had signed winger Howard Gayle from Liverpool in January 1980. Far from resenting

Howard, I welcomed him into my home as a lodger. The club had already asked Joyce and me to look after a couple of apprentices, so we were happy to squeeze Howard into the one remaining spare bedroom. I took him under my wing, and we used to go sprint training together.

In one appalling sequence, from 15 December 1979 to 15 March 1980, Fulham picked up just four points from draws in a thirteen-match sequence. The other nine matches all ended in defeat, and our gates dwindled to 4,000. By the end of February, Campbell had told me he was only prepared to play me in home games, and I was very disappointed. He thought I was a bit lazy and a luxury item in away games, where Fulham required 100 per cent effort to get any sort of reward. I didn't have a strong work ethic but I always believed I could be a match-winner, creating goals for others. Our relationship deteriorated. He tried to needle me, humiliate me as a ploy to get my back up and make me come out fighting. He sometimes sang a few bars from that Kenny Rogers hit 'Coward of the County' within earshot. But I was stubborn and cynical. The next time I started playing, seriously playing again, it would be a long way from Stevenage Road, SW6.

George Best made a fleeting reappearance at Fulham, but rarely on days when the training schedule involved anything more strenuous than five-a-sides. One Thursday morning George and I were playing for the reserves and youth team select XI against Saturday's first team. Obviously, there was an away match on the horizon. Twice George threaded through magnificent passes from midfield, and I ran on and scored. Campbell was furious, halted the practice match and barked, 'Right, you Scottish bastard. That's you finished for the game. Go and have a shower.' What had I done wrong? What was I supposed to do? Miss those chances?

Then there was the time before an away match when Campbell was apparently 'too busy' to pin up the teamsheet as was his custom each and every Friday. Mike Kelly told me the first-team squad was unchanged. I took that to mean I would be travelling, as I had played in the previous match, and dashed home to pack a suit and my playing gear. I had a quick bite to eat and walked back to join our transport bound for a 12.30 p.m. departure to the Midlands, only to be challenged by Campbell, sneering, 'Peter, have you seen the teamsheet?' I said I hadn't because there wasn't one. 'There is now, son. And I suggest you go and have a look at it.' I did as I was told, noticed my name was conspicuous by its absence and suffered the huge embarrassment of climbing back on to the coach to retrieve my gear and go home.

My last recorded appearance for Fulham came on 8 March 1980 in a 2–1 home defeat by Chelsea. I started only twenty-five league matches over fifteen months for the Cottagers in two fractured seasons through a depressing combination of my mercurial form, injury, managerial preferences and Joyce's health – although I would never, ever apportion any blame to my wife. It was simply a factor in another two seasons of professional under-achievement.

There were several smashing characters with me at Craven Cottage, including Mr Mischief and joker-in-chief, Les Strong, who frequently had us in stitches. On one hilarious occasion, a local rascal brought a blow-up doll to a match and, for some reason, she ended up in the groundsman's hut. Les liberated Little Miss Latex and smuggled her into the dressing-room where 'she' was kitted out in a white Fulham shirt, black pants and a long curly blonde wig and positioned in one corner moments before Campbell came in to deliver his serious regular Friday team-talk after training. Bobby had been expounding his views on our opponents for a full three minutes before he became aware that four of us were giggling hysterically. Mike Kelly saw the funny side of it, but poor Bobby went potty. Les also enjoyed dishing out nicknames and dubbed me 'Toby' because of my fondness for the odd bottle of Toby light ale, rather than any suggestion I was developing a beer belly and resembled a Toby jug.

I never could understand why John Beck became such a devotee of the long-ball game when he went into management. Granted, he was so successful with the ploy at Cambridge United they very nearly made it all the way up into the Premiership, but the Beck I fondly remember was the talented long-haired guy pulling the strings in midfield with flair and precise little one-twos. John became my room-mate on away trips, and we shared a love of tennis. We were so good, I swear we could almost have played doubles for England. Or Scotland in my case!

In the heart of our defence you could find Richard

Money, when he wasn't at the bookies. Richard was a good player, similar in some respects to Alan Hansen, but he cost me a fortune. I lost quite a lot with Richard on ante-post bets, but I kept giving him money. We stood to win a small fortune if Tromos won the 2,000 Guineas for example and, believe me, this horse was an absolute flying machine. I must have had at least £400 riding on Tromos at anything from 8–1, when the books opened, to the starting price of 6–4 favourite. Richard and I waited and waited for Tromos to make his move, and it never happened. He finished just about last, and the jockey, Willie Carson, later announced that Tromos had been got at, definitely nobbled. Tromos never ran again.

Partnering Richard was Kevin Lock, looking like Goldilocks with his long, curly blond hair. With his elfin, angelic looks, I always thought of Kevin as a dead ringer for Mozart – but looks can be deceptive. He was a hard, hard player who had come from West Ham, and I thought he could easily cut it at the top level again.

Tony Gale was another good centre-half on the books. Never flustered, he used the ball well, and some judges thought he could have become the second Bobby Moore. In goal was Gerry Peyton, a big, quiet, dependable lad in the Bob Wilson mould who went on to represent the Republic of Ireland. Like most goalkeepers and fine wine, he improved with age.

Ray Evans at right-back was an Edmonton boy who began his career down the road in north London at Tottenham before arriving at Fulham via Millwall. He was good at his job and liked overlapping as well as a laugh and a drink after matches. Ray was sold to Stoke City in August 1979, a big mistake as far as I was concerned because he, John Margerrison and I formed a very tidy triangle going forward down the right.

Little Terry Bullivant had a good engine on him in midfield and was another sociable character who enjoyed a laugh, a joke and a drink, while John Evanson had been about a fair bit at Oxford and Blackpool and proved himself to be another sound drinking companion. When I was either off form, injured or absent, my place on the wing might be taken by Brian Greenaway, a fast Cockney lad – but nice and honest with it.

Around Easter, I took a phone call from Motherwell. It was Peter Millar, telling me that he and Willie Watson had signed agreements to play for Phoenix Inferno in the fledgling Major Indoor Soccer League (MISL), which had taken over from the Northern American Soccer League in the United States. The guy in charge of the new franchise at Phoenix just happened to be Norman Sutherland, who hailed from Edinburgh, and they had recommended me to him. Fulham were not prepared to let me go for nothing. My mind raced back to an occasion during the brief purple patch at the start of my time down by the Thames when Campbell boasted he'd turned me into a £150,000 player, and now he told me, 'I don't want you to go, you'll help us get out of the Third Division.' I took a phone call from Sutherland, established we were in business and he asked: 'How much do you think Fulham will take for you?' I said

I thought £40–50,000 at the most, yet Campbell was demanding £60,000, and things got very heated between us. Campbell told me no one had been in for me. There was stuff going on behind my back that I was suspicious of, and I brought matters to a head by complaining to the Fulham chairman, Ernie Clay, a bluff Yorkshireman. I was in the manager's office and we were both sitting down to begin with. Words were exchanged and the situation quickly escalated out of control. I called him a liar as we were leaving the room, and he saw red and grabbed me against the wall and said, 'OK, you're on your bike – you've got your transfer.'

Two or three days later I was on my way, my pit stop at Fulham over. Mike Kelly wished me the best of luck when I popped into Craven Cottage for the last time to pick up my boots and say cheerio. I got the impression Kelly thought I'd been given a raw deal by Campbell, but I didn't bear the manager any grudges, even if things went on between us at the end which meant it would have been impossible for us to work together again. I suppose the pressure got to Campbell in the end. We had an up-and-down relationship but, ultimately, I don't bear him any malice because he was brilliant at the beginning and very understanding over Joyce's crisis.

As one door slammed shut, another was opening in America . . . where the Mafia had my Scottish 'mob' running scared – and the Baptist Church, of all people, put the squeeze on me.

CHAPTER 17

Phoenix Nights

I kissed goodbye to Joyce and the boys and jumped into the taxi waiting to take me to Heathrow airport in May 1980 for the beginning of another adventure – in America this time. Needless to say, the beers soon started flowing in the departure lounge, and backs were heartily slapped as I caught up with olds pals and new Phoenix Inferno team-mates Peter 'Doomie' Millar, who was to be club captain and became part-time coach, and Willie Watson. We were like excited kids on a big school outing on that jolly trip over the pond to St Louis and a connecting flight to Phoenix, Arizona.

Quite apart from the prospect of six-a-side indoor football on the distant horizon in November, I knew it was all going to be very different the moment the three of us got off the plane and were almost knocked out by the heat from a desert sun. 'We're going to have to take a bit more water with it now,' I joked to Peter and Willie.

Norman Sutherland, the Inferno general manager and a dead ringer for Stan Flashman, greeted us, and we soon got down to brass tacks in the air-conditioned comfort of our temporary headquarters, a plush hotel in downtown Phoenix. Peter and Willie had both left Motherwell on free transfers and were delighted to receive cheques of $10,000 apiece as their signing-on fees. That suited me, too, although I could tell Norm was surprised I didn't ask for more, as the team's so-called star player who had cost the club a not inconsiderable transfer fee. But I wasn't greedy and I didn't want Peter and Willie to think I thought of myself as anything special, and besides, the basic salary on offer was nothing to complain about.

We were to enjoy a few days completely at our leisure, taking in the sights and country sounds of Phoenix, before Norm contacted us again, and his parting shot was a plaintive: 'Just try and keep the tab reasonable, will you, lads?' Meanwhile, he informed the curious Phoenix public: 'I believe Peter will be the straw that stirs our drink.' Phoenix was Elvis Presley territory, as well as a big holiday town, and we certainly did enjoy ourselves. Our drinks tab alone was $600 for the first week, and Norm ordered us to trim it to under $200 in future.

It was a bizarre existence. The three of us plus Roger Verdi, a Nairobi-born Sikh who had played for Phoenix Fire in the North American Soccer League when they went belly up, were the elite, and every few days we were expected to put trialists through their paces and decide between us whether they would cut it in the Major Indoor Soccer League. Roger was a very interesting character who moved to England when he was seven, changed his name from Rajinder Singh Virdee and impressed Bobby Robson sufficiently in a trial to win himself a three-year contract at Ipswich Town. He had a good pedigree in the States, too, having played against Pele, Franz Beckenbauer and Johan Cruyff. A host of would-be soccer stars turned up in low-grade motels from places such as Milwaukee, Boston and Denver, and we'd take them out on a park for a pick-up match. Norm could sign seven non-US citizens, but only play four at any one time. Peter, Willie and I applied a strict criterion: if they could drink, they got a contract.

By July I had been joined by Joyce, Paul and Jon after a hairy trip over from London. The airline they flew out with went bust, and they found themselves stranded overnight in Boston before completing the journey. Our new home in Glendale, roughly a dozen miles from the centre of Phoenix, was a luxury apartment in a complex with a swimming pool and tennis courts. I was a king on those courts and played a wicked trick on Peter, our strong, disciplined German defender. He also fancied himself with a racket, so I involved him in a marathon tennis session in temperatures which must have touched 100 degrees in the fiendish heat of an August Arizona afternoon. Peter was bald, my main tactic was the lob, and by the end of the match he was suffering from sunstroke and blisters were forming on his scalp. He was not a happy man.

Our Russian goalkeeper with American citizenship, Nico, was a colourful combination of Danny Kaye, Max Bygraves and Walter Mitty. He wore the sort of flashy tracksuits in shades that forced you to wear sunglasses and he had his own fan club. At least, I believe he thought he did, because Nico never went anywhere without a huge bundle of signed action photographs of himself, which he was keen to distribute to all and sundry.

The quickest player on the books was undoubtedly Leroy, who claimed to be thirty-seven and a Jamaican international. He could leave me standing, and I was still very sharp. Leroy was always a bit vague about the number of caps he had won and also his age, which we subsequently found to be officially forty-two. Leroy could most certainly play and sometimes displayed such skill he reminded me of Pele, but he was a mercenary, basically in it for the money, and already had a long track record with a string of American college soccer teams. Leroy was never going to earn top-dollar anywhere, so he had to be content with drifting from club to club.

A career in the porn industry would have made defender Daniel, our man from Haiti, world famous. He was fantastically well endowed, and several of the squad were extremely keen to share a room with Daniel on the road. His pulling power was legendary, he had birds in every port of call, and there were always spin-off opportunities for his friends. Daniel had a secret, though. He was on the run having done a bunk in Miami after playing for the Haitian Under-23 international team. The reason became clear when Daniel confessed one evening that life back in Haiti had become rather too hot for him after he'd got a police inspector's daughter pregnant. We sympathised, nodded gravely . . . and got another round of beers in.

There was a vast gulf between the $30,000 or so I was collecting for the season and the $8–12,000 being earned by Daniel and others in the same boat. The rank-and-file members of the club were always having money problems, and one night Daniel turned up at my house with a sob story about his financial plight. In the end, the senior players simply had a whip-round to give Daniel a big enough pot to leave town and try his luck elsewhere.

We also had a couple of Mexicans in the squad plus an another foreign player, who supplemented his wages as a male stripper. That sort of thing, refined in later years by the Chippendales, was going down a storm among the matrons of North America at the time, and the players' wives regularly went out in a group for a good ogle and a giggle. Most of the squad were on cut-contracts, which meant if they didn't perform they were out on their ear. After every defeat, the select few would run a book on who would get the boot. Cruel, I know, but true.

Our stadium was the Colisseum, also home to the Phoenix Suns basketball team. They pulled in 14,000 spectators, while our gates were usually between 6,500 and 8,000.

I vividly recall before one match in Cleveland when some dodgy characters with bodyguards accosted a group of our players. It was clear the heavies were armed – I could see the bulge of pistols in shoulder holsters underneath their jackets. We saw them talking and the mood among the rest of the squad was quiet and concerned. Then one of the guys who'd been spoken to announced with a half-smile, 'There's $3,000 for you to split this evening if we win. Don't ask me what happens if we lose!' That was just the incentive we needed to come out on top.

Later, when I was at Hearts, Peter Millar phoned to tell me that same chap had died in a car crash in supposedly mysterious circumstances. 'What happened?' I asked Peter. There was a short pause before he replied, 'Draw your own conclusions.'

Peter himself received a couple of death threats at one stage from someone accusing him of having a dalliance with the man's wife. In the normal course of events, 'Doomie' would have probably laughed off the menacing notes as emanating from an individual who was all mouth and no trousers. But they bore the postmark of Marina del Rey, a holiday resort in southern California and reputed hangout of Mafia hitmen. Certainly, the relevant authorities took the threats seriously, and for a couple of our matches there were undercover police in the crowd because they feared Peter might be shot by a sniper. We wound him up something rotten that he had to keep moving on the pitch because he was getting a bit thin on top and that made him an easy target for a sniper. The captain suddenly became the fittest player you've ever seen.

Despite the rampant socialising, I was always up fit and early for work. I needed to be because we trained at six o'clock in the morning, such was the heat later in the day. Norm constructed a replica pitch in a car park, and I soon got to grips with the Astroturf. I was lean, fit and buzzing just before the season kicked off in November when we played a practice match against a college team, who were reinforced by our own Argentinian beefcake. He was a fierce, pocket-sized firebrand, a little like Alan Ball, with calves on him like tree-trunks, and when we contested a block tackle, I heard the medial ligament in my right knee snap. It was a cruel injury, but it would have been far worse had it been the career-threatening cruciate ligament. The damage meant an operation. I missed the opening five or six weeks of the season, and that gave me plenty of time to show my dad around Phoenix.

It's ironic that Dad was there for that practice match, because that was the first time he'd ever been to see me play football as a professional and I only lasted twenty minutes before being crocked. Psychiatrists might read something hugely significant into the fact Dad had never previously watched me, but it never bothered me in the slightest. He lived and breathed his job at the Old Coach Inn in Edinburgh and was firmly convinced the whole place would collapse without him. He always worked weekends – it was his busiest time – and it's a tiring game running a pub, as I would discover for myself in due course. Dad told me he'd been something of a goalkeeper in his younger days, and I know he did follow my fortunes, thanks to the Saturday night punters in the pub who regaled him with tales of how well or how badly I'd played that particular afternoon. Then he'd read a match report and tell me, 'Buck your ideas up, son, you had a nightmare,' to which I'd reply, 'Have a look at this paper instead, Dad. I'm man of the match here!'

America was also the first time Dad had been to stay with us and the first time he'd ever used a passport to venture abroad. Usually, it was always Mum who visited and she was a regular guest when I played at Arsenal, Portsmouth and Fulham – especially welcome when Joyce was poorly. I'd phoned Mum to invite her over, pay for her ticket naturally, and was totally surprised a few days later when she called to reply, 'It won't be me this time, Peter, your father's coming instead.' He got on extremely well with Joyce and the boys. I think it was the holiday of a lifetime for him, better than Butlin's at Ayr. Dad took only one week off a year then in my childhood. He came for three weeks and was particularly smitten by the go-go dancers in bars and insisted on tucking his dollars away in their garters. I enjoyed his company, too. Sadly, Dad passed away a fortnight before Christmas 2006 at the ripe old age of 89. I hope I make it that far.

His presence in America took my mind off the injury. More formal rehabilitation came in the shape of whirlpool baths. The injury would have been encased in plaster back home, but here they favoured water – and I suppose it did the trick. When Inferno wanted to press me back into action after just five weeks, I thought to myself, 'This is fucking ridiculous,' but I wasn't in any position to argue. I had arrived in Phoenix billed as their top player, and the Americans do like to see their star names playing, rather than on the sick list. I was obliged to play wearing a very expensive contraption on my dodgy knee, made out of thick rubber with metal hinges. It enabled me to run OK in straight lines, but whenever I tried anything fancy, the twisting or turning which was always my hallmark, the knee popped out alarmingly and I had to click it back into position. One seriously false move and my career could have ended there and then.

We were poor to begin with, losing something like ten of the opening fourteen matches – despite the last-minute arrival of another familiar face, Vic Davidson, to join our band of brothers from Scotland. Vic had plied his trade at Celtic, Blackpool and Motherwell, and soon took over from me as the star turn. He proved to be a prolific poacher of goals, and mastered the art of beating opponents by firing the ball against the wall and collecting the rebound.

Inferno caught fire in the second half of the season, winning maybe twelve of our last fifteen games to top the Western Division ahead of clubs based in cities such as Wichita, Denver, St Louis and San Francisco. It had taken us some time, but we'd eventually sussed out the best way to play. With fifteen players stripped and ready for fast and furious action, it made sense to make maximum use of the roll-on, roll-off substitutes, and sometimes we'd find ourselves being hauled off for a breather after a high tempo burst of as little as ninety seconds. When the season started we'd been playing for up to ten minutes each, and that was useless in the hour-long matches split into four quarters of fifteen minutes.

I was also intrigued to see the sin bin in operation, but not altogether surprised to see Peter Millar and Willie Watson spending half the season in it. Willie's nickname, 'The Whale', followed him from Scotland, and he became the man rival fans loved to hate. Yanks loved the fast pace of indoor soccer, although it was never going to make that much of an impression on a nation where sport was dominated by baseball, American football and basketball – in that order. Twenty goals a match was something supporters could appreciate. They never could get their heads around a good, solid 2–0 win. That was, like, 'boring, man' and undoubtedly the reason professional football has never taken a grip on the hearts and minds of the American sporting public.

Eastern Division kingpins New York Arrows, back-boned by some more than useful Canadian players, provided the opposition for our semi-final in the MISL play-offs. The match was televised by HBO, and I disting-uished myself by achieving the rare feat of scoring a header as we won 13–8 in Phoenix. It was precisely the same score in the return leg in the Big Apple – only this time in favour of the Arrows, and we lost the toss for the venue for the decider. We stayed overnight in a very plush hotel in Long Island and were unfortunate to go down 6–5 the following evening. Our efforts had been well received at home, however, and a crowd of 1,500 Inferno supporters were at the airport to welcome us back. The inaugural year of the Phoenix Inferno franchise could be classed as a great success.

Some of our opponents were among the biggest names in the game. Paolo Rossi, the Italian legend, was playing for Buffalo as part of his rehabilitation through FIFA after being caught up in a bribery scandal – and being banned for three years in 1980. Rossi always protested his innocence and must have got time off for good behaviour for he went on to become top goalscorer and was voted most valuable player in the 1982 World Cup finals in Spain, where he netted the opening goal in Italy's 3–1 victory in the final over West Germany. Portugal icon Eusebio also played a few games in the MISL, as did his fellow countryman, the winger Simoes.

My contract stipulated I spent the summer coaching, and I was delighted to spread the gospel to some of the 50,000 kids learning how to play the game in schools and special soccer camps in the Valley. Joyce and I got friendly with a couple whose son played with our Paul for Marinello's Marauders Under-10s. One Sunday, they invited us to accompany them to their Baptist church, a monstrous brick and glass building with padded velvet seats and kneelers to match. It was a far cry from the traditional well-worn wooden church pews from my Catholic childhood as an altar boy. To be honest, I'd much rather have spent the morning in a reclining chair with a cool bottle of beer or two around the pool. Joyce went to church regularly in America, but religion didn't do much for me. And I was even less impressed after witnessing a service in which members of the congregation took to hurtling down the aisles, crying, 'Save me,' and 'Bless me,' and hurling themselves into the arms of an evangelical minister, who had been preaching fire and brimstone. What crap. As we were filing out into the foyer, the husband and I were suddenly ushered into a small side room by a minder, while his wife and Joyce went into another cubicle. 'Do you feel you want to make the commitment?' he asked me. 'Do you believe, because we would like you to commit to the church.' Then came the small print, so to speak. They wanted me to commit one-sixth of my income to their church. I felt anger and resentment welling up inside me. We had only gone to church out of courtesy to them, and now here we were being press-ganged into some kind of sect. I let him know in no uncertain terms that I wasn't signing. Even if I had been marginally interested, I was disturbed that in what must have been a congregation of 2,000, I had not cast eyes on a single black face. Now, you tell me, what denomination deserves to be that exclusive? Our friendship with the couple dissolved after that unfortunate episode. They both looked distraught at failing in their mission to recruit us. Maybe they had lost kudos or some brownie points with the Baptists.

There were more ructions behind the scenes at Phoenix Inferno among the foreign contingent after one player left his lovely wife for a cheerleader, who was like Sharon

Stone, Marilyn Monroe and Doris Day all rolled into one.

Although the club was in financial difficulties, and Fulham were applying pressure for £20,000 still owed them over my transfer, I was given a pay rise, taking my salary to over $38,000. Peter Millar was relieved of his coaching duties and replaced by Adrian Webster, who had enjoyed a successful career as a full-back with Seattle Sounders. I think the added responsibility of effectively running the side as well as playing had got to Peter. I can't imagine the death threats helped much either.

Things eventually settled down but it wasn't long before my future was in the melting pot again. Norman Sutherland called me in and related the news that the club had severe financial problems. Although I'd happily signed a new contract with Phoenix with the intention of staying at least a second season, Fulham had been on to FIFA arguing the case that they were owed another £20,000 instalment on my transfer fee. Fulham apparently threatened that, if they didn't get their money, they would ask FIFA to have Phoenix banned from playing football. Norman told me that, unless I wanted to pay Fulham the £20,000 out of my own pocket, which I was wealthy enough to do, there were three clubs prepared to sign me – Motherwell, Hearts and Portsmouth. 'If you go, Peter, we can afford to pay Fulham off. It squares everything and gets everyone out of the shit,' he said simply, putting everything into perspective.

I had no genuine desire to leave Phoenix because I'd finished the season buzzing, but good old me, I thought a move would make everybody else happy. Inferno would be able to pay Fulham, and my new club would get what they wanted – me. And when Norman mentioned the choice of teams, I thought simply, 'Why not go back to Edinburgh?'

CHAPTER 18

Hearts Attack

Hearts meant a move back to my hometown, Edinburgh and the opportunity to play for the first club I ever supported as a kid. The deal was done and dusted in an instant. Wallace Mercer, the Tynecastle chairman, put in a transatlantic phone call, after agreeing to pay a £30,000 transfer fee, but quickly established that he couldn't match the dollars I was raking in personally and asked, 'How much money would you like to sign on, Peter?' When I replied ten grand and Wallace said, 'Done,' I felt as if I had been! The speed with which he agreed to give me £10,000 made me feel sure I could have got £15,000 had I driven a hard bargain. I should have known Hearts had a bob or two because the previous month they paid a club-record fee of £100,000 to sign my old pal Willie Pettigrew from Dundee United.

I flew home in late October 1981 with all the family in

tow plus Norman Sutherland, who was coming to Edinburgh on business, and Mercer generously offered to install the entire family in a hotel while I found us a house, but we were quite content to pitch in at Mum and Dad's until I bought a flat in Edinburgh New Town.

I knew Mercer wanted me at Tynecastle to operate on the left wing, with Pat Byrne running the right flank, but I wasn't sure about the manager, Tony Ford, a big Englishman, or the fans. To them, it would always be a case of once a Hibee always a Hibee, but I was guaranteed a warm welcome from Pettigrew and Stewart McLaren, who had been with me at Motherwell in the mid-1970s. And it was always going to take me a little while to get back into the swing of things, playing in the second tier of Scottish football, the First Division. The standard of indoor soccer was high in America, but playing in two-minute bursts on astroturf before retiring for a breather was a totally different game to ninety minutes slogging through the mud at Morton. I hadn't worn a proper pair of football boots with studs for eighteen months, and my fitness wasn't great either.

The season in America had finished in April and, since then, I'd only managed about fifteen days' training. Apart from the coaching, most of the summer had been spent lazing around the swimming pool in Glendale, enjoying rather too much of the good life. Ford made no bones about the fact he didn't consider I was in good enough physical shape after watching me play fifty minutes of a friendly against St Mirren at Love Street on a Thursday night, although one reporter reckoned, 'Marinello had a most pleasing debut. His speed, ball control and precision centres with both feet were highlights. He could be a decided asset to the Tynecastle attack.'

I began on the bench in two losing matches, scoring in a 3–1 defeat at Dumbarton on Saturday 28 November, before making my first start in the Scottish Cup against Queen's Park at home in a 1–1 draw. It felt good to be back in Edinburgh, if a little strange to be running out in a maroon jersey, rather than the green of Hibs. There were very good kids coming through the ranks, such as John Robertson and Gary Mackay, whose father, Peter, had been influential in my early development at Salvesen boys' club.

However, my early promise at Tynecastle was shattered by a torn hamstring, and it wasn't too long before Ford resigned, to be replaced by little Alex MacDonald, who arrived from Rangers as player-manager with my good friend Sandy Jardine as his assistant. I liked Alex, and after training we would often go into a little café and chat about our business plans for the future. I suspected football wouldn't be detaining me for very much longer if I kept getting injured.

Hearts should have won promotion in 1981–82, but we could only manage to draw a crucial game we needed to win at the end of the season and reluctantly had to settle for third place.

The 1982–83 league campaign started promisingly on 4 September when, with Hearts trailing 1–0 at the interval against Queen's Park at Hampden, I came on as a substitute and scored the equaliser in a 2–1 victory – even if there were under 2,000 souls there to witness the event. But, already, I feared for my future because the previous month had seen us competing in the group stages of the Scottish League Cup, and I had lost my place in the side.

That goal against Queen's Park was never going to be enough to keep me in contention for a role after Willie Johnston was signed to play on the wing. Willie had been sent home from Scotland's World Cup squad in Argentina in 1978 for having failed a drugs test but had recovered from that nightmare ordeal, leaving West Brom to play for Birmingham, then Rangers, before arriving at Tynecastle with the season barely a month old. Wee Willie was still a great little player and fitted in well to the 4–3–3 MacDonald deployed to take the Jambos to promotion in second place. I thought I still had a part to play, but maybe that was just me.

There was a tried and trusted method of determining where your future lay. Around the end of March and beginning of April, you told the club your boots were knackered and you needed a new pair. If new boots arrived, all was well. If the reply was of the 'make do and mend' variety, you knew you were in big trouble. I never had the opportunity to put that theory to the test at Tynecastle. Alex and Sandy broke the news I had been fearing, quietly and professionally, one bright spring morning. They were letting me go on a free transfer at the end of the season. They thought the future at Hearts lay with youth. We shook hands. I couldn't really argue. I had scored five goals in two seasons for the Jambos after twenty-eight appearances including substitutions. I was. thirty-three, and it was not exactly the sort of playing record which suggested it would improve with age. Mind you, if my football was on the wane the same couldn't be said for my enthusiasm for gambling and drinking. I was about to start combining those two to my heart's content.

CHAPTER 19

Juggling with Jags

There was no queue of clubs falling over themselves for my services, so I busied myself building up the profile of a bar I bought in Leith called Copperfield's and rechristened it, with all due modesty, Marinello's. But I was still thrilled to take a call from Peter Cormack at Partick Thistle. We went all the way back to our formative years as teenagers together at Hibs, and now the Jags manager wanted me to come and give his team at Firhill Park the benefit of my experience. It was only part-time stuff, Peter was quick to point out, and he could only afford to pay me £60 a week, but was I interested? The money side of football was of little concern now, because the game had treated me well – better than I deserved – and I was comfortably off.

By this stage I'd gone into a partnership with a view to developing my business interests. I'd paid £24,000 to sign a twenty-one-year lease on Marinello's, and we soon branched out into property and formed a limited company. I financed the whole operation with £40,000 for us to buy an old house outside Edinburgh, and my partner supplied the business acumen which led to a conversion of the building into flats. We took one each and sold the other three for a tidy profit.

I was so busy, sometimes my feet never rested that summer. One minute I seemed to be working behind the bar of Marinello's, the next I was jumping in the car to round up all Partick's Edinburgh contingent and drive them to training in Glasgow every Tuesday, Wednesday and Thursday night. Then I'd drop the lads back off at home and maybe, if I was lucky, get back to the bar by 10.30 p.m. and close at midnight. Partick were paying me £60 to play football, but I must have been on another £120 a week in expenses. I joked to Peter Cormack: 'I know I've got a red and yellow shirt, but when is my chauffeur's uniform going to arrive?'

Maurice Johnson was emerging as a teenage striker of rare promise at Partick, and I considered him the brightest prospect I'd clapped eyes on in many a year. I phoned Arsenal's chief scout, Steve Burtenshaw, and said, 'Quick, Steve, we've got a lad here at Partick who is really going to be some player,' but I don't think the Gunners followed up my hot tip. Maybe Highbury thought they'd had their fingers burned once before by a young Scottish starlet!

Partick looked like having a fair old season. So did I, and life was good, if hectic, until I did my Achilles tendon. I had caught the eye in a couple of pre-season friendlies but was soon restricted to hobbling around Marinello's with one leg encased in plaster. I came back after the injury to make my first appearance in late November, but balancing bar work with club commitments became just too much, and after six games without a goal for the Maryhill Magyars, I called it quits with Partick after coming on as a substitute in a 2–1 home win over Meadowbank Thistle. There were 1,732 fans there on 10 March 1984, privileged to witness what turned out to be my final match in professional football. I didn't think it was farewell that day, however, so there was no great sense of emotion, just a quiet sense of satisfaction that the team had picked up the points. Although I knew at the back of my mind that things were coming to an end, and the workload at the pub was hectic, I retained an appetite for football and clung to the belief I still had something to offer someone, somewhere.

Ever since making my debut for Hibs as a naive, wide-eyed seventeen-year-old, I had been cocooned in the little shell that is professional football, where everything gets done for you – whether it's arranging a mortgage, buying a house or getting a loan if you're broke. If you were really skint, you could always get a transfer providing you had talent to spare. I had left school at fifteen without a single certificate worth a candle. At thirty-four, I still felt vulnerable. I wasn't prepared to become an ex-professional footballer.

Meadowbank boss Terry Christie refused to let me go quietly and tempted me to play a couple of friendly matches for Edinburgh's third professional club. I thought I performed proficiently enough to earn a contract, and

Christie was enthusiastic before announcing he was signing Arthur Duncan. I had to smile, remembering Arthur from many years before as the winger Hibs signed to replace me when I went to Arsenal, the man who picked me up in his car at a bus stop and told me I was away to the bright lights of London, while he was heading to sign on at Easter Road.

When Meadowbank didn't give me a contract, I was approached by Broxburn Athletic, a Scottish junior club, and joined them on 2 November 1984, making my debut at home in a 3–0 cup defeat by Kirkintilloch Rob Roy FC. Their terms were pretty good – £700 to sign on, plus £100 a game. I started quite promisingly, but almost immediately became a prime target for the boot boys. The pitches were not the greatest, and I could sense opposing tough guys sizing me up and licking their lips at the prospect of regaling punters in their local pub that night with tales of how they kicked Peter Marinello off the park. I'm no coward, but it suddenly dawned on me, as if an electric lightbulb had been switched on inside my head, that I didn't have anything left to prove as a footballer. I walked away with my legs intact after three or four matches and later returned the signing-on fee to Broxburn.

The pub work was hard and demanding. I became increasingly required behind the bar as my partner concentrated on looking after the books. For two years the arrangement worked quite well. Marinello's was basically a fairly smart lounge bar with an L-shaped function room upstairs. It was situated about a ten-minute drive from my home, but I'd often walk instead because Edinburgh was a nightmare for parking with permit zones dotted all over the place. In a bad week, my Opal Cadette and I could easily collect four or five tickets. My punters were ordinary, working-class folk, including young Hibs supporters who made Marinello's their headquarters. We ran darts and football teams . . . and plenty of scams. Although Ladbroke's had a shop over the road, I ran an operation from behind the bar, with an ex-bookie from Humberside. The regulars would come in for a pint and a £2 punt on, say, the favourite in the 2.30 at Newmarket. If I thought they'd lost too much, like £20, I always made sure they got a free pint and a pie – which is more than could be said for Ladbroke's, Joe Coral or William Hill. Of course, we were strictly small-time, but you'd be amazed how those little bets added up, especially the losing ones, and after eight months my bookie pal confided we were £8,400 in profit. Hotshots, such as the stranger who took us for £800 with three straight wins at Cheltenham, were very much the exception rather than the rule, thankfully.

Inevitably, word reached Ladbroke's about our operation, and I received a personal visit from their security officer, who marked my card in no uncertain fashion. We had to watch our step now, and I informed all my crew to speak in whispers when they wanted to place a bet over the bar. There were other 'non-official' books rooming in the city of course, which we could turn to if a punter wanted to place a bet that was too steep for us. We'd just advise them to go elsewhere – provided we could track down where the operations were running from at any given time. On one occasion, I remember, we were stuck on our own. The 'bookie-snatcher' seemed to have visited Edinburgh the night before, because we couldn't locate anyone when this flash guy walked in and demanded £400 on a short-priced favourite. My pal and I argued over whether to take it. I said no, he said yes. He won, and less than two minutes before the off I shot over the road to lay off £200 at Ladbroke's, but the place was heaving. I failed to get the bet on, but stayed to watch with mounting pleasure as the horse in question finished fourth.

French Day at Marinello's was rather special because we hired a big-screen television to watch the Prix de l'Arc de Triomphe meeting from Paris. Entry was £10, an absolute bargain, as it covered a limitless supply of quality French wine and a high-class buffet including chicken, ham, turkey, French loaves and fifty of my mum's special garlic-flavoured meatballs in an Italian sauce. While the serious business of betting took place upstairs in the function room, several gourmets were attracted purely by the food and wine. Mtoto was European racehorse of the year in 1988, and a large proportion of our guests fancied him to win that year's Arc with Michael 'Mouse' Roberts on board. I warned my pal, 'We're going to have to do a runner if this thing comes in, or find two grand to pay out.' I think we were the only two people inside the place that afternoon smiling when Mtoto was rather unluckily beaten by a fast-diminishing neck by Tony Bin.

I was always a sucker for a hard-luck story, a fact borne

out by the size of my weekly tick bill, which regularly reached £200. We never got it all back, and I could get tapped up for a loan four times a day. I was too soft. There must have been eighty pubs at least along Leith Walk, from the top of Princes Street to the dockland area, so it didn't pay to let your punters get too heavily in debt. You never knew if you'd ever see them again, let alone the money they owed you. A few customers were well down the slippery slope and beyond salvation. One old guy used to piss himself, and I'd end up carrying him home, cleaning him up, putting him to bed and arranging for social services to keep an eye on him. I suppose I could have barred him – but that would have been very cruel because his drinking cronies were all there. You can't put a price on friendship in life.

I was drinking too much myself, missing the excitement of football, and increasingly turning to booze and betting to get my adrenalin rush. The hours at Marinello's could be gruelling. After arriving at 8.30 in the morning to supervise the cleaning and sort the post, I would have a pint and a half of cider with a couple of bacon and egg rolls for breakfast. It wasn't unusual for me to drink another five or six pints of cider steadily throughout the day, and at night it would be half a dozen vodkas. Sometimes I wouldn't get to my own bed until 3.30 a.m. after ensuring all the part-time staff had got safely home. In my opinion, you've got to be either teetotal or an excessive drinker in the licensed trade. There don't seem to be any half measures. On several occasions when Joyce was suffering bad spells and hospitalised, I'd organise an after-hours session until three or four in the morning and doss down in the pub. On really heavy days, when the pressure of business and Joyce's illness became overpowering, I'd lose count of how much I'd had to drink. I always subscribed to Dean Martin's view on drinking: if you wake up with a hangover, at least you can look forward to feeling better as the day wears on.

Joyce and Paul warned me I was heading for a heart attack and had to calm down. I felt in a hole, I wanted to escape, sell up. I wished we'd never left America, where the sun always shone and life seemed so simple and undemanding. I was a professional sportsman, I'd never known anything else and now I was being asked to cope with other stuff. There had been so much freedom as a footballer, but now I sometimes felt as if I was a prisoner, working seventy to eighty hours a week, always expected to be on show, always on parade. Even on my night off, I would come down and lock up the pub.

The very nature of running a pub means you come across all sorts of characters who can offer you all sorts of 'good deals'. One bloke, who worked for a whisky bonding company, lost his pension and went to jail for smuggling out bottles of export-only scotch which he'd sell to us at less than half-price, but I wasn't that interested because Marinello's tended to appeal to a younger crowd much more heavily into vodka and Bacardi. One scam we did employ, however, was to keep all the slops and slip them along with a sly £12 to a dodgy drayman, who would come off his regular route to pay us a visit, in exchange for a fresh barrel of beer. I never did discover the next pub on that drayman's route, but they must have bombarded their brewery with complaints about the quality of the stuff they were receiving. Neither was I averse to taking in a crate or two of cheap vodka through the back door, but I drew the line at watering down drinks. You've got to have certain principles! No half measures, as I've said.

Once Marinello's was up and running successfully, my partner and I paid £85,000 in 1984 for the freehold of a more arty, trendy pub in the city centre. £70,000 was required in a loan from the brewery to complete the deal, which, once signed, had me installed and leaving Marinello's in the hands of a capable manager. This new place catered for an entirely different crowd plus hen and stag night parties. We couldn't fail to be a popular watering hole because our restaurant licence meant we were the only pub in the city open until 2 o'clock in the morning. I'm sure the authorities thought we were serving steak and chips with a decent red wine into the early hours, but the reality was we'd slip customers a slice of pizza with their pints to keep everyone sweet. My tactful doorman, Davie, built like Mike Tyson, and I were desperate to get a big bet on Dancing Brave on one occasion, but we were skint. Davie's other significant role was as president of the darts team, and we raided the kitty of £600 Christmas club money. Dancing Brave duly delivered, and we repaid the loan with a 'mystery donation' on top. Every gambler thinks he wins, of course, yet all but a handful end up losing in the long run. They boast about the winners and rarely mention the losers. I was lucky because all my large bets seemed to come off, although I could just as easily go through £30 to £40 several days running on losers, and that soon adds up and eats into your winnings.

Ready cash was also sometimes a problem for employees of a local massage parlour. I cashed cheques for the girls, even though one bounced for £300. She smiled sweetly and tried to pay her debt in kind. Years earlier, as a single man, I would have been tempted, but I had developed a moral conscience and declined her offer. The two main girls at the massage parlour were a big hit at our Tuesday-night disco, where they would climb on the bar and leave nothing to the imagination in their erotic interpretation of 'Je t'aime' by Jane Birkin and Serge Gainsbourg.

I was still drinking heavily at times in the new place, a considerable amount each day. All that cider and vodka added up to a lot of units – over 100 a week, easily. How many are you supposed to have? Seven or eight, is it? I never knew what the safe limit was, and I didn't care. I never needed to see a doctor about my drinking, but I got an unpleasant surprise the first time I consulted him about a sore throat which wouldn't go away. We had three Expelair extractor fans in our arty watering hole – but I never turned them on. My customers relished the fuggy atmosphere, and the smokier it became, the better it was for trade. It wasn't just tobacco smoke either because the crowd loved their marijuana, too. I was quite liberal-minded about that, perhaps too liberal. When I explained my working environment and the fact I was cleaning about fifty ashtrays a night, my doctor said, 'You might as well smoke yourself, Peter, because I've never met a bigger passive smoker in my life!'

Meanwhile, I felt we should have accepted an offer of just under £60,000 to sell Marinello's, but we tried to hold off for a bit more, and it never happened. The original offer would have netted us a handsome profit on a business with high rent and rates, but I was persuaded against it. The road ahead was beginning to worry me and it was about to become much darker and more dangerous.

CHAPTER 20

Dirty Rotten Scoundrels

If I never realised my full potential on a football pitch, the story of my disastrous life in business is a truly distressing tale. Maybe it was my fault, being too naive and trusting, especially with people I considered to be friends. In football, I had done everything on a handshake, and I fondly remember how Ally MacLeod honoured the £3,000 which he promised me when we shook hands before I left Motherwell shortly before Christmas 1978. The trust I showed to a succession of people I considered pals was abused. I never wanted to become a millionaire or a big-time Charlie, just to be able to enjoy a comfortable existence, sharing a laugh and a drink with friends and family, with the odd spot of tennis and charity football thrown in. That would have been enough. Evidently, fate had other plans for me.

I put up more money for the company to buy a big place

on the coast. The plan was for another lucrative conversion job on a house there, but the venture turned sour. I signed a personal guarantee, using my home and two flats I owned as collateral, when we took out the loan to purchase the place, but we couldn't get planning permission for some reason and lost a bundle on a deal which became messy and confusing. I recall there was some talk about the property being a listed building, which certainly didn't help matters.

On the pub front, we got ourselves into all sorts of bother with paperwork. And I mean bother. For whatever reason, it turned out that our accounts weren't up to date and this meant that we were struck off the companies' list. It was a shambles and, needless to say, my partner and I had words. How had we let things slip to this point? It was my name on the guarantees, and if everything went tits up, I knew the authorities would come gunning for me. I felt as if I was running in quicksand, the situation was becoming desperate and, sadly, in Scotland at that time it was easier to divorce your wife than your business partner. He probably felt the same. And my sense of impending doom increased when a solicitor informed me, 'You do know it's your neck on the line for this, don't you, Peter?' Out of the blue, I got a phone call from an old friend who casually asked, 'How would you like to earn £20,000, Peter?'

The idea was to convert a magnificent old building down south into a swanky nightclub. Now that appealed. My role was to be the 'face' to apply for the licence for the proposed venture. Apparently, because of the nature of the conversion and some previous history with my new colleagues, the backers needed someone who was squeaky clean in terms of licence application. There would be £20,000 for me if I succeeded – or a stake in the nightclub, whichever I preferred. The £20,000 I had been promised was, I understood, purely to ensure the nightclub received the all-clear from the licensing authorities.

Just for once I was giving it the superstar treatment, the big-name professional footballer who ran two successful pubs in Scotland – and the court saw no reason to decline the application. Truth be told, I was facing financial meltdown in Edinburgh, and this project felt like closing time in the last-chance saloon for me.

The licensing authorities gave me the green light, and then it was off to a solicitor's office for me to autograph various documents. What they were, I wasn't too sure. As I've mentioned, I simply trusted people.

Converting an ancient building with bags of character and charm into a swinging hotspot was a monumental task, not your overnight lick-of-paint job. The overall plan catered for shops on the ground floor, a disco and bars on the first floor with a piano bar and restaurant at the top. The sound system alone cost £40,000. From that first fateful phone call that got the ball rolling until the night we opened must have been eighteen months and involved three massive separate loans as the extensive renovation work gobbled up funds and we transferred our mounting debts from one company to another. Being the nominal head of the enterprise, my fellow entrepreneurs sent me a chequebook, and I'd think nothing of signing a dozen blank cheques and posting them back to them down south. Little wonder, then, that I ended up £300,000 in the red.

Finally, after much soul-searching and agonising, we were ready to open – but not before a last-minute hitch when Health and Safety refused to grant us the all-clear because a staircase was out of alignment by two or three millimetres. The pettiness of some people, I ask you. That problem alone cost me £27,000 for a team of specialist carpenters to work throughout the night installing a brand new set of stairs.

We got in touch with a number of big names to come along to the opening night – not least my old mate George Best, whom I asked if he'd like to come along to christen the nightclub. Is the Pope a Catholic? We opened in a blaze of publicity with all sorts of celebs, including Eddie Kidd, the motorcycle stunt rider, and Vicki Michelle, the knicker-flashing star of the hit TV comedy series 'Allo 'Allo also in attendance. An old mate of mine agreed to come along as my guest and act as chauffeur.

We met George and his minder in a hotel at 5 p.m. It was one of his periods of apparently trying to kick the booze with the help of patches or implants, but there was no way this evening would be a dry run for Bestie. We both went up to our respective rooms to change for the grand opening, and when I reappeared George was waiting at the bar for me with vodkas for the pair of us and a big smile. I thought George and I were supposed to be the stars of the show – but the lads who were meant to be looking after us kept us waiting for ages while they preened themselves upstairs in preparation for the ladies to come. George and I laughed at this little role reversal and ordered another drink. George, bless him, was on board for a cut-price £600 appearance fee as a favour to me alongside the model Mandy Smith, who looked like a million dollars, absolutely gorgeous, although you would have thought her mother was the main attraction, the way she was bossing people around. True to form, George ended up in bed with a beautiful woman – a scene I inadvertently witnessed when I knocked on his hotel room door and slipped a bottle of champagne inside.

Earlier that night we chewed the fat with bigwigs from the brewery. They must have thought the sun shone out of my backside. Here I was fronting one of the most opulent nightclubs in the area, and they thought I was flourishing because they only ever phoned me on Saturday nights at Marinello's when we were rammed solid with punters. We were quiet during the week – it was a working man's area – but hectic from Friday to Sunday. Truth is, the moneymen in Edinburgh had lost patience and called in the liquidators. I had the bailiffs knocking on the door every Monday, Tuesday and again on Friday demanding £400, £500 or threatening to shut the place. 'Take it, take it all, take the fucking lot,' I'd shout, ushering them towards the spirits and till. The liquidators were travelling from Glasgow first class by train at my expense and paying me £150 a week to manage the place. I was desperate to sell

Marinello's and had brochures printed, but the accountants wouldn't have it. They were running me into the ground and refused to let us stay open until 2 a.m. at the weekends, which we were perfectly entitled to do. It was commercial suicide, and the takings collapsed from £3,000 a week to under £2,000.

The biggest relief was 5 p.m. on a Friday, when I knew I'd have those parasites off my back for the weekend, and then I could relax with a good drink. I was so desperate for cash, I opened the back door for long, illicit Sunday-afternoon sessions. If this was breaking the law, then we were only copying local custom, and I wasn't getting rich on the proceeds because the vast proportion of our takings was going to servicing debts, while the brewery no longer wanted to know us unless we paid cash on delivery. We should have shut up shop at 2.30 p.m., but I'd happily keep twenty or thirty punters in until 7 p.m., when we would legally trade again and everything would go strangely quiet. Along Leith Walk the publicans had a system of 'jungle drums'. If the licensed police were on patrol and raided one, word would quickly spread for everyone else to keep their heads down.

As for my nightclub, the dream died after little more than a week because bills and running costs had spiralled out of all control, forcing us to close. The place went up for auction and we got £425,000. Just £40,000 of that was profit and it went into my bank account to reduce a massive overdraft.

In Edinburgh, things became extremely tense within the

partnership. It was my personal guarantees against all the money owed. I dreaded the moment I would have to face up to reality and buried myself in gambling and pints of cider with the punters. I was always convinced there was hope, that I possessed some deep inner strength which would rescue me, pull me back from the brink, no matter how deeply involved I became with drink, gambling or debt. Now I was having second thoughts because there was no way out of this hole I was in.

An ex-bookie mate of mine of the old school – skint one minute and flush the next – took over the lease at the city-centre bar, paying us £350 a week, a sum which made no impact whatsoever on a mountainous debt. He was a loveable rogue and would have been ideally cast alongside Michael Caine and Steve Martin in *Dirty Rotten Scoundrels*, the film about two rival swindlers on the French Riviera. I once had a £1,500 bet on Reference Point with him . . . and I'm still waiting for all of my winnings. He was the sort of guy you'd go to see, determined to get your money, and end up so bamboozled by his charm and scheming that you felt you had to lend him another £200. A little team of half a dozen of us were sitting in the bar the night it reopened after refurbishment, agreeing that he'd done a really smart job, when it dawned on the six of us that we'd paid for all the decorating out of our own pockets. The place was worth in excess of £100,000, and I really needed my mate to buy the place, but he couldn't afford it.

I got involved with another bloke – I'll call him Simon –

who struck me as a responsible family man who invested in stocks and shares. Things were becoming very messy so, to try and dig us out of trouble, Simon and I set up a new company. By this stage my original partner and I had split – at the cost of £750 in cash, the empty pub safe from Marinello's for sentimental reasons and a couple of kegs of beer. My side of the bargain was that we wouldn't pursue him for any debts. He was well out of it because, unknown to him, his well-being was under serious threat from an Edinburgh gangster I dubbed 'Benny from the Bronx' due to a close physical resemblance to a character in the Al Pacino film *Carlito's Way*.

My partner had asked me to ban Benny after he first began to frequent Marinello's, purely on the basis that he didn't like him. I remonstrated: 'That's madness. The guy's our best customer. He spends over £200 a week in here.' I was quite taken aback one evening when Benny casually informed me he had learned of my partner's views and wanted to shoot him. With the change in circumstances, however, Benny asked if he could either work behind the bar or as a doorman. 'Better than that,' I told him, 'why don't you come in with us and have a share?' He liked the idea and said he had £12,000 to invest immediately. I wasn't altogether surprised because Benny was a huge gambler and also extremely generous. But the following day when he turned up with £12,000 in cash, I wondered if it came from a dubious source, although I thought it prudent not to ask any questions.

Benny was a loose cannon, and the following week he

requested £2,000 back. He had either had a bad run on the horses or maybe he'd heard the whispers that the business was in a perilous state. It wasn't long before our chief creditors began turning the screw still tighter, and I was obliged to return another £4,000 of Benny's short-lived investment. Benny became more than a little agitated when it dawned on him that I wouldn't be able to pay him back the full £12,000, although his girlfriend did ring to reassure me: 'Don't worry about it, Peter. The money is down to me.'

Meanwhile, in a fifteen-month period I must have paid Simon over £110,000 towards our bolt hole. This was my big get-out – a little bar which we were going to buy, run by a couple of English brothers, in Spain. Don't laugh, but Simon suggested a way out until he firmed up the Spanish operation – do a runner to Butlin's holiday camp. I rather fancied South America myself or maybe the South of France, but my business partner thought Skegness was more suitable. It was a fitting comment on my fall from grace, I suppose.

I contacted a few friends to scrape together £2,500 and even thought about having my car torched to claim the insurance money. I went as far as to give this shady character I knew £60 to 'lose' the motor after parking it round the back of Marinello's one night. He drove it away to Dalkeith, but the car proved a stubborn customer. Back in the bar, the police walked in just as my pal with the singed black hair and eyelashes was explaining how he'd done his best but failed – managing only to ignite the can of petrol. Fortunately, the boys in blue never put two and two together on that occasion.

With Joyce and the boys I jumped on a train to Skegness and our new home for six weeks. I got to know all the jokes and cabaret acts off by heart. Butlin's almost offered me a job as a Redcoat while Paul, a handsome teenager by now, was enjoying a wonderful life with a new girlfriend every week. Joyce was suffering very badly, however. Her condition required tranquillity, stability and routine while I had plunged the whole family into a frenetic, hand-to-mouth existence.

My money was starting to run out, inevitably, and each week seemed to be a charade of Simon promising me that we could go to Spain and start a new life as soon as the English brothers had found property back home they wanted, while I went to a pay phone near reception at Butlin's and rang the girl sitting a few yards away from me to book us in for yet another seven days' self-catering, quoting a special number which earned us a 30 per cent discount. It might sound odd, but that was the way it worked. You couldn't get the same deal face to face at the desk, but had to quote a number from an advert in one of the tabloid newspapers.

Desperate times called for desperate measures, and I knew my luck had finally run out when the £50 bet I had riding on a Steve Cauthen horse went down by a short head. I was down and out.

It was Saturday, change-over day, and our suitcases were packed. We were standing outside Butlin's, ready to go home and face the music in Edinburgh, where Joyce was at least hopeful a friend would take in her and Jon. Now I had eight lousy quid in my pocket – nowhere near enough to buy the train tickets to Scotland. We repaired to the bar at Butlin's, where salvation arrived in the most unlikely form – a six-a-side touring football team from Liverpool. There was a live match on the TV, and Paul started talking to one of the Scousers on the next table about football. Drink flowed, I got involved, and out came the full sob story. Those eight or nine lads from Merseyside were unbelievably generous. Not only did they all chip in and raise £140 to help us financially, they even said they would change their sleeping arrangements and bunk in together so we could stay with them, which we did for four or five days.

I thought my luck really had changed when I walked into the gents and spotted a bulging leather wallet lying on the floor. In normal circumstances I would have taken it straight to lost property, but these were not normal circumstances. I kicked that wallet under the door of a cubicle and followed it inside, secure in the knowledge the contents would amount to a small fortune. The wedge turned out to be nothing more than a long string of credit cards inside a plastic sleeve, and I took the wallet to reception. Honesty is the best policy, because there was £20 awaiting me the following day as a reward.

Joyce's friend was having personal problems of her own and couldn't provide any temporary lodgings. My wife had the breakdown she had been threatening and was admitted again to the Andrew Duncan Clinic in the Royal Edinburgh Hospital. I was virtually living like a tramp now, with a wife in hospital and two sons to provide for. What could I do? I decided to turn to Simon as that was where my investments had gone – to fund the Spanish enterprise. He had a nasty surprise when I turned up uninvited on his doorstep to confront him and was very keen on getting me back to Edinburgh and away from his nice, comfortable family. I got a night in a bed-and-breakfast, £300 in cash and a lift back to the railway station the following day. Simon promised 'on his life' he'd give the English brothers the hurry-up and complete the Spanish deal.

Meanwhile, I was homeless, and Simon's next bright idea was that I should return to Skegness and stay in a caravan in a field. You couldn't make it up! Before long I was heading back to the south coast with my sons, and trying to be both mum and dad to them. Instead, I acted like a big kid myself. I suppose it was some relief from the day of reckoning I knew would have to be faced sooner or later.

CHAPTER 21

Clinging to the Wreckage

Help arrived from an unexpected source in the shape of Frank Tate, an old friend who had helped me run the St Mary's School and Salvesen boys' club football teams in Edinburgh several years earlier. I had known Frank's wife Helen even longer, as she had grown up in the Canonmills district of the city when I was a boy. Frank had often popped into Marinello's for a drink, but by that stage promotion with British Telecom had won him an executive position in Bournemouth and a nice home to go with it in St Catherine's Hill, Christchurch. As luck would have it, the Tates, with sons Colin and Graham, were on a month-long touring holiday of Scotland when they popped in to see my mother and check how we were getting on. We were still trying to negotiate the last exit from Skegness Butlin's, and Frank, bless him, left his house keys with my mum to pass on with the message that there was £400 cash in the pocket of a jacket hanging up in his bedroom for me to use if things got desperate.

Phone calls were duly exchanged, in which I confessed the full extent of my financial plight, and I could visualise Frank shaking his head in despair. Sometimes it takes an outsider to see how stupid you have been. Frank knew I had to leave Edinburgh fairly abruptly, because the business pressures were mounting, and my gangster friend Benny from the Bronx was sick and tired of waiting for the remainder of his £12,000. At least I always knew where I stood with Benny. I was still clinging to the hope Simon would come through with the Spanish deal. It's the sort of thing you do when you trust somebody, but at the back of my mind I suppose I knew it was hopeless.

I accepted Frank's generous offer to stay at his house in Dorset, scraped a few bob together and caught the train south with Paul and Jon. Sadly, there was no question of Joyce coming with us because she was still in the clinic. We had the place in Christchurch to ourselves for a few weeks, but things got rather cramped and heated with seven of us living together and the four boys starting to fight among themselves. Helen was working like a Trojan in the kitchen, knocking out delicious home-made pizzas, despite suffering quite badly from rheumatoid arthritis. I didn't need Frank to quietly suggest the time had come to move on. I would have hated to become an imposition after he had so generously rescued me from the hole I'd dug for myself. It wasn't long before I picked up the

Bournemouth Evening Echo, saw an advert for a bedsit and moved into the place.

Paul, Jon and I basically lived in one big room. We shared the bathroom and toilet with other occupants in the property, but I didn't pay any rent. The caretaker, a Londoner, was a big football fan and simply got me to sign a few pieces of paper and said it wouldn't be a problem claiming for me. Years earlier I had rented out property myself and now I knew, for sure, the boot was on the other foot.

I went on the dole and felt a right fucking prick, to be brutally honest. I had lost all my businesses and property in Scotland and gone from being well off to totally skint. When I had tried to draw benefit from the DHSS back home in Edinburgh, I received incredulous looks from staff, who told me, 'But, Mr Marinello, we already pay cheques to you.' That was true because I had people on benefit living in flats I owned. It was too complicated and awkward to explain that money wasn't mine any more, so I walked away empty-handed. I'd paid my dues, tax by the bucketload when I was a player, so there was no sense of shame or degradation in signing on. Joyce was in hospital, I had two boys to bring up as best I could and, after getting a couple of grand from two insurance policies I cashed in, no other source of income.

Jon began secondary school; Paul got a job and started an accountancy course, while the caretaker took me drinking most nights in a lively local boozer, opposite a very convenient, good Indian takeaway. Although the kids were very adaptable, this was no place to raise them, my caretaker friend insisted. It could be noisy and dangerous at certain times and, after a couple of police raids for drugs, I had to agree. One weekend he suddenly appeared at the door with two black plastic carrier bags crammed full of frozen food and explained, 'It's my going-away present to you, Peter. I've found you and the boys somewhere better to live.'

We moved a few miles away, nearer Bournemouth town centre, to a lovely big house where I was asked to oversee the other occupants and collect the rent. Life there with five young Cockneys was like a scene out of the *Big Brother* house. We all liked a drink and football, but I soon insisted on doing the weekly £80 shop in Asda myself after discovering a couple of the lads had a tendency towards kleptomania. On a previous expedition they had emerged from another supermarket with about £80 worth of food alone crammed into various jacket pockets.

One of the likeable young Londoners was a chef working locally in a hotel and he ensured we dined well, happy to knock up duck à l'orange, beef stroganoff and a succession of curries. When we weren't scoffing I seem to recall we were starving ourselves, on purpose. One drunken night I had a bet with two of the lads that I could lose more weight in three weeks than they could. We chipped in £30 apiece, and I collected the winnings after shedding 20 lbs having pushed the slim-in to the limits. A temporary lifestyle of tap water, three Brussels sprouts for tea and ridiculously early nights had caused me to become very light-headed and dizzy. One of the losers had to pay a fine for being spotted sneaking into McDonald's, and we celebrated the end of the fast with a big slap-up meal in one of Bournemouth's best Italian restaurants. The only problem was our stomach capacity had shrunk so much that after a couple of pints we couldn't manage anything more than a prawn cocktail apiece for starters.

I got friendly with our landlord, a great guy. He and a character known as Big Red called themselves 'the Pirates' and enjoyed a highly lucrative sideline 'working' the beaches. They had the illegal ice-cream business stitched up for seven miles with walkie-talkies to keep one step ahead of the beach patrol units. A little trip to Portsmouth during the height of summer would see the Pirates make bulk purchases of choc-ices for 5p and lollies for 10p. Back on the beaches, those choc-ices and lollies were being knocked out for 50p and 70p. In a good weekend, with the thermometer touching seventy degrees, the boys master-minded an operation which could net them as much as £4,000. My sons, Paul and Jon, were willing recruits, and I'm sure they enjoyed looking at the topless girls queuing up to buy their wares almost as much as their very generous wages at the end of the weekend.

It may sound as if Bournemouth's sunshine scene was one long laugh and a joke, but I was flying by the seat of my pants and still had huge financial worries haunting me in Scotland, where Joyce was hospitalised. It seemed as if I didn't have two pennies to rub together – and it wasn't long before I had murder in mind.

CHAPTER 22

Gangsters and Guns

Collecting the rent money on behalf of the owner of the house in 1990 was a piece of cake compared to contacting my so-called business partner Simon. He wrote to me occasionally, very occasionally, but every time I called him on his mobile phone he was mysteriously unobtainable.

My chef housemate was very taken with the idea of providing meals and snacks at our bar in Spain, and Simon agreed he should come on board. Months passed before we got down to the nitty-gritty. Joyce was still undergoing treatment for her psychiatric condition in Edinburgh, and the plan was for her to improve before flying out two or three weeks later to join us. One tea-time found my sons Paul, Jon, myself and the chef all with our cases packed outside the house waiting excitedly for transport arranged by Simon to take us to Birmingham airport where, he had assured us, we had been booked on the 10.35 p.m. flight to Spain. Thirty minutes passed with no sign of a car, then another thirty minutes before a familiar feeling of betrayal and dread began to seep through my body. Simon's number was dead, and when I called Birmingham airport, not only was the last flight to Spain at 8.35 that evening, they had no reservations whatsoever in our names for any flight that day.

I knew then that was it. In my mind all I could think of was that I'd been turned over by a rip-off merchant. I became hell bent on revenge against a man who I felt had salted away £110,000 of my money. Chasing my dream in Spain, I had given him a lump sum of £40,000 plus the takings from Marinello's of between £600 and £1,200 each week plus the rent from the arty pub and the flat I owned in Leith, which together amounted to another £450 a week. I had been purely 'existing' with my family, rather than living in any great style or splendour, all the time pinning my hopes on that bloody bar in the Spanish sunshine. Now I was stranded on the south coast with next to nothing.

The biggest of the Cockneys where I was living was Adam, 6ft 7in, built like Arnold Schwarzenegger and keen to be of any assistance. We went to London to meet an underworld contact of mine from my Arsenal days in a Kentish Town pub. This fellow had been a contemporary of the Krays and the Richardsons, a distinguished gentleman who had served time for jewel thefts and stealing mail. Hardened villain though he was, I had a soft spot for him, and when I played at Portsmouth I'd popped over to visit him in prison. As I regaled my mate with the full story of my lost fortune, he just stared at me coldly before saying slowly, 'How can you be so fucking stupid, Peter?' before offering to arrange to have Simon shot for £30,000.

I didn't want Simon murdered; a proper kneecapping would have sufficed for the mental anguish he had put me through. I wasn't thinking straight, but I could quite happily have pulled the trigger on Simon there and then and served the time. When my underworld contact established I could possibly scrape together £30,000 by tapping up every remaining friend on this planet, he proposed an alternative major-league crime which, he promised, would turn that £30,000 into £60,000. He and his associates were apparently bribing an African chief into letting them illegally export diamonds, which were then transferred to Amsterdam and exchanged for drugs being smuggled into this country. I had known him for an awfully long time and had no reason to doubt the truth of what he told me – even if it did sound far-fetched.

Adam and I left the pub, went outside, looked at each other and shook our heads. We needed a plan but, more than that, we needed to confront Simon because I was down to my last £400 in cash. Our next stop was a snooker hall, where we handed over £120 for a handgun that had been deactivated. Now it was time to head north and put the frighteners on Simon. We booked into a motel near where he lived and, with money running out, Declan Murphy obliged at 7–2 on a hurdler for me when I gambled £40 in a fit of inspiration, or desperation. Take your pick.

The following morning we drove to his home, only to find it empty with no recent signs of life whatsoever as we peered through the French windows. One neighbour told us we weren't the only people looking for Simon and also that he'd never owned the house, merely rented it, before doing a moonlight flit with his wife and son.

As we drove away, another car entered the cul-de-sac and blocked our path. The driver got out, approached and said, 'Are you looking for him, too?' It turned out Simon had taken this chap's brother for £4,000 in a bogus taxi business. 'He got off lightly,' I told the driver before exchanging addresses and phone numbers.

I knew my erstwhile partner ordered plenty of booze, and when we spied an off-licence down the road, Adam and I pulled over on a hunch, and – what do you know? Surprise, surprise – the lad running the shop told us Simon had an outstanding account with him totalling over £600 and, suddenly, he couldn't be contacted.

Simon's son played rugby, and we turned up at the club to discover they had been conned as well. He had done a bunk with hefty deposits after promising to provide match tickets and a coach to take parents and children to see the massive Grand Slam decider between Scotland and England at Murrayfield.

Our next stop was the private school attended by the boy – and paid for by me. I didn't know exactly what I expected to find skulking around the lockers but I was apprehended by the janitor and security, and marched into the headmaster's office. I explained who I was, why I was there, and he smiled. Simon owed the school for two or three terms. 'Can I get you a cup of tea, or maybe a coffee?' inquired the kind gentleman in a black gown before scribbling down an address on a sheet of paper and leaving his study. His parting shot was: 'I do hope you can get some joy.'

Armed with Simon's last-known address, Adam and I staked out the property but, again, it was empty. Then, at last, we struck lucky with a tip-off where Simon would be watching his son play rugby that weekend. We drove to the place staging two or three matches and, bingo, there he was among a couple of hundred spectators – this big, well-dressed man, looking his usual smug, arrogant self. Adam hung back 100 yards as I approached my business partner, who was visibly shaken as I yelled in his face, 'Where's my fucking money, you fat bastard!' Oh dear, that didn't go down too well with Simon's friends and fellow parents among the green-welly and sheepskin-coat brigade. 'Shush, shush,' he hissed. 'We can sort all this out. Trust me.'

We walked and talked urgently until we reached an isolated corner of the playing field, where there was a building. Up against the wall, Simon visibly relaxed and became his usual composed self again. He was much bigger than me, and I was never going to physically intimidate him. What he had no way of knowing, however, was that Adam was about to make a dramatic entrance. The big Londoner suddenly pounced from out of nowhere, grabbed Simon around the neck and stuck our gun to his head. Now Simon was squealing like a stuck pig, and I had not a single ounce of sympathy for the man who had gambled and drunk away my money, sent his son to an expensive private school, stayed in fancy hotels and enjoyed foreign holidays.

'Let me batter the fucker,' pleaded Adam, but Simon talked his way out of that extremely tight spot by promising to meet me with £10,000 cash the following day at a nearby hotel. I fell for it, of course, but there wasn't any real alternative as I saw it. The gun didn't fire bullets and if Adam and I had battered Simon we would have faced GBH charges with plenty of witnesses in green wellies.

Sitting in the hotel the next morning, checking my watch every five minutes and fearing the worst, I received a message via the receptionist that Simon had called, apologising for running late because he'd been held up in traffic. He turned up eventually, looking a haunted man, as well he might after Adam's performance the previous afternoon, and promised he would get £10,000 to me within a week. I left him in no doubt that we knew where to find him now if he didn't keep his end of the bargain. But in my heart of hearts, when I watched him walk out of the door, I knew I'd never see a penny of what he owed me. The funny thing is he wasn't living the life of a millionaire, just spending money as quickly as he got it. I reckoned if I could get £10,000 out of him I would be doing well.

Back in Bournemouth several days later, there was a

knock on my front door at five in the morning. Bleary-eyed and stubble-chinned, I opened up to discover two policemen who were quite insistent I join them there and then down at the police station to help them with their inquiries. I was none too keen at that hour and replied pithily, 'Bollocks to that idea,' to which they said if I didn't go voluntarily I would be arrested under suspicion of attempted murder. Put like that, they had made me an offer I couldn't very well refuse.

It was noon before I had chance to speak to a solicitor, a nice guy, who shook his head as I told him the bulk of the story – carefully managing to leave Adam out of the picture. If anyone was going down for this little escapade it was me, and me alone. That afternoon there were five of us in the interview room at Bournemouth Central police station – me, my solicitor, a woman police officer and two members of CID. I related the full story, at least my version of it, from start to finish and got a bit emotional. As far as the gun was concerned, it was Simon's word against mine, but I did say that if he died tomorrow, I would be delighted and get pissed to celebrate.

I was released at 4.30 p.m. without charge, and, as I headed for the bus stop, one of the visiting CID officers called across, 'Mr Marinello, we know what you did. Don't ever pull a stunt like that again but, rest assured, that bastard will get his come-uppance one day.' Shortly afterwards, the police were back at my house, this time bringing good news. No action to be taken against me. Case closed.

CHAPTER 23

Smack in the Face

Heroin: how low can you go? I thought it was the six months I spent driving my youngest son Jon to his dealer's house, near our home, parking up, taking £20 notes, tenners and fivers from my back pocket and watching him disappear inside to buy the smack he craved, the drugs which would kill him if he didn't stop. But I was wrong, however diabolical that made me feel, however much that was a fucking nightmare. No, the lowest point in the unequal fight against heroin came after all Jon's veins were so badly damaged he had to inject himself in the groin. Jon, Joyce and I presented ourselves at the doctor's surgery. If we hadn't received a positive response that day, I was ready to encourage Jon to commit the sort of crime guaranteed to get himself locked up – either in prison or a mental institution – where the authorities would be obliged to help him. If our doctor hadn't helped,

I wanted Jon to go berserk in a shop, trash the place.

How had it come to this? I had been one of the luckiest teenagers in the world, born with a talent that earned me a £100,000 transfer to Arsenal – a passport to fame and fortune. Now I was the father of a teenager with a death wish. I reminded Jon of everything I'd had by his age: marriage, kids, money, a home and car. I would try and shame him into confronting his demons, and Jon tells me the truth hurt because drugs had taken such a complete hold on his life and he knew he was messing up big time. Sometimes our relationship degenerated to the extent he would sidle up to me in the bookies and I would slip some money to him, our eyes never meeting, no words exchanged. That's no way for a father and son to behave. How on earth can you avoid looking someone you love in the eyes? I don't know which of us was the more ashamed.

Guilty? Of course I felt guilt. I had been lax and lazy with Jon, a lovely, bright, bubbly lad who had been more into *Star Wars* and computers than football. My elder son Paul had adapted to our nomadic existence, but poor Jon, the baby of the family, had been pulled from pillar to post. I indulged him and always tried to give him what he wanted to make up for the tough times he'd been forced to endure through no fault of his own.

It brought a few things home to me after Jon had been through rehab and told me he hadn't felt in tune for seventeen years, between the ages of eight and twenty-five. He would have been still in short pants in Edinburgh, helping with the early-morning bottling up in my pubs when I'd open the door for the tramps and dossers to come in to warm themselves up – and I'd drink cider for breakfast. Maybe I was wrong to have exposed him to things like that. It didn't help, of course, when we moved to Bournemouth, his mum still in hospital in Scotland, and lived in a bedsit with next to no money.

No drug addict to my knowledge starts off using heroin. Cannabis is almost certainly the gateway drug, and I freely admit I was not overly concerned when Jon first started dabbling. There had been a local scandal at his comprehensive school when some prefects were expelled for selling cannabis to younger pupils. As Jon was on the periphery of this dodgy group, I was summoned by the headmaster and given a warning. At that stage, I believed cannabis was fairly harmless, even beneficial for some people, as it does have some medicinal properties. When I was playing in America for Phoenix Inferno, it was the drug of choice along with a glass or two of wine in the evening for many of our friends, who had openly smoked it in high school. Cannabis was their social lubricant while mine was alcohol, and I have always been a very social kind of guy. I had a few smokes in my days in America too, but I was never a proper smoker because I didn't like inhaling any kind of smoke. I always had vodka, lager and gambling to give me a buzz. My opinion of cannabis has changed. If you are easily led with an addictive nature there's a genuine danger of it leading to far more harmful substances, especially if you're young, with a rebellious streak and get a thrill from experimenting. The temptation will always be there to go higher and higher, particularly in a crowd. With a group, I imagine drugs never seem so bad, with everyone else getting their kicks.

One day Jon had a ferocious argument with his girlfriend, and the next thing I knew the police were on our doorstep in Southbourne asking if they could have a look upstairs. You could have knocked me down with a feather when one of the cops said, 'Do you know you've got cannabis plants growing up there, Mr Marinello?' 'No,' I replied, straight-faced. 'I'm not an expert in botanical matters.' Jon was cautioned and got rid of those plants, although I later learned he and his group of friends found a discreet patch of land out in the New Forest to start cultivating the plants.

Too many people started coming round to our house for comfort, and on occasions I had to throw some of them out. I didn't like their attitude but still I had no inkling of how far Jon had descended into drug-taking.

Jon was nineteen and on holiday with his brother Paul in Spain when he discovered he was a drug addict. They went for a fortnight, but he spent the first five or six days shaking and shivering from withdrawal symptoms. They returned, and Paul told me starkly, 'Jon's got problems, Dad. It's heroin.' That was after Jon collapsed at home with terrible stomach pains, which saw me rushing him to hospital because my immediate thought was appendicitis. I should have known something was wrong when the doctor started questioning him about various things he might have ingested, and Jon quietly asked me to leave the cubicle. I was so naive then, I thought you had to inject the stuff, but suddenly things started to click – like all the silver foil that had gone missing from the kitchen cupboard. Jon was smoking the heroin. Silver foil was the least of our worries, I could replace that for pennies from the corner shop, but cash was taken too, along with a television and two video recorders.

All the thieving, lies and deceit led to fist fights between us. I thought junkies were down-and-outs, but through a large proportion of his time on drugs, Jon successfully managed to hold down jobs in banking and financial institutions in Bournemouth, although he ended up with me driving him to work on building sites after he'd had a morning smoke to get him through the day. Jon was one of half a dozen school friends who were all hooked on heroin after graduating from cannabis. They had just experimented at first, seeking a bigger buzz, a greater high and now all of them were in trouble, serious trouble, with habits costing them anything up to £70 a day to feed. The war in Afghanistan was raging at the time – and that was particularly bad news for local junkies, because their smack was coming in from the Afghans. Demand locally was outstripping supply, so much so that I heard how one couple were turned over in Boscombe when they paid a dealer £100 for some gear that turned out to be mostly brown curry powder. You have to laugh, or else you'd cry.

I threw Jon out of the house a couple of times, and he and his girlfriend fled to St Issey in Cornwall to work in a bar after Paul and I discussed kidnapping him and taking him to a country cottage to kick the habit and go cold turkey. He had run up a £1,000 debt on his credit cards, which I paid, while Paul sorted out some problems Jon had in Portsmouth, where he had been dealing drugs. I was still soft, I suppose, and regularly sent Jon £60 a month while he was down in the West Country.

Jon returned to live with us but was soon back to his bad old ways, and things reached a stage when Joyce and I even discussed leaving the area and not telling him. There was no way on earth Jon could sustain a £70-a-day heroin habit, and I tried my best to wean him off it to a level of £20–30, which was just about affordable. That's the period when I drove him to see the local dealer two or three times a week. The business going on inside that property sickened me to the pit of my stomach, and I told the police what was happening, but word came back to me that they already knew and weren't prepared to put that particular dealer out of business because it would merely transfer the problem somewhere else in the locality.

Jon was prescribed Methadone and visited the local chemist on a daily basis for the heroin substitute, but it didn't suit him. Meanwhile, one of his pals was admitted to the Priory in Roehampton, where his father splashed out £35,000 to get him off heroin, but it was money down the drain as far as I was concerned. I went to a 'family and relatives' meeting at the Priory and thought it was a soft regime geared to pampering celebrities from the world of showbusiness. In any case, the boy wasn't ready to stop. He had not hit rock bottom.

Jon had, though, and the turning point came when I told our doctor, 'Listen, you've got to help. This has to end.' We had an agonising three-hour wait at the surgery with Jon sweating profusely and shaking while the doctor, bless him, sought guidance from a superior before prescribing Jon a course of heavy duty DFS tablets designed to cure anxiety and, more importantly, getting him booked into the Providence Projects, a local drug and alcohol dependency unit.

I received an invitation to travel with the Arsenal old boys to Rimini on an eight-day tour for a veterans tournament. I was torn between going and staying to ensure Jon started at the Providence. Joyce encouraged me to go, stressing I had done all I could for Jon, and the night I arrived in Italy she phoned me with the wonderful news that Providence had delivered and the National Health would meet the £8,000 costs of his six-week rehabilitation.

I was always there for him, always with the best intentions even if I was a bit tactless meeting Jon the day he completed rehab with the suggestion we go and celebrate in the nearest pub. I needed a pint more than he did.

Jon is clean, but he knows a lot of people still struggling with drugs. He says he's lucky to survive and just wants to get on with the rest of his life, which would inevitably have taken another turn for the worse had he succumbed to the wiles of a local villain who fancied branching out from dealing drugs to robbing the bank where Jon worked. I'm relieved Jon retained the mental strength to say 'no' in the pub that night when the villain and two heavies lent on him to give them the security numbers and access codes to the bank. Jon tells me he feared the nutter might 'top him' so it was a brave thing he did. It can't have been easy.

CHAPTER 24

Home and Dry

I was declared bankrupt in Scotland in 1991, but I swear word never reached me because I was living in Bournemouth by then. Three years later, however, the past caught up with me. I came home to discover Joyce entertaining a complete stranger in our living room with tea and cake. I had never clapped eyes on this guy before but, not wishing to appear rude, I simply held my hand out and said: 'Hello, I'm afraid I don't know you.' He rose from his chair and replied, 'Hello, Peter,' before grabbing my shoulder and pressing a piece of paper on me. 'What's this?' I asked. 'It's a bankruptcy order,' he explained. 'What do you mean!' I exploded. 'And you can bugger off right now, using false pretences to come into my house.'

I manhandled him down the stairs, and there was a comical moment when his wig got pushed askew. This was swiftly followed by another bit of farce. Out on the pavement, I took the writ, screwed it up tightly into a ball and threw it as hard as I could, with a glint of satisfaction in my eye as I shouted, 'This is what you can do with your bloody writ.' We stood there and watched as that ball of paper came rolling down a roof before landing right at my feet. That told me all I needed to know – I wasn't going to run away from this financial crisis.

My creditors were after me for something like £18,000, an amount that had mushroomed out of all proportion from an initial unpaid £7,000 wet stock bill at Marinello's for barrels and crates of beer over about six weeks. The legal side of this sad affair, court costs, hiring solicitors from Southampton who, in turn, employed private detectives to track me down, plus interest, was responsible for that additional £11,000.

Joyce and I were living quietly in a modest flat above a shop in a lane, which was also home to a couple of small garages and an electrician's. It was hardly Park Lane, yet those who were after my cash evidently believed I was rolling in money. The reality was that I was skint and very soon on legal aid. The bankruptcy order was not actually against me in person, but the company I had fronted with Simon when my previous company was dissolved, and the word from my legal people was that it was impossible to be declared bankrupt in both Scotland and England. I could go to Scotland and fight the case, but a barrister suggested it would be much simpler just to declare myself bankrupt in England, which is what I duly did.

For a few weeks I was actually looking forward to my

big day in court, where I was going to name and shame a few characters, but as the day drew closer I began to shy away from the prospect of all the negative publicity and the effect it would have on the rest of the family, particularly Joyce. I wasn't obliged to attend in person, and four days later, a letter arrived informing me of my official status as a bankrupt and requesting my attendance at a receivers court. What followed were two-and-a-half days of farce as I went through my entire, disastrous business history for the benefit of the wide-eyed receivers, who didn't know whether to laugh or cry. It was hilarious, ludicrous stuff. I got the impression they firmly believed it was a complete waste of time. In fact, they were quite sympathetic. Obviously, I had lost two houses, two businesses and any assets, yet my creditors had pursued me for £7,000, which had become £18,000, while I had ceased trading in 1987. I was living in rented accommodation, I had no job and was claiming Social Security benefits. I offered the receivers my car, an old Vauxhall Viva worth £250, but it was politely refused. Instead, they took two insurance policies – but these were only payable on my death, so relatively worthless to them, and I paid £125 to retrieve them several months later.

My next big match was against the Inland Revenue, who pulled me, claiming I owed them £16,000 in unpaid income tax. I offered to pay at £2.50 a week and the chap said, 'Are you taking the piss? At that rate, it will take you 350 years to repay us.' I've never stopped to discover if his mathematics were correct, but after the Inland Revenue heard my full circumstances they said any judge would laugh the matter out of court if legal proceedings were instigated against me.

Up until a couple of years ago I received phone calls keeping me in touch with Simon's movements and, on occasions, informing me that he would be eating in a particular restaurant at a specific time. I frequently think about what I could have done with that £110,000, but you have to move on in life, and I don't want to end up emotionally crippled by bitterness and resentment.

Some things never change, however, and I still have no difficulty attracting con artists. I was scouting around, seeking fresh talent for Parkbury, the Bournemouth Sunday League team I help coach, and this good-looking feller in his mid-to-late twenties appeared a great find after I bumped into him at the bookies. He was new to Bournemouth and it was clear from a couple of training sessions that he had obviously played at a decent level. In fact, he told me he'd played for a Premiership side, only to be bombed out of there for taking the banned steroid nandrolone.

Well, I must admit, it all rang true as far as I was concerned and I thought to myself how keen he was arriving an hour before kick-off one Sunday morning. I wasn't too impressed after the match, however, to learn that a few weeks later Parkbury would be without six of our main players, who were off to see Manchester United tackle Chelsea. Our 'star' man had spun them a line about his dad doing a lot of printing work for a character with an executive box at Old Trafford, and how he could get tickets for the glamour match against Chelsea. He promised them return travel from Bournemouth to Manchester, executive box seats and signed shirts – all for £100 a head. A very good friend of mine, Guiseppe, handed over £500 on behalf of himself and four pals, but it all sounded too good to be true and, inevitably, it was. Three of the lads pulled out when I told them Parkbury would be so short of players that Sunday I'd have to pull my boots on again. But two others paid £100 cash each and one lad got a text message telling him to place £100 in some girl's account in Poland. Our 'star' ended up stealing £700 from local footballers and honest, decent football fans who just thought they'd struck it lucky – only to get taken for a sick ride.

Luck was conspicuous by its absence the day my playing career came to an abrupt halt at the ripe old age of fifty-four in a freak accident. Of course, I had finished as a serious footballer many years before, but I still lived for matches with the combined Arsenal veterans and showbiz personalities, plus the odd twenty minutes here and there as a second-half substitute if Parkbury were short. It was a pre-season friendly in the summer of 2004 when I was our sponge man, running to tend an injured player, and getting both my feet tangled up in the opposition's string ball-bag. I fell to earth like a sack of potatoes, catching my right hip on the edge of a hard rubber bucket. The pain was agonising, I felt as if I'd been struck by a car, and both sets of players were doubled up too – in laughter. That hip had already been causing me some grief, and that night my old Arsenal pal Eddie Kelly tried to reassure me over the phone that I was merely suffering from arthritis. But my doctor's diagnosis was swift and to the point as he studied an x-ray. A hip replacement operation was called for as soon as possible. I contacted the Professional Footballers' Association and the chairman, Gordon Taylor, wrote back immediately telling me to get the job done privately at the PFA's expense, for which I was extremely grateful.

Mind you, I wish I hadn't gone private because they said I was still too young and fit to have that sort of major surgery. A course of heavy-duty steroid injections were prescribed instead, for which the PFA kindly paid £1,200. For a week after the jab I felt like death warmed up, really lousy with hot flushes and indigestion. Once those side effects wore off, I'd feel brilliant for four or five weeks, able to run, shoot and kick all over the park and thinking, 'This is magic.' But those injections were only a short-term solution to a serious handicap to my mobility. I was struggling to walk to the bookies every morning, things were that bad!

The PFA very generously promised me £7,500 towards the £9,500 I was quoted for a private operation in England, although my son Paul discovered via the internet that similar surgery in Germany was available for £5,500, while in Turkey it was as low as £4,500. I was rapidly weighing up all my options while downing a dozen industrial-strength painkillers a day and day-dreaming about beautiful nurses in Istanbul when I got the thumbs up from the National Health Service. November 2004 saw me go under the knife at the Royal Bournemouth Hospital, and Brett, my young Aussie surgeon, was brilliant – as were all the staff. Mind you, I suspect this isn't the end of the story because my left hip is starting to give me grief.

Despite everything I've taken from life and everything that's been chucked back at me, which has sometimes left me feeling like a peasant in the stocks having garbage hurled at his head, I'm still smiling, happy and as content as a man has a right to be. Joyce and I live in a beautiful part of the world, and I will always be there as her husband and carer. I have a simple, uncomplicated life, and it suits me, with a few little bets on the dogs and horses – plus a few jars with the Parkbury lads on a Sunday lunchtime after the local park football, which still has the capacity to give me a big lift or leave me down in the dumps. I'm still a born optimist, whose first nature is to trust others. That's cost me, I've been hurt, but I'll never change. It's in the blood.

The fit, healthy, muscular Jon Marinello I see bears no resemblance to the deeply troubled character reliant on a daily fix for his kicks. He's learning a noble trade as a plumber, works out regularly in the gym and lives for the summer when he can indulge his major passion for surfing among friends at the beach that is virtually on their doorstep. Jon looks more like a male model than an ex-junkie – and I am eager to make that point because I'm sure there will be a fair few readers of this book going through the hell of living with someone addicted to drugs or alcohol. Maybe they see no light at the end of the tunnel. But never give up, things can turn around quite dramatically. Jon is living proof of that. He made it in the end because he was sick and tired of feeling sick and tired. And am I proud to call him my son? You bet.

Paul, Jon, Joyce and I are very much a family unit, and there's so much to look forward to, especially a grandchild or two to kick a ball with on the beach once my sons get cracking in that department. Hopefully, it won't be too long before I'm teaching that first grandchild to dribble on the sand, reading bedtime stories and maybe regaling the little 'un with the tale about a teenager from Scotland who scored at Old Trafford on his debut for Arsenal.

Career Statistics

PETER MARINELLO
Born Edinburgh, 20 February 1950.

Career
St Anthony's Secondary School, Salvesen BC, Hibernian 1966, Turned professional 1967. Transferred to Arsenal January 1970 £100,000. Transferred to Portsmouth July 1973 £100,000. Transferred to Motherwell December 1975 £25,000. Loaned to Canberra City May 1978. Transferred to Fulham December 1978 £30,000. To Phoenix Inferno 1980. Transferred to Hearts October 1981 £30,000. Transferred to Partick Thistle 1983. To Broxburn Athletic 1984.

Honours
Scotland Under-23
1969 v France (sub) with Hibernian
1970 v England (sub) with Arsenal (match abandoned 62 minutes; snow)

Scottish League
1978 v Irish League

Season	League S/Cup		FA Cup SL Cup		Lge Cup/ Cups		Other	
	Apps	Goals	Apps	Goals	Apps	Goals	Apps	Goals
HIBERNIAN								
1967–68	12	–	2	–	–	–	–	–
1968–69	19	1	–	–	9	3	2+	1
1969–70	14	4	–	–	4	1	–	–
ARSENAL								
1969–70	14	1	–	–	–	–	4+	–
1970–71	3	–	–	–	–	–	1+	–
1971–72	8	1	–	–	1	–	2*	1
1972–73	13	1	1	–	4	1	–	–
PORTSMOUTH								
1973–74	39	3	6	–	2	–	–	–
1974–75	39	2	1	1	2	1	–	–
1975–76	17	2	–	–	4	1	–	–
MOTHERWELL								
1975–76	18	3	6	3	–	–	–	–
1976–77	22	3	3	–	5	–	2#	–
1977–78	35	5	2	2	1	–	3#	1
CANBERRA CITY (loan)								
1978	11	1	–	–	–	–	–	–
MOTHERWELL								
1978–79	14	1	–	–	4	3	2#	–
FULHAM								
1978–79	9	–	3	–	–	–	–	–
1979–80	18	1	–	–	2	–	–	–

Season	League S/Cup		FA Cup SL Cup		Lge Cup/ Cups		Other	
	Apps	Goals	Apps	Goals	Apps	Goals	Apps	Goals
PHOENIX INFERNO								
1980 & 1981								
HEARTS								
1981–82	18	2	2	1	–	–	–	–
1982–83	4	1	–	–	4	1	–	–
PARTICK THISTLE								
1983–84	6	–	–	–	–	–	–	–
TOTAL	333	32	26	7	42	11	16	3

+ Fairs Cup
* European Cup
# Anglo-Scottish Cup

BLACK AND BLUE

Paul Canoville

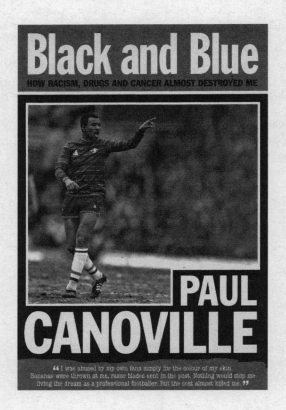

£12.99

SPORT/AUTOBIOGRAPHY 978 0 7553 1644 1

Now you can buy any of these other bestselling
non-fiction titles from your bookshop
or *direct from the publisher*.

FREE P&P AND UK DELIVERY
(Overseas and Ireland £3.50 per book)

Being Gazza   Paul Gascoigne   £6.99
Footballing hero Gazza, in the company of his therapist,
confronts his demons and examines the reasons behind his
depression and addictions.

John Greig: My Story   John Greig   £6.99
'The greatest Rangers player of all time' recounts the highs and
lows of his career and relives classic moments on and off the
pitch with both club and country.

Hail Cesar   Billy McNeill   £7.99
Celtic's greatest hero and captain of their 1967 European Cup-
winning side recalls his glory days with the club and beyond,
in this remarkable autobiography.

Gazza: My Story   Paul Gascoigne   £7.99
The No. 1 bestselling and award-winning autobiography of the
biggest football star of his generation.

True Grit   Frank McLintock   £7.99
A captivating story of Arsenal's Double-winning captain,
spanning 45 years of fabulous highs and shattering lows, told
with humour, honesty and passion.

Pointless   Jeff Connor   £7.99
An inside, in-depth story of a season with East Stirlingshire,
Britain's worst football club, as they struggle to climb to second
bottom of the Scottish Third Division.

To order, simply call 01235 400 414
visit our website: www.madaboutbooks.com
or email orders@bookpoint.co.uk

Prices and availability subject to change without notice.